MW01482512

A Sampler of Chinese Literature

From the Ming Dynasty to Mao Zedong

Sidney Shapiro

A SAMPLER OF CHINESE LITERATURE

From the Ming Dynasty to Mao Zedong

Translated, Compiled and Edited by
Sidney Shapiro

Panda Books
Beijing

First Edition 1996

Published by CHINESE LITERATURE PRESS
Beijing 100037, China

ISBN 7-5071-0345-5
ISBN 0-8351-3181-5

Distributed by China International Book Trading Corporation
35 Chegongzhuang Xilu, Beijing 100044, China
P.O. Box 399, Beijing, China

Printed in the People's Republic of China

CONTENTS

Prologue

This is a collection of literary gems, complete or extracts from larger works, created between the Ming dynasty (14th to 17th century) and the era of Mao Zedong, which ended with his death in 1976. I translated them into English during the past thirty years and all were published, but for cold war reasons had very limited circulation in the West. They are particular favorites of mine, and I have put them together now so that you may share in my pleasure, and the pleasure of thousands of Chinese over a 600 year period, in reading them.

Their tightly constructed plots and subtle characterizations dispel to some extent the strangeness of a distant land and different culture. The human qualities of their personae seem remarkably familiar. But they are, after all, Chinese stories about China and the Chinese, and these have special attributes which may puzzle Westerners. Rather than wrench the reader out of the narrative flow and mood with burdensome footnotes, I have inserted occasional comments, in italics within parentheses, wherever clarification seems called for.

For general background I tell a bit about the development of Chinese literature, describe the main historical periods during which it evolved, and introduce the authors and the circumstances under which they created our particular selections. Over-all, I let the pieces speak for themselves.

What has come down to us today as written Chinese literature dates from long before the Ming dynasty. The *Book of Songs*, compiled in the seventh and eighth centuries BC, vividly depicts social conditions in those times. It contains songs, poems, myths and legends, gathered together, much as were the *Hebrew Psalms* and the *Song of Solomon*, and have a simple charm of their own.

The Tang dynasty (7th to 10th century) is famed as the golden age of Chinese poetry. One old anthology contains over 48,900 poems by 2,200 poets, whose numbers included courtiers, soldiers, painters and priests. Of such beauty are Tang verses that they are still memorized and recited today.

They have been translated in many languages. During the Yuan dynasty (13th and 14th centuries) when the Mongols ruled China, Han intellectuals, prohibited from taking part in the civil service examinations, turned to writing plays. A number of fine dramas were created.

Wood block printing was used in China in the tenth century, but it was a slow process, and most literary creations were still painstakingly transcribed by hand. Then, in the eleventh century printing with movable type was invented — four hundred years before Gutenberg printed his bible by that process in Germany — and mass production of books in China became possible.

Concurrent with this technological advance, new Chinese cultural forms were evolving. Growing out of the ancient fables, moral parables, tales of the miraculous and supernatural, myths and legends, came short stories, and the elaborate recitals of the professional yarn spinners. These men were real artists, enthralling audiences at fairs and markets and other places of public gatherings with dramatic accounts of historic events, imaginatively exaggerated and much embellished, and accompanied by grimaces, gestures, and self-created sound effects. The story tellers would stop suddenly at the tensest moments and request financial contributions from their captivated listeners before continuing with the next episode.

To remember the details of their involved plots, they kept prompt books, which were quite long. These proved to be ideal raw material for China's first novelists. During the Ming dynasty a few intellectuals took the prompt books and fashioned them into smoothly crafted novels, while retaining the earthy "cliff-hanger" style of the originals. The Ming dynasty marked the flowering of Chinese feudal fiction, and saw the creation of the classics *Outlaws of the Marsh*, *Romance of the Three Kingdoms*, and *Journey to the West*.

Printing with movable type brought these books to thousands. Lengthy works of Chinese literature for the first time became available to the reading public in large number. An extract from *Outlaws of the Marsh*, published in the early fourteenth century, starts our Sampler under the heading *Feudal Fiction*.

There was little change in Chinese social structure for

hundreds of years. It remained feudal, patriarchal, autocratic, inward-looking. But then in the twentieth century internal strife coupled with foreign invasion cracked the old complacent shell. War followed war — among regional tyrants scrambling for territory and power, against foreign exploiters, between the controlling dictatorial government and the people struggling for emancipation. It was inevitable that authors should use war as a background for many of their tales. From the thirties to the sixties, novels and short stories of this nature appeared in profusion.

Our next section is called, therefore, *War and Revolution*. It includes three short stories and three extracts from novels. The short stories by Mao Tun describe the impact of the Japanese invasion on differing individuals. Extracts from three novels were written against a background of three other types of warfare in three separate areas.

With old China crumbling all around them and the whole world in ferment, the Chinese people in the twentieth century were shaken out of their conviction that their hoary traditions were best. Resentment of feudal ways and feudal rulers had been brewing for many years, and at times burst forth in open opposition. The rebellion against what had been the accepted standards, and the search for fresh new approaches, both prior and after the establishment of the People's Republic, are reflected in Chinese fiction.

The third section of our Sampler is entitled *Transition*. Two short stories and extracts from two novels graphically demonstrate the intellectual complexities and ethical conflicts in an era of revolutionary China.

We end with a few satirical verses on domestic and international affairs composed between 1943 and 1960 by the master of that genre, Yuan Shuipo, better known as Ma Fan Tuo. They were included in his *Soy Sauce and Prawns*, published in 1962.

We hope, while demonstrating the variety of styles and the artistry of leading Chinese authors, to afford insights on the people and their society during three major periods of Chinese history.

Spelling, except for a few personal names too well-known to be changed, is in the *Hanyu pingyin* romanization adopted by the People's Republic of China.

FEUDAL FICTION

China's earliest major novels were created during her feudal era, which lasted roughly from the second century BC to well into the twentieth century. Feudalism was based on the control by a small landlord minority of the vast majority who tilled the soil in an agricultural society. In medieval China these were mainly tenants or serfs. The tenants, who had to pay the lion's share of the yield as rent, were compelled to borrow seed or food grain at exhorbitant interest from the landlords to tide them over after bad harvests. Usually, it was only a question of time before a crushing burden of debt reduced the tenant to serfdom or beggary, or forced him to sell his wife or his children.

This was the economic foundation of a political pyramid which extended upward through layers of bureaucratic officialdom, bolstered by armies and courts and police, all the way to the emperor. He was China's biggest landlord, since theoretically he owned all the land, run for him by sufference to lesser landlords.

He was also the infallible fountainhead of justice and wisdom, modestly known as the "Son of Heaven". Every few hundred years, when China slid into chaos, popular uprisings might remove a particular emperor, but only because he was deemed to have "lost Heaven's Mandate". Another emperor was quickly put in his place. Feudalism as an imperial political and social system was never questioned.

Prevailing religious beliefs and philosophic concepts praised submissiveness and respect for authority as the supreme virtues in a male chauvinist world. Women, at the bottom of the ladder, had to obey their husbands who took their orders from the local magistrates — euphemistically called "the parents of the people". The magistrates were under the command of the provincial governors who were ruled by the emperor. He had a direct pipeline to God — whose popular label was "the Old Lord of the Sky".

It was an autocratic, paternalistic society in which the average Chinese respected the traditional ethical values and was generally law-abiding. At the same time he recognized the venality of the bureaucracy and the corruption of the clergy, and harbored no illusions about many who called themselves his superiors. If they harried him beyond endurance, he might rationalize resistance or even crime, always in the name of upholding righteousness and opposing immorality.

China's creative writers were of course thoroughly saturated with the concepts and attitudes of feudal China. This is very evident in the extract from *Outlaws of the Marsh*, the most popular of the Ming novels, with which we start our Feudal Fiction section. A rip-roaring tale, even the violence and carnage of its protagonists are always presented as manifestations of the purest virtue.

Shi Nai'an (1293-1368) and Luo Guanzhong (1330-1400)

Shi Nai'an and Luo Guanzhong, Jiangsu province literati, are credited with having been the authors of Outlaws of the Marsh, *although there is some dispute over which of them wrote the novel and who made the additions and revisions. During the Ming and Ching dynasties it appeared in numerous editions ranging from seventy to 124 chapters, the denoument changing with the political temper of the ruling monarch. Arguments over the authorship and the authenticity and dates of the various editions continue to this day. The prevailing opinion is that Shi Nai'an and Luo Guanzhong should be credited with the original creation.*

During the final years of Song emperor Hui Zong, who reigned from 1101 to 1125, one hundred some-odd men and women fled persecution to band together on a marsh-girt mountain in what today is Shandong province. They became the leaders of an outlaw army of thousands and fought bold and resourceful battles against the powerful military forces of the corrupt ministers who, the outlaws alleged, were deceiving the emperor. While the outlaws used no-holds-barred tactics against the establishment, they ran their internal affairs in a strictly "correct" manner, and took a high moral benevolent tone in their relations with the local populace.

The trials and triumphs of these brigands became the fabric of one of the best-loved episodic thrillers of the professional story tellers, and their tale was polished and elevated into the 14th century Ming dynasty novel Outlaws of the Marsh. *Most of the events actually occurred, and most of the personae actually existed, although much liberty was taken by the authors.*

They committed many inaccuracies. Fourteenth century dress, weapons, government offices are superimposed on the twelfth. Some time sequences and place locations are wrong. The authors often put their native Jiangsu province colloquialisms in the mouths of Shandong province characters...

But this is of little consequence to any but the most nitpicking scholars, for the novel is intriguing and beautifully constructed. In spite of its enormous cast, the characters come across as distinct personalities, convincingly and in depth. The reader finds it difficult to remain objective and neutral as he becomes increasingly enmeshed in the complexities of Song dynasty society.

In many respects it was the most advanced society in the twelfth century world. China was already using inventions like gunpowder, the compass and movable type. Her great merchant ships plied trade routes between China and southeast Asia and northern Africa. The arts flourished. There was heavy commerce between the cities and the countryside.

But the court and the bureaucracy were corrupt. By the late twelfth century the empire was beginning to crumble, hammered by continuous attacks by tribal nations from the north. Internal disturbances gave rise to the formation of bandit gangs, such as the one described in our novel.

Outlaws of the Marsh *has fascinated Chinese readers, young and old, for six hundred years. It has been adapted for stage and screen, for television, for puppet theatre, for picture books. Children know the tales by heart. Commented upon by decades of literati, it has been frequently quoted by eminent personalities, including Mao Zedong. In Japan it has long been appreciated in translation, and has exercised a considerable cultural influence. A few translations are also available in English and in European languages. The one presented here is the first to have been done in China under the direct guidance of Chinese scholars.*

It was formed by adding the final 30 chapters of the 100 chapter version to the 70 chapter edition. In the original, each chapter is headed by a rhymed title, and concludes with a "cliff-hanger" ending. These we have kept. The headings also include introductory verse, which we have cut. Not only are they inferior doggerel, but they also reveal the denoument, thus ruining the suspense of the chapter which follows.

Our sample starts in the middle of Chapter Forty-Four. It tells how an encounter with a cuckolding wife and a lecherous monk sets a young man on the road to joining the rebels in a mountain fortress.

OUTLAWS OF THE MARSH

Elegant Panther Meets Dai Zong on a Path; Yang Xiong Meets Shi Xiu on an Avenue

Dai Zong, the Marvellous Traveller, a member of the famous rebel band on Mount Liangshan, has been sent down to look for another member, a Taoist known as Master Gongsun, who has unaccountably failed to return from a visit home. Dai meets Yang Lin, a young man called the Elegant Panther. Eager to join the band, Yang volunteers to help him look.

Travelling by day and resting at night, Dai Zong and Yang Lin soon reached the outskirts of Qizhou Town. There they put up at an inn.

"Brother," said Yang Lin, "Master Gongsun is a student of Taoism. He's probably in some mountain grove. He wouldn't live in town."

"You're right," Dai Zong agreed.

They walked around the outskirts of Qizhou, inquiring about Master Gongsun, but no one knew him. They went back to the inn. The next morning they tried more distant villages and market-places, again without any success. They returned to the inn once more.

"Could there be someone in town who knows him?" Dai Zong wondered on the third day.

He and Yang Lin went looking in Qizhou. Every reliable person they asked said, "Don't know him. Are you sure he lives in town? He's probably in some famous mountain monastery in an outlying county."

They came to a large street. Further down, muscians were welcoming an approaching man. Dai and Yang stopped to watch. First came two prison guards. One toted colorfully wrapped gifts. The other carried bolts of satin and brocade. Behind, shaded by a black silk umbrella, walked a prison executioner. A fine figure of a man, he wore a gown of embroidered blue indigo. His long eyebrows extended into his sideboards, his eyes turned up at the corners, his complexion was pale brown, and he had a whispy mustache. He was from the province of Henan, and his name was Yang Xiong. He had come to Qizhou with a paternal cousin who had been appointed prefect, and had remained ever since. The prefect who succeeded his cousin also knew him, and had made him warder of the town's two prisons, as well as the official executioner. Yang Xiong was a first-rate man with weapons, but his complexion was rather pale, and so he was nicknamed the Pallid.

To his rear another prison guard carried a sword with a demon's head hilt. They were returning from an execution, and friends, who had bedecked Yang Xiong with red ribbons and offered him their compliments, were seeing him home.

As the procession was passing Dai Zong and Yang Lin, a group of people, wine cups in hand, stopped it at an intersection. Seven or eight soldiers emerged from a side street, headed by a certain Zhang Bao, better known as Kick a Sheep to Death. He was part of the garrison guarding the town walls. His cronies were impoverished idlers from in and around the town who were always extorting money. Zhang had been reprimanded several times, but to no avail. It irked him that Yang Xiong, not a local man, should be feared and respected.

Now, seeing the Henanese showered with gifts, and himself backed by a gang of half-drunken knaves, he decided to vent his spleen. He pushed his way through the crowd of well-wishers at the intersection.

"My respects, Warden," he cried.

"Come and have a drink, brother," said Yang Xiong.

"It's not wine I want from you, but a hundred or so strings of cash!"

"Although I know you, brother, we've never had any financial dealings. How can you ask me for money?"

"You've squeezed plenty of riches out of the people today. Why not share some with me?"

"It's only that others wanted to give me a bit of face. I didn't squeeze anything. What are you trying to provoke? You're military and I'm civil administration. One has nothing to do with the other."

Zhang Bao did not reply, but called to his men, who rushed forward and seized the gifts and brocades. "Mannerless rogues," shouted Yang Xiong, incensed, advancing to intervene. Zhang Bao clutched him by the front of his robe, while two scamps grabbed his arms from behind. The mass attack was too much, and the guards turned and fled. Yang Xiong, held powerless, could only fume, unable to break free.

While all this turmoil was going on, a big fellow carrying a load of brushwood on a shoulder-pole approached. He saw the scoundrels holding Yang Xiong, and his sense of fairness was offended. He set down his load and pushed through the crowd.

"Why have you attacked the warden?" he demanded.

Zhang Bao glared. "Miserable wretch of a beggar, what business is it of yours?"

The big fellow was enraged. He lifted Zhang by the hair and flipped him to the ground. Before Zhang's ruffians could come to his defence, one punch apiece from the big fellow sent them reeling. Yang Xiong, freed, brought his own skill into play. His fists flew like shuttles, knocking rascals flat left and right. Things looked bad for Zhang Bao. He crawled to his feet and scooted. The furious Yang Xiong pursued with large strides, Zhang following the men who had snatched the bundles, Yang Xiong chasing after Zhang. They disappeared into a lane.

The big fellow was still slugging away at the intersection. Dai Zong and Yang Lin watched in admiration. "Quite a man," they said. "Truly, 'He sees injustice and leaps into the fray.'" They went up to him.

"Bold fighter," they urged, "for our sakes, desist." They hauled him into a lane, Yang Lin, carrying his brushwood, Dai Zong holding his arm and guiding him into a tavern. Yang Lin set down the load and followed them inside. The big fellow clasped his hands together gratefully.

"Thank you, brothers, for getting me out of that predicament."

"We two are strangers," said Dai Zong. "While we admired your gallantry, we were afraid you might hit someone too hard and kill him, so we pulled you away. Please have a few cups with us. Now that we've met, let's be friends."

"You not only help me, you invite me to wine. It's really too much."

"'Within the bounds of the four seas, all men are brothers. You mustn't speak like that," said Yang Lin. "Please be seated."

Dasi Zong urged him to sit at the head of the table, but the young fellow wouldn't consider it. Finally Dai Zong and Yang Lin sat there and their guest seated himself opposite. They summoned the waiter. Yang Lin gave him two pieces of silver.

"Never mind asking what we want. Just bring us anything that goes with wine, and put it all on one bill."

The waiter took the money and left. He returned with vegetable dishes and various tidbits to consume while drinking. The three men downed several cups.

"What is your name, sir? Where are you from?" asked Dai Zong.

"I'm called Shi Xiu. My home is the prefecture of Jiankang, in Jinling. Since childhood I've been fond of weapons. Whenever I see injustice I feel I must lend a hand, so I've been nicknamed the Rash. I was travelling with my uncle, who was selling sheep and horses, but he died on the road, and I soon lost our capital. I couldn't go home, and I remained here in Qizhou, selling brushwood for a living. Since you've honored me with your acquaintance, what I tell you is the absolute truth."

"A certain matter has brought us here," said Dai Zong, "and that has enabled us to meet you and witness your courage. But you'll never prosper, selling brushwood. Why not join the gallant fraternity, and be happy the rest of your days?"

"I have some skill with arms, nothing more. How can I aspire to happiness?"

"In these times it doesn't pay to be too proper. The addle-pated emperor is kept in the dark by corrupt officials. My understanding wasn't terribly clear, but on impulse I joined Song Jiang's band in Liangshan Marsh. Now we all get fair shares of gold and silver, and receive whole sets of clothing. Sooner or later the imperial court will declare a general amnesty and we'll all be given official posts."

Shi Xiu sighed. "I'd love to go, but I don't know how to get in."

"If you really would like to join, I could write you an introduction."

"May I have the temerity to ask you two gentlemen your names?"

"My name is Dai Zong, and this brother is called Yang Lin."

"Not Dai Zong the Marvellous Traveller, famed among bold men?"

"I am that humble person," Dai acknowledged. He told Yang Lin to take ten ounces of silver from the bundle and give to Shi Xiu for his business.

Shi Xiu had to be urged repeatedly before he would accept the money. Now that he knew who Dai Zong was, he was eager to talk about joining the band. But just then a search party was heard outside the tavern, making inquiries. Dai and other two looked. It was Yang Xiong and more than twenty policemen. They started coming in. Startled by the large number, Dai Zong and Yang Lin took advantage of the excitement to slip away.

Shi Xiu rose and greeted Yang Xiong. "Warden, where are you coming from?"

"I've been looking all over for you, brother, and you've been here drinking wine. Those oafs were holding my arms and I couldn't go into action until you rescued me. I ran after them to get my packages and had to leave you behind. When these brothers saw me pummelling them, they pitched in to help, and I got my gifts and brocades back. By the time I returned, you were gone. Someone said, 'A couple of travellers pressed him to drink with them, and so we've been searching taverns."

"They're from out of town, and they invited me to have a few cups. We were just chatting. I didn't know you were looking for me."

Yang Xiong was very pleased to have found Shi Xiu. "What is your name, sir?" he asked. "Where is your home, and what are you doing here?"

Shi Xiu related the same story he had told Dai Zong and Yang Lin.

"Where have the travellers gone?" asked Yang Xiong.

"They saw you coming in with a large party and thought there might be trouble, so they left."

Yang Xiong spoke to the policemen. "Let the waiter bring two jugs of wine and give each of your men three large bowlfuls. Then you can leave me here. I'll see you again tomorrow."

The men drank and departed. Yang Xiong turned to Shi Xiu.

"You mustn't treat me like a stranger. I imagine you have no relatives here. Let's pledge each other blood brothers. What do you say?"

Shi Xiu was delighted. "May I ask your age, Warden?"

"Twenty-nine."

"I am twenty-eight. Please be seated and accept my kowtows as your younger brother."

Shi Xiu kowtowed four times. Yang Xiong was very pleased. He instructed the waiter to bring wine and tidbits and said to Shi Xiu, "Today we must drink till we're good and soused."

While they were indulging, Yang Xiong's father-in-law, Master Pan, entered with half a dozen men. Yang Xiong rose.

"What are you doing here, father-in-law?"

"I heard that you were in a fight, and came to help."

"Thanks to this brother, I was rescued. He gave Zhang Bao such a drubbing that the rogue's afraid of his shadow. Shi Xiu and I have pledged each other blood brothers."

"Fine. Excellent. Give these brothers who've come with me some wine."

Yang Xiong ordered the waiter to serve them three bowls each. The men drank and left. Yang then asked his father-in-law to be seated at the side of the table. He himself sat at the head, with Shi Xiu opposite. The waiter poured the wine. Pan saw what a big, heroic type Shi Xiu was, and he liked his looks.

"My son-in-law won't go wrong with you two helping each other," he said. "No one will dare pick on him now as he goes about his official duties." And he asked, "What is your line of business?"

"My father was a butcher."

"Do you know how to slaughter?

Shi Xiu laughed. "Of course. I was raised in a butcher's family."

"I used to be one, myself, but I'm too old. I've only this one son-in-law, and he's an official. So I've had to give it up."

The three drank until they were mellow, then had the bill added. Shi Xiu gave the tavern the brushwood to cover the wine bill. All went home with Yang Xiong.

"Wife," he called, when they entered the door, "come and meet your young brother-in-law."

From behind the portiere a voice retorted, "Since when have you had a younger brother?"

"Don't ask. Just come out."

The door curtain was raised and a young woman emerged. She had been born on the seventh day of the seventh month, and she was called Clever Cloud. Formerly she had been married to a petty official in Qizhou Prefecture named Wang. After two years, he died, and she married Yang Xiong. They had been husband and wife for less than a year. Shi Xiu hailed her respectfully.

"Sister-in-law, please be seated." He dropped to his knees to kowtow.

"I'm much too young," Clever Cloud protested. "How can I accept your courtesy?"

"I've acknowledged him my blood brother, today," said Yang. "That makes you his sister-in-law. You may receive half the full obeisance."

Like pushing a golden mountain, like a falling pillar of jade, Shi Xiu kowtowed four times. The young woman returned him two curtsies. He was invited into the parlor while a room was prepared, after which he was urged to rest. But enough of idle chatter.

The next day, as Yang was leaving for his office, he instructed his household, "Have clothes and headgear made for Shi Xiu." He also told them to fetch his guest's luggage and bundles from the inn.

As to Dai Zong and Yang Lin, on leaving the tavern they returned to their inn outside the town and rested, continuing their search for Gongsun the following morning. But in the two succeeding days they met no one who knew him, nor had they the slightest clue as to where he had gone. After talking it over, they packed their luggage and left Qizhou for Horse Watering Valley. There they rejoined Pei Xuan, Deng Fei and Meng Kang who had volunteered to take their band of five hundred brigands and three hundred horses and join the outlaws on Mount Liangshan. All disguised themselves as government officers and set out for the stronghold that same night.

Dai Zong made an impressive contribution, bringing such a

large force of men and horses to the mountain. A feast was laid in celebration. Of that we'll say no more.

Master Pan offered Shi Xiu a proposition. He said, "At the rear of a dead-end lane behind our house we have an empty building. There's well water conveniently at hand. It would make a good butcher shop and you could live there and look after everything."

Shi Xiu inspected the place. It was indeed an ideal spot. Pan found an old skilled assistant of his to do the heavy work. He said Shi need only keep the accounts. The young man agreed. He had the assistant decorate the tables, the tubs and the chopping blocks in black and green, sharpen all the knives and arrange the counters. Shi Xiu put the pig pens in order and drove in a dozen fat swine. On an auspicious day, he formally opened the shop. Neighbors and relatives arrived to offer congratulations and hang streamers of red. This was followed by two days of festive drinking.

Yang Xiong and his family were happy to have Shi Xiu running the shop. Of this, there's nothing much to be told. Pan and Shi did the buying and selling, and time passed quickly. Soon, two months had gone by. It was late autumn and the beginning of winter. Shi Xiu changed into brand new clothing, inside and out.

One morning, he rose at the fifth watch and went to another county to buy hogs. (*The night is divided into five watches of two hours each, starting at 7 in the evening. The "fifth watch", from 3 to 5 in the morning, means around dawn.*) Returning three days later, he found the shop closed and the chopping blocks and knives all put away. Shi Xiu had a subtle mind. He was a man who kept his own counsel.

"As the old saying goes: 'Good times don't last forever, all flowers fade,'" he thought. "Brother is often away on official business and doesn't bother about home affairs. Seeing that I've bought new clothes, sister-in-law must be saying things behind my back. And certain persons are sure to be spreading stories about me because I've been gone a couple of days. They're suspicious of me, so they've closed the shop. Why should I wait for them to say it openly? I'll just resign and go home. As the old saying goes: 'Who wants to do the same things all his life?'"

He drove the hogs into the pens, changed his clothes, packed his belongings, wrote out a detailed account, and entered the family house through the rear door. Master Pan had laid out a modest repast. He invited Shi to sit down and drink.

"You've had a long, hard trip, bringing in those hogs," said Pan.

"I did no more than my duty, old sir. Here are my accounts. May

Heaven strike me dead if I've kept a penny for myself."

"What kind of talk is this? There's no question about it."

"I've been away from home for six or seven years. It's time I went back. I'm handing in my accounts. Tonight, I'll take leave of brother and tomorrow morning I'll depart."

The old man laughed. "You've misunderstood. You must stay on. Let me explain."

Pan spoke only a few words. And as a result, in gratitude to his benefactor, a warrior with his three-foot blade dispatched a wicked monk to the depths of Hell.

What were the words which Master Pan spoke to Shi Xiu? Read our next chapter if you would know.

Yang Xiong, Drunk, Berates Clever Cloud; Shi Xiu, Shrewdly, Kills Pei Ruhai

"I know what you're thinking," said Master Pan. "You come home after an absence of two days and find that all the butcher's implements have been put away. Of course you assume we've closed down, and so you want to go. Even if our business wasn't as good as it is now, even if we really did close down, we'd still keep you in our home. The fact of the matter is this: Today is the second anniversary of the death of Wang the Scribe, my daughter's first husband. We're going to have some prayers said for him, that's why we shut the shop for a couple of days. We've asked monks to come tomorrow from the Grateful Retribution Monastery to conduct a service and we'd like you to look after it. I'm too old to stay up all night. I thought I'd talk to you about it, first."

"In view of what you've said, old sir, I'm willing to remain a while longer."

"Don't let your imagination run away with you in the future. Just do what's proper according to your station."

They drank several cups of wine and ate a few vegetables dishes, and that was the end of it. (*Devout Buddhists are vegetarians.*)

The next morning lay brothers arrived bearing scriptures, and set the scene for the ceremony. They installed idols and sacrificial implements; drums, gongs, bells and chimes; incense, flowers, lamps and candles. In the kitchen, meatless dishes were prepared.

Yang Xiong came home late in the afternoon. "I'm on duty at the prison tonight," he said to Shi Xiu. "I can't be here. May I trouble you, brother, to take care of matters?"

"Don't give it a thought. I'll keep an eye on things for you."

Yang Xiong departed, and Shi Xiu posted himself at the front door. Just as dawn was breaking the following day, a young monk pushed aside the gate screen and entered the courtyard. Palms piously together in the Buddhist fashion, he bowed deeply to Shi Xiu, who returned the courtesy.

"Please be seated, Reverend."

A lay brother carrying two boxes on the ends of a shoulder-pole had come in behind the monk.

"Old sir," Shi Xiu called, "there's a monk here to see you."

Master Pan emerged and the monk hailed him: "Godfather, why haven't we seen you at our monastery?"

"I haven't had time since opening this shop."

"I've brought some paltry gifts to commemorate the scribe's passing away. Just some noodles and a few packets of dates."

"*Aiya*, Reverand, there's no need for you to spend any money," said the old man. But he said to Shi Xiu, "Please take them for me."

Shi Xiu carried the packages inside. He instructed a servant to bring tea and serve it to the monk.

Meanwhile, the girl came downstairs. She wore only light mourning attire and make-up, since more would not be appropriate to a woman who had remarried.

"Who are the gifts from?" she asked Shi Xiu.

"A monk who calls your father 'godfather'."

The girl smiled. "That must be Pei Ruhai, who's known as the Preceptor, a very honest monk. He used to run his family's silk-thread shop before he joined the order in the Grateful Retribution Monastery. Because his superior is a secular prelate, Ruhai is able to call my father godfather. He's just two years older than me. I call him my reverend brother. His name in the order is Master Hai. Wait till you hear him chant tonight. He has a beautiful voice."

"So that's how it is," Shi Xiu thought. He already had a one-tenth inkling of what was brewing.

She went out to meet the monk. His hands clasped behind his back, Shi Xiu followed as far as the door and watched them from behind the curtain. The monk rose when the girl emerged, placed his palms together and bowed.

"You had no right to spend money on presents," she said.

"They're only small things, sister. Not worth mentioning."

"How can you say that? We shouldn't take gifts from a man who's renounced the world."

"We've built a new Hall for the Spirits of the Departed on Land and Sea. We wish you would honor us with a visit and look it over. But perhaps the warden would disapprove."

"He's not so petty. When my mother was dying I promised to have prayers offered for those who died in childbirth. I've been meaning to go to your temple and trouble you to have this done."

"But such prayers are my duty. No trouble at all. Whatever you wish me to do, you've only to ask."

"Then please chant a few scriptures for my mother."

A little maid served tea. Clever Cloud wiped the rim of a cup with her handkerchief, then proffered it respectfully in both hands to the young monk. He started boldly and greedily into her eyes, and she gazed back at him, smiling.

"Lust engenders boundless audacity," as the saying goes. Shi Xiu observed all this from behind the door curtain. By now he had guessed two-tenths. "'Believe not that in straightforwardness there is only honesty. Beware, rather that evil lurks beneath the guise of virtue,'" he said to himself. "That girl has dropped me hints several times, but I've treated her strictly as a sister-in-law. So that's the kind of a wench she is! If I catch her, don't think I won't act on Yang Xiong's behalf!"

He thought about it, three-tenths sure. He raised the door curtain and went outside. The monk hastily set down his teacup and addressed him.

"Sir, please be seated."

"This brother-in-law is a new blood brother of my husband," the girl explained.

"Where are you from, sir?" the monk queried with polite gravity. "What is your name?"

"Shi Xiu, from Jinling," was the curt reply. "Because I fight injustice, even when it's no affair of mine, I'm known as the Rash. I'm a crude fellow without any manners. Forgive me."

"Not at all, not at all! I must fetch some more monks for the ceremony," the young man said hastily. He headed for the gate.

"Come back soon, reverend brother," the girl called.

He hurried away without reply. The girl saw him as far as the gate, then returned to the house. Shi Xiu stood outside the door, his head bent in thought. He was by this time four-tenths sure.

Later, a beadle came and lit the candles and the incense. Shortly after, Hai the Preceptor returned with several monks. Master Pan asked Shi Xiu to receive them. After they drank their tea, they began beating drums and gongs and singing verses in praise of the departed. Hai and another young monk conducted the ritual — ringing bells, burning prayers to the gods (*smoke from the burnt paper wafts the prayers to Heaven*), offering sacrificial food to the Defenders of Heaven and Chief Watcher of the Celestial Altar, entreating that the spirit of the departed Wang the Scribe be allowed to enter Heaven soon.

The girl Clever Cloud, simply adorned, entered the garden. She lit a stick of incense, inserted it in a small burner which she held in her hands, and prayed before the idol of Buddha. This aroused Hai the Preceptor to greater fervor. He rang his bells and gave full vent to his voice. The sight of the luscious Clever Cloud, piously undulating, caused the other monks to reel and stagger.

When the prayers of entreaty for the dead ended, the monks were invited inside for a meal. Hai sat behind the others. He turned his head, looked at the girl and smiled. She put her hand over her mouth to smother a laugh. Their eyes exchanged loving glances.

Shi Xiu observed it all. He was five-tenths annoyed. The monks were each served a few cups of wine before their vegetarian meal, and were given some money. Master Pan said he was weary, and retired. When they had finished eating, the monks went out for a stroll to aid digestion, then returned to the ceremonial arena. Shi Xiu's irritation had reached six-tenths. Claiming to have a stomach ache, he lay down in a room behind the partition wall.

Clever Cloud, her passions stirred, didn't care whether anyone was watching her or not. She brought tea and fruit and cakes to the monks, who were once again beating drums and gongs. Hai abjured them to concentrate on their prayers and supplications. The ritual continued. By midnight the other monks were exhausted, but Hai was only getting into stride. He chanted loud and clear. Clever Cloud, who had been standing for a long time by the door curtain, was inflamed with desire. She instructed the little maid to tell Reverend Brother Hai she wished to speak to him. The scoundrel hastened over. She put her hand on his sleeve.

"When you come for the memorial service money tomorrow you can talk to papa about those prayers for mama. Don't forget."

"I won't. I'll say: 'If we're to fulfil her wish, we should do it promptly,' said the young monk. And he added: "That brother-in-law of yours looks tough."

The girl tossed her head. "Don't pay any attention to him. He's not a real relative."

"I won't worry, then," said Hai. He slipped his fingers inside the girl's sleeve and squeezed her hand.

She made a pretense of pulling the door curtain between them. That rogue of a shaven-pate grinned and went off to continue his prayers for the dead.

Shi Xiu, feigning sleep behind the partition, had missed none of this. He was seven-tenths positive. The ceremony ended at the fifth watch. After the idol was removed and the paper money burned (*paper replicas of gold or silver ingots designed to provide spending money for the deceased*), the monks thanked their hosts and departed, and clever Cloud went upstairs to bed.

"Brother Yang Xiong is chivalrous, but that wife is a sexy bitch," Shi Xiu said to himself indignantly. Repressing his anger, he went to sleep in the butcher shop.

The next day Yang Xiong came home, but Shi Xiu didn't say a word. After eating, Yang again left and Hai the Preceptor, wearing a fresh cassock, returned once more. On hearing of his arrival, the girl quickly descended the stairs. She hurried out to greet him, invited him into the house and ordered tea.

"You must be exhausted from all those ceremonies last night, reverend brother," said the girl. "And we still haven't paid."

"Not worth mentioning. I've come about those prayers your mother wanted read. Just write out what you want me to say and I'll include it while reciting scriptures at the monastery."

"Excellent," said Clever Cloud. She told the little maid to ask her father to join them.

Master Pan entered and thanked the monk. "I couldn't stay up so late last night, and had to leave you," he said apologetically. "I didn't expect Shi Xiu to develop a stomach ache. You were left with no one to look after you. I'm very sorry."

"Think nothing of it, godfather."

The girl said: "I want to fulfil mama's wish to have prayers said for women who died in childbirth. Reverend brother says he can include them in the scriptures which will be chanted in the monastery temple tomorrow. I suggest he go back now, and tomorrow, after breakfast, you and I will visit the temple and attend the prayers. We'll have done our duty."

"All right," said Master Pan. "But I'm afraid we'll be busy at the butcher shop tomorrow, with no one to handle the money."

"You've got Shi Xiu. What's there to worry about?"

"Your wish is my desire, daughter. Tomorrow we'll go."

Clever Cloud gave Hai some silver and said: "Please don't scorn this as too small. Perhaps you'll have some meatless noodles for us when we call at your monastery tomorrow."

"I shall respectfully await your coming to burn incense." Hai stood up. "Many thanks. I'll divide this money among the other monks and look forward to your visit."

The girl saw him off to the outside of the gate.

Shi Xiu, in the butcher shop, rose and slaughtered hogs and attended to business. That evening, Yang Xiong returned. When he had finished supper and washed his feet and hands, the girl had her father speak to him.

"When my wife was dying," Master Pan said, "my daughter promised her to have prayers said at the Grateful Retribution Monastery for women who died in childbirth. I'm going there with Clever Cloud tomorrow to see it done. I thought I'd let you know."

Yang said to the girl: "You could have spoken to me about this directly."

"I didn't dare. I was afraid you'd be angry."

Nothing more was said that night, and all retired. The next day at the fifth watch Yang got up and went to sign in at the office and commence his duties. Shi Xiu also rose and set about his butcher shop business.

The girl, when she awakened, made herself up seductively and put on her prettiest clothes. Carrying an incense burner, she bought some paper money and candles and hired a sedan-chair. Shi Xiu was busy in the shop and didn't pay much attention.

After breakfast, Clever Cloud dressed up Ying'er, the little maid. At mid-morning Master Pan changed his clothes. He went over to Shi Xiu.

"Can I trouble you to keep an eye on our door? I'm going with my daughter to fulfil a prayer wish at a temple. We'll be back later."

Shi Xiu smiled. "I'll look after the house, you look after sister-in-law. Burn plenty of incense and return soon." He was eight-tenths sure.

Master Pan and Ying'er walked along with the sedan-chair as it proceeded to the Grateful Retribution Monastery. It was solely because of Clever Cloud that Hai the Preceptor, that sneaky shaven-pate, had adopted Master Pan as his godfather. But due to Yang Xiong's vigilant eye, he had been unable to get to her. Although he and the girl had been exchanging languishing glances ever since she became his adopted "sister", it hadn't gone beyond that. Only the night of the memorial service did he feel he was beginning to get somewhere. The date for their meeting had been fixed and the tricky shaven-pate had, so to speak, sharpened his weapons and girded his loins.

When his visitors arrived he was waiting outside the mountain gate. Beside himself with joy at the sight of the sedan chair, he came forward to greet them.

"I'm afraid we're imposing on you," said Master Pan.

Clever Cloud, as she stepped down from her sedan-chair, said: "Thank you so much for your trouble."

"Not at all," replied Hai. "I've been reciting scriptures with the other monks in the Land and Sea Hall since the fifth watch without a break. We've been waiting for you, sister, so that we could burn the prayers. It will be a virtuous deed."

He escorted the girl and her father into the hall. Incense and candles and other such paraphernalia had been prepared, and the monks were busy at their scriptures. Clever Cloud curtsied to them in greeting and paid homage to the Three Treasures — the Buddha, his teachings, and their propagators. The wicked shaven-pate led her before the idol of the God of the Nether Regions, where she burned the prayers for her departed spouse. Paper money was then also burned, after which the monks were given a vegetarian meal, paid for by Clever Cloud.

Hai summoned a couple of novices to act as servants and asked Master Pan and Clever Cloud to his own apartment to dine. He lived deep within the monks quarters. Everything was ready.

"Bring tea, brothers," he called when they entered his rooms. Two novices served tea in snow-white cups on a vermillion colored tray. The leaves were delicate and fine.

After they finished drinking he said: "Please come and sit inside, sister." He led the girl and her father to a small inner chamber containing a gleaming black lacquer table and, on the walls, several paintings by famous artists. On a little stand fragrant incense was burning. Master Pan and his daughter sat at one end of the table, Hai at the other. Ying'er stood to one side.

"Ideal quarters for a man who's renounced the world," the girl commended. "So quiet and peaceful."

"You're making fun of me, sister. How can it compare with your fine home?"

"We've wearied you all day," said Master Pan. "We must be getting back."

The monk wouldn't hear of it. "Godfather, it hasn't been easy to get you here, and we're not exactly strangers," he said. "The simple meal I'm offering has already been paid for by sister. Have some noodles before you go. Brothers, hurry with that food!"

Before the word were out of his mouth, two platters were brought in laden with rare fruits, unusual vegetables and all sorts of tidbits, and placed on the table.

"What a spread," the girl exclaimed. "We're being too much of a nuisance."

The monk smiled. "It doesn't amount to anything. Just a small token of my esteem."

The novices poured the wine and Hai said: "You haven't been here for a long time, godfather. You must try this."

Master Pan sipped. "Excellent. A very strong bouquet."

"One of our patrons taught us how to make it. We've put to brew four or five bushels of rice. When they're ready we'll send your son-in-law a few bottles."

"You mustn't do that."

"I've nothing really suitable to offer. Sister, at least have a cup of this wine."

The novices kept filling the cups. Hai also pressed Ying'er to down a few.

"That's enough for me," said Clever Cloud finally. "I can't drink any more."

"You come so seldom," said Hai. "You must have one more."

Master Pan called the sedan-chair carriers and gave them each a cup of wine.

"Don't worry about them," said the monk. "I've already ordered that places be laid for them outside for wine and noodles. Relax and enjoy yourself, godfather. Have some more wine."

As part of his scheme to get the girl, the wicked shaven-pate had served a wine that was particularly good and potent. It was too much for Master Pan. A few more cups and he was drunk.

"Put him to bed and let him sleep it off," Hai instructed the two novices. They supported him to a cool, quiet room and made him comfortable.

"Have no fears, sister," the monk urged Clever Cloud. "Another cup of wine."

The girl was willing enough, and the wine was stirring her senses. "Why do you want me to drink so much?" she asked huskily.

In a low voice the monk replied: "Only because I think so well of you."

"I've had enough," the girl said.

"If you'll come to my room I'll show you Buddha's tooth."

"That's why I'm here, to see Buddha's tooth."

Hai took Clever Cloud upstairs to his bedroom. It was very neat and clean. The girl was half enchanted already.

"How nice. You certainly keep it spic and span."

The monk laughed. "All that's missing is a wife."

Clever Cloud smiled. "Why don't you choose one?"

"Where could I find such a patroness?"

"You promised to show me Buddha's tooth."

"Send Ying'er away and I'll take it out."

"Go and see whether father is still drunk," Clever Cloud said to the little maid. Ying'er went downstairs to Master Pan. Hai closed the door at the head of the stairs and bolted it. The girl laughed.

"Why are you locking me in?"

Lust surged up in the wicked shaven-pate, and he threw his arms around her.

"I love you. For two years I've been racking my brains how to get you, and today you're here at last. This chance is too good to miss."

"My husband is a hard man. Do you want to ruin me? If he ever finds out, he won't spare you."

The monk knelt at her feet. "I don't care. Only have pity on me."

"Naughty monk." The girl raised her hand. "You know how to pester people. I'll box your ears."

Hai chuckled."Hit me all you like. I'm only afraid you'll hurt your hand."

Inflamed with passion, Clever Cloud embraced him. "You don't think I'd really hit you?" she murmured.

He picked her up and carried her to the bed. Then he disrobed her and had his heart's desire. Only after a long time did the clouds expend their rain.

Holding the girl in his arms the monk said: "As long as you love me, though I die for it I won't care. The only flaw is that while today you're mine, our joy is quickly past. We can't revel all night together. Long waits between meetings is going to kill me."

"Calm yourself," said Clever Cloud. "I've thought of a plan. My husband is on duty at the prison twenty nights out of the month. I can buy Ying'er's co-operation. I'll have her watch at the rear gate every night. If my husband isn't home, she'll put a stand with burning incense outside. That will mean you can come. Find a friar to beat on a wooden fish at the fifth watch near our rear gate as if summoning the faithful to prayer. Then you won't oversleep and will be able to slip away. The friar can both keep watch and see to it that you're gone before dawn."

The monk was delighted. "Very clever. Take care of your end. I have just the man. He's a mendicant friar called Friar Hu. He'll do whatever I tell him."

"I'd better not stay too long, or those oafs will get suspicious. I must go home at once. Don't miss our next appointment."

The girl got up, straightened her hair, re-applied make-up, opened the stairway door and went down. She told Ying'er to awaken Master Pan, and quickly left the monks' living quarters. The sedan-chair carriers had finished their noodles and wine and were waiting at the monastery entrance. Hai the Preceptor escorted them as far as the mountain pass, where Clever Cloud bid him farewell and mounted the sedan-chair. With Master Pan and Ying'er she returned home.

Of that we'll say no more.

Hu had formerly worked in the monks' quarters, but he had retired and now lived in a little temple behind the monastery. He was known as Friar Hu because he rose at the fifth watch every day and beat on a wooden fish to announce the coming of dawn and urge the Buddhist faithful to prayer. After daybreak he would beg alms for food. Hai summoned him to the monks' quarters, treated him to three cups of good wine, and presented him with some silver.

Hu stood up and said: "I've done nothing to merit this. How can I accept? You're always so kind to me."

"I know what an honest fellow you are. One of these days I'm going to purchase a religious certificate for you and have you accepted into our order. This silver is just to let you buy yourself new clothes."

Hai the Preceptor frequently instructed his monks to send Hu lunch. Or to include him when they went out to perform a religious service, so that he could also receive a small fee. Hu was very grateful.

"He's given me money once again," thought Hu. "He must have some need of me. Why should I wait for him to bring it up?" And he said: "If there's anything you want, I'd be glad to do it."

"Since you're good enough to put it that way, I'll tell you the truth. Master Pan's daughter is willing to be intimate with me. She's going to have an incense stand put up outside her rear gate whenever it's safe for me to call. It wouldn't be wise for me to check, but it doesn't matter if you go and have a look. Then I can risk it. Also I'd like to trouble you, when you're calling people to prayers near dawn, to come to her rear gate. If there's no one around, bang on your wooden fish and loudly summon the faithful, and I'll know I can leave."

"Nothing hard about that," said Friar Hu. He fully assented.

The next day he went begging alms at Master Pan's rear gate. Ying'er came out and said: "What are you doing here? Why don't you do your begging at the front gate?"

He began chanting prayers. Clever Cloud heard him and came to the rear gate. "Aren't you the friar who heralds the dawn at the fifth watch?" she asked.

"That I am. I tell folks not to sleep too much and to burn incense in the night, so as to please the gods."

The girl was delighted. She instructed Ying'er to run upstairs and get a string of coppers for the friar. When the little maid had gone, Friar Hu said: "I'm a trusted man of Teacher Hai. He's sent me to get the lay of the land."

"I know about him. Come tonight. If there's an incense stand outside, tell him."

Hu nodded. Ying'er returned with the copper coins and gave them to him. The girl went upstairs and confided in Ying'er. The little maid saw this as a chance to gain some advantage, and was glad to help.

That day Yang Xiong was on duty at the prison. Before evening, he left with his quilt. Ying'er, who had already received a small emolument, couldn't wait till nightfall, and put the incense stand out while it was still dusk. Clever Cloud hurried to the rear gate and waited. Around the first watch a man, his head bound by a kerchief, suddenly appeared.

Startled, Ying'er called out: "Who's there?"

The man did not reply. Clever Cloud reached out and yanked off the kerchief, revealing a shaven pate. She cursed him fondly.

"Wicked baldy. You really know what you're about."

Arms around each other, they went up the stairs. Ying'er took in the incense stand, bolted the gate and went to bed.

That night the two lovers were as close as glue and turpentine, sugar and honey, marrow and bone juice, fish and water, indulging merrily in licentious pleasure. Just as they were falling asleep, they heard the rap-rap-rap of a wooden fish and a voice loudly calling believers to prayer. The monk and the girl were instantly wide awake. Hai the Preceptor threw on his clothes.

"I'm going. See you tomorrow."

"Come whenever the incense stand is outside. If it's not there, stay away."

The girl tied the bandanna round his head. Ying'er opened the rear gate and let him out.

From then on, Yang Xiong had only to be on duty at the prison, and the monk came. Master Pan was at home, but he went to bed early. Ying'er was part of the conspiracy. There remained Shi Xiu to be deceived, but by then the girl was so intoxicated with sex she didn't care. As for the monk, from the time he began savoring the charms of Clever Cloud, his very soul seemed to have been snatched away. The moment the friar reported that the coast was clear, the monk would leave the monastery. With the collusion of Ying'er, Clever Cloud would let him in. Joyous love-play went on in this manner for more than a month.

Shi Xiu every evening, after cleaning up the butcher shop, retired to an adjacent room. The problem of Yang Xiong's wife was still troubling him, but he had no proof. He hadn't seen any signs of the monk. When he awakened at the fifth watch each morning he would sometimes jump up and peer outside. There was only a friar in the lane herarlding the dawn by beating on a wooden fish and shouting a call to prayers.

Young Shi Xiu was clever. Already nine-tenths sure, he analyzed the phenomenon coolly. "This lane is a dead-end with no other families," he mused. "Why should a friar come here, of all places, to summon people to prayer? He's definitely up to something."

It was then the middle of the eleventh month. One morning, when Shi Xiu woke as usual at the fifth watch, he again heard the friar beating on the wooden fish as he entered the lane. At the rear gate of the house the friar shouted: "May the gods save all living things from misery and hardship."

Shi Xiu hopped out of bed and glued his eye to a crack in the door. A man with a kerchief binding his head slipped out of the shadows and departed with the friar, after which Ying'er closed the gate. Shi Xiu now had the whole picture.

"Brother Yang Xiong is chivalrous, but he's picked himself a wanton for a wife," he thought angrily. "He's completely deceived, and she's playing her own little game."

At daybreak he hung the hog carcasses in the shop and commenced serving the early morning customers. After breakfast he went out to collect some accounts. He headed for the prefectural office at noon to see Yang Xiong, and met him coming over the bridge.

"What brings you here, brother?" asked the warden.

"I've been collecting accounts in the neighborhood. I thought I'd drop by."

"I'm always so tied up on official business, I seldom have time to drink with you and relax. Let's go and sit down for a while."

Yang Xiong took him to a tavern, chose a secluded room upstairs and told the waiter to bring good wine and some fresh tidbits. They downed three cups. Shi Xiu sat with lowered head, deep in thought. Yang Xiong was an impetuous man.

"You're unhappy about something," he asserted. "Has anyone at home said anything to offend you?"

"No, it's not that. I'm grateful to you, brother. You've treated me like your own flesh and blood. I've something to tell you, but I don't know whether I dare."

"How can you act as if I were a stranger? Whatever it is, speak out."

"When you leave the house every day, your whole mind is on your official duties. You don't know what's happening behind your back. Sister-in-law isn't a good person. I've noticed signs of it several times, but I didn't dare tell you. Today it was so obvious I had to come and speak frankly."

"I haven't got eyes in the back of my head. Who is the man?"

"When you had the memorial service at home, Hai the Preceptor, that knave of a bald-pate, was asked to officiate. I saw him and sister-in-law making eyes at each other. Two days later, she and her father went to the monastery temple to hear the prayers her mother wanted said, and they both came home smelling of wine. Lately, I've been hearing a friar beating a wooden fish and calling people to prayer in our lane. I thought there was something peculiar about the villain, and this morning I got up at the fifth watch to have a look. Sure enough, there was the scoundrelly bald-pate, a bandanna over his head, coming out of the house. A hussy like that, what do you need her for!"

Yang Xiong was furious. "The bitch. How dare she!"

"Control yourself, brother. Don't say anything tonight. Just behave as usual. Tomorrow, say you're on duty, but come back at the third watch and knock at the front gate. The knave is sure to sneak out the back. I'll be there to catch him, and then you can dispose of him."

"A good idea."

"Be careful what you say tonight."

"I'll meet you there tomorrow, then."

The two drank a few more cups, paid the bill, went downstairs, left the tavern and prepared to go their separate ways.

Four or five captains hailed Yang Xiong. "We've been looking all over for you, Warden. The prefect is waiting in his garden. He wants you to joust with us with staves. Come on, hurry it up."

"The prefect wants me. I'll have to go," Yang said to Shi Xiu. "You go back first."

Shi Xiu returned home, put the butcher shop in order, and retired to his room.

Yang Xiong went to the rear garden of the prefect and fought a few demonstration rounds with staves. Mightily pleased, the official rewarded him with ten beakers of wine. When the gathering broke up, the others invited Yang out for more imbibing. By evening he was very drunk and had to be supported home.

Clever Cloud thanked his escort. She and Ying'er helped him up the stairs, lit a lamp and turned it on brightly. Yang sat on the bed as the little maid removed his padded shoes and his wife took off his bandanna and cap. The sight of her reaching for the head covering stirred a surge of rage within him. "Sober thoughts become drunken words," as the old saying goes. He pointed at her and cursed:

"Baggage! Strumpet! I'm going to finish you off, come what may!"

The girl was too frightened to reply. She eased Yang down on the bed. He fell asleep the moment his head touched the pillow, but he continued muttering. "Wretch. Dirty whore. Your lover dares to spit in the tiger's mouth. You... You... You'll pay for this!"

Clever Cloud didn't dare breathe. She stayed with him while he slept. At the fifth watch he awoke and asked for a drink of water. She scooped up a bowlful and gave it to him. The lamp was still burning on the table. Yang drank.

"Why haven't you undressed and come to bed?"

"You were stinking drunk. I was afraid you'd want to vomit. How could I take off my clothes? I lay at the food of the bed all night."

"Did I say anything?"

"You're not bad when you're drunk. You only go to sleep. But I couldn't help worrying about you during the night."

"We haven't had brother Shi Xiu in for drinks in some time. Prepare a few things at home and I'll invite him."

Clever Cloud did not reply. She remained seated on the step of the bed, her eyes swimming with tears. She sighed.

"I was drunk last night, wife, but I didn't give you any trouble. Why are you so upset?"

The girl put her hands over her tear-filled eyes. Yang pressed her for an answer. Clever Cloud, covering her face, pretended to weep. Yang raised her from the step to the bed, insisting that she speak.

"When my parents gave me in marriage to Wang the Scribe I hoped it would be for life. Who expected him to die so soon?" she sobbed. "Now I'm married to you, a chivalrous, bold hero, and you don't even protect me."

"This is crazy. What do you mean I don't protect you? Who's picking on you?"

"At first I wasn't going to say anything, but I'm afraid you'll be taken in by him. I've been wanting to tell you, but I'm also afraid you'll swallow it and not do anything."

"What the devil are you talking about?"

"I'll tell you. But promise me you won't be too hurt. For a while, after you brought Shi Xiu home and recognized him as a blood brother, everything was all right. But later, he began dropping hints. The nights you were on duty he would say: 'Brother's not coming home again. Won't you be lonely, sleeping by yourself? I ignored him, though he made such remarks more than once. But never mind about that. Yesterday morning, I was in the kitchen washing my neck when that rogue came up behind me. Seeing that there was no one around, he slipped his hand under and fondled my breasts. He said 'Sister-in-law, are you pregnant? I pushed his hand away. I was going to yell, but I was afraid the neighbors would laugh and mock you. Then, back you came, soaked to the gills. How could I speak? I hate him so I could tear him apart with my teeth, and you ask sweetly after 'brother Shi Xiu'!"

Yang was consumed with rage. "'A tiger's picture shows its pelt but not its bones; you can know a man's face but not his heart! That villain had the nerve to come to me with a lot of stories about Hai the Preceptor, and all the while there was nothing to it! The lout is scared. His idea was to smear you before you could speak!"

Angrily, Yang said to himself: "He's not my real brother. I'll drive him away, and that'll be the end of it."

At daylight he went downstairs and spoke to his father-in-law. "Salt the animals that are already slaughtered. From today on, we won't do any more of this business," he said. He smashed the counters and tables in the butcher shop.

Shi Xiu, when he was bringing out meat to hang at the front of the door and open the shop, saw the wreckage. A shrewd fellow, he understood at once. He smiled.

"Of course. Yang got drunk and let the cat out of the bag. His wife turned the tables by accusing me of getting fresh, and got him to close the shop. If I argue, it will only be washing Yang's dirty linen in public. I'd better retreat a step and try to think of another plan."

He went in and collected his belongings. Yang Xiong, not wanting to embarrass him, left first. Carrying his bundle, his dagger at his waist, Shi Xiu bid Master Pan farewell.

"I've imposed on your household too long. Today, brother has closed the shop and I must go. The accounts are written out in detail. If they're so much as a penny off, may Heaven strike me dead."

Master Pan had received orders from his son-in-law and couldn't ask Shi Xiu to stay. He let him depart.

Shi Xiu found an inn in a nearby lane, rented a room and moved in. "Yang Xiong is my pledged blood brother," he thought. "If I don't clear this matter up, I may be sending him to his death. He believes his wife and blames me. At the moment, I'm in no position to argue. I must be able to prove it to him. I'll find out when he's on duty again at the prison, get up at the fourth watch, and see what the score is."

After a couple of days at the inn, he hung around outside Yang Xiong's front gate. That evening, he saw a young guard from the prison taking off with the warden's quilt.

"That means he's on duty tonight," Shi Xiu said to himself. "I can do a little work and see what happens."

He return to the inn and slept till the fourth watch. He rose, hung on his dagger, quietly left the inn, and concealed himself in the shadows of the lane near Yang Xiong's rear gate. Around the fifth watch a friar, with a wooden fish tucked under his arm, came to the head of the lane and peered stealthily around. Shi Xiu darted behind and grabbed him, pressing his dagger against the friar's neck.

"Don't move. One sound and you're a dead man. The truth, now. What are your orders from Hai the monk?"

"Spare me, bold fellow. I'll speak."

"If you're quick about it, I'll let you live."

"Hai the Preceptor is mixed up with Master Pan's daughter. He comes every night. When I see incense burning at the rear gate, that's the signal to tell him he can 'slip it in'. At the fifth watch I beat on the wooden fish and call to prayers. That's to tell him to 'pull it out'."

"Where is he now?"

"In the house, sleeping. When I bang on this fish, he'll leave."

"Give it to me, and your clothes."

Shi Xiu snatched the fish. As the friar was undressing, Shi Xiu drew the dagger across his throat and killed him. He put on the friar's cassock and his knee-length stockings, sheathed the dagger, and entered the lane, tapping the wooden fish.

At the sound, Hai hurriedly got out of bed, flung on his clothes, and went downstairs. Ying'er opened the rear gate and the monk darted into the lane. Shi Xui was still loudly clobbering the fish.

"Must you make such a racket?" the monk hissed.

Shi Xiu did not reply, but let him walk to the head of the lane. Suddenly he flung the monk down and pressed him to the ground.

"If you raise your voice, I'll kill you. I'll have your clothes, first."

Hai the Preceptor recognized Shi Xiu. He dared not struggle or cry out. Shi Xiu stripped him and left him without a stitch. Silently, he pulled the dagger out of his stocking and finished the monk with three or four stabs. He placed the knife beside the body of the friar, tied the clothes of the two men into a bundle and returned with it to the inn. Softly, Shi Xiu opened the inn gate. Quietly, he closed it. Then he went to bed. Of that we'll say no more.

An old man called Master Wang who sold gruel in the district was carrying his pots on a shoulder-pole at the fifth watch and holding a lantern, followed by a little boy. They were out to catch the early morning trade. The old man stumbled over the corpses and fell, spilling the gruel.

Because someone talked loosely,
Death came to Hai the Preceptor.

Everyone in Qizhou was discussing the matter, and Clever Cloud was scared stiff. But she didn't dare say anything, and could only lament inwardly.

Yang Xiong was in the prefectural office when the murder of the monk and the friar was reported, and he had a pretty good idea of how it happened. "This must be the work of Shi Xiu," he thought. "I was wrong to put the blame on him. I've got some spare time today. I'll find him and get the true story."

As he was crossing the prefectural bridge, a voice hailed him from behind. "Brother, where are you going?"

Yang turned around. There was Shi Xiu. "Brother," said Yang, "I was just looking for you."

"Come to my place, and we can talk."

Shi Xiu took him to a small room in his inn. "Well, brother, was I lying?"

"Don't hold it against me. I made a stupid mistake. I got drunk and let something slip. She fooled me. She said a lot of bad things about you. I was looking for you today so that I could apologize."

"I'm an unimportant fellow of no talent, but I'm absolutely clean and honest. I'd never do anything underhanded. I came to you because I was afraid she'd harm you. I have proof." Shi Xiu brought out the clothes of the monk and the friar. "I stripped this from their bodies."

Yang Xiong looked and rage flamed in his heart. "Forgive me, brother. Tonight, if I don't pulverize that baggage, I'll burst!"

Shi Xiu laughed. "There you go again. You work in a government office. Don't you know the law? You can't kill her unless you catch her in the act. Besides, I may be just making this up, and you'll be killing an innocent person."

"But I can't let her get away with it!"

"Listen to me, brother, and I'll tell you how to behave like a real man."

"How is that?"

"East of town is Jade Screen Mountain, a secluded place. Tomorrow, you say to her: 'I haven't burned incense to Heaven in a long time. Let's go together. Trick her into going with you up the mountain, and have her bring Ying'er. I'll be there, waiting. We'll have it out face to face and get the facts straight. You can then write a declaration of divorce and drop her. Isn't that a good plan?"

"There's no need. I know you're clean. She told a pack of lies."

"But that's not all. I'd like you also to hear how she managed their assignations."

"Since you're so wise, brother, I can't go wrong taking your advice. Tomorrow, I'll definitely bring the slut. Don't fail me."

"If I'm not there, you'll know everything I said is false."

Yang Xiong returned to his office. That evening when he came home he spoke only, as usual, of ordinary affairs. He rose the next morning at daybreak and said to Clever Cloud: "Last night in my dreams I met a spirit who berated me for not having kept my vow to burn incense in that Yue Temple outside the East Gate. I have time today, so I can do it. I'd like you to go with me."

"You can go yourself. What do you need me for?"

"I made the vow when we were courting, so we must go together."

"All right, then. We'll have a vegetarian breakfast, take warm baths, and depart."

"I'll buy incense and paper money and hire a sedan-chair. You bathe and fix your hair. I'll be back soon. Tell Ying'er also to get ready."

Yang Xiong went to the inn and spoke to Shi Xiu. "We leave after breakfast. Don't be late."

"Have the sedan-chair bearers wait halfway up the slope, and you three come the rest of the distance alone. I'll be waiting in a quiet spot. Don't bring any outsiders."

Yang then bought the paper money and candles, returned home and had breakfast. The girl had no suspicions, and made herself up neatly and attractively. Ying'er would accompany her. Bearers were waiting with the sedan-chair at the front gate.

"Please look after things here," Yang Xiong said to his father-in-law. "I'm going with Clever Cloud to burn incense."

"Burn plenty and come home early," said Master Pan.

The girl mounted the sedan-chair and set out, followed by the little maid, with the warden bringing up the rear. After they passed through the East Gate, Yang said to the porters in a low voice: "Go to Jade Screen Mountain. I'll pay you extra."

In less than two watches, they were climbing the slope. Jade Screen Mountain is twenty *li* outside of Qizhou's East Gate. On it are many scattered graves. Further up you see nothing but green grass and white poplars, but it's devoid of any nunnery or monastery.

Halfway up, Yang told the bearers to halt. He opened the latch, raised the curtain and asked the girl to step out.

"What are we doing on this mountain?" Clever Cloud said.

"Just start walking. Porters, stay here. Don't come up. In a little while I'll give you wine money."

"No problem. We'll await your orders."

Yang led the girl and Ying'er up four or five levels. He could see Shi Xiu sitting above.

"Why haven't you brought the incense and the paper money?" Clever Cloud asked.

"I've sent someone ahead with them."

He helped the girl to an ancient tomb site. Shi Xiu, who had placed his bundle, dagger and staff at the foot of a tree, came forward.

"My respects, sister-in-law."

"What are you doing here, brother-in-law?" Clever Cloud hurriedly replied, startled.

"Waiting for you."

Yang said to the girl: "You told me that he made remarks to you several times, and felt your breasts and asked if you were pregnant. There's no one here but us. You two can get the story straight."

"Aiya! It's past. Why bother?"

Shi Xiu stared at her. "Well, sister-in-law, what do you say?"

"Have you nothing better to do than rake that up now?"

"Sister-in-law, look." Shi Xiu opened the bundle, took out the clothes of Hai the Preceptor and the friar and flung them at her feet. "Do you recognize these?"

The girl blushed. She was unable to speak. Shi Xiu whipped out the dagger and handed it to Yang Xiong.

"Question Ying'er."

Yang seized the maid and forced her to her knees. "The truth, little hussy," he shouted. "How did she start her lechery in the monk's quarters? What about the signal with the incense table? And the friar beating on the wooden fish? Tell me, and I'll let you live. One lie, and I'll hack you to mincemeat."

"It wasn't up to me, sir," cried Ying'er. "Don't kill me! I'll tell you everything! We all had wine at the monk's quarters. Then we went upstairs to look at Buddha's tooth, but she sent me down to see whether Master Pan had recovered from his drinking. Two days later a friar came begging alms at the rear gate. She told me to get him a string of copper cash. She must have made the arrangement with him then. Whenever you were on duty at the prison, she had me put a table with incense outside the rear gate. That was the signal for the friar to tell the monk the coast was clear. Hai the Preceptor disguised himself as an ordinary man and wore a bandanna on his head. The mistress snatched it off, and I saw his shaven pate. Every morning at the fifth watch, when we heard the sound of the wooden fish, I had to open the rear gate and let him out. My mistress promised me a bracelet and new clothes. I had to obey. He came dozens of times, before he was killed. She gave me some hair ornaments and instructed me to tell you that brother-in-law had made wicked remarks and got fresh with her. I hadn't seen it myself, so I didn't dare. This is the whole truth, every word!"

"Well, brother," said Shi Xiu, "there it is. This isn't anything I've told her to say. Now please question sister-in-law."

The warden grasped Clever Cloud. "Bitch, the maid has confessed everything. Don't try to deny it. Tell me the truth and I'll spare your wretched life."

"I was wrong. For the sake of what we once were to each other as husband and wife, forgive me."

"Brother, don't let her gloss this over," said Shi Xiu. "Make her confess in detail."

"Speak, bitch," Yang barked. "Be quick about it."

Clever Cloud had no choice but to relate how she and the monk became lovers, beginning with their flirtation the night of the memorial ceremony, and all that followed.

"Why did you tell brother I tried to get fresh with you?" Shi Xiu demanded.

"When he came home drunk the other night and swore at me, he hit very close to the mark. I guessed that you knew, and had told him. Two or three nights before that, Hai instructed me what to say if this should happen. So the following morning, I had a story all prepared. Actually, you hadn't done any such thing."

"Today, the three of us are here together and the facts are clear," said Shi Xiu. He turned to Yang. "What to do about it is up to you."

"Take the ornaments from the wanton"s hair, brother, and remove her clothes. I'll attend to her."

Shi Xiu did as bidden. Yang cut two ribbons from the girl's skirt and tied her to a tree. Shi Xhi also ripped off Ying'er's hair ornaments. He took up the knife.

"Why leave this little tramp? Get rid of the weeds, roots and all," he said.

"Of course. Brother, give me that blade. I'll do it myself."

Ying'er opened her mouth to scream. With one blow Yang cut her in two.

"Brother-in-law," pleaded the girl at the tree, "reason with him."

"Sister-in-law," said Shi Xiu, "brother will deal with you personally."

Yang Xiong advanced on Clever Cloud, pulled out her tongue and cut it off, so that she wouldn't be able to shriek. He pointed at her in a rage.

"Harlot, you had me confused. I nearly fell for your lies. You've sullied my brother's name and you're sure to kill me if you get the chance. My best bet is to strike first. What kind of heart has a bitch like you? I want to see for myself!"

He sliced her open from breast to belly, hauled out her organs, hung them on the tree, and cut her into seven parts. Then he wrapped her hair pins and ornaments into a bundle.

"Come here, brother," Yang said to Shi Xiu. "We need a long-range plan. A treacherous male and a lecherous female have both been killed by us. The question is where can we find refuge?"

"I have a place. We'll go together."

"Where is it?"

"You've killed a person and so have I. We'll join the band in Liangshan Marsh. Where else could we go? Everyone in the gallant fraternity has heard that Song Jiang, the Timely Rain from Shandong, is recruiting bold fellows from all over. Who doesn't know that? You and I are both good with weapons. Of course they'll accept us."

"It's always better to expect the worst. In that way you don't run into trouble. I'm an official. They'll be suspicious of me, and won't want us."

Shi Xiu laughed. "Wasn't Song Jiang a county clerk? I tell you there's nothing to worry about. Do you remember those two men I went drinking with in that tavern the day we met? Well, one of then is Dai Zong the Marvellous Traveller. The other is Yang Lin the Elegant Panther. They're both from Liangshan Marsh. Dai gave me a ten-ounce ingot of silver. I still have it in my bundle That means I can go to him."

"I'll go home for some money, then, and we'll leave."

"You mustn't dither so, brother. If you go back into town and are arrested, how will you get away? You've those hair pins and ornaments, and I have some silver. Even if there were three of us, it would be more than enough. Why try to take more? How could I rescue you if anything went wrong? This business will be out in the open soon. We mustn't hang around. I say let's get to the other side of the mountain."

Shi Xiu shouldered his bundle and picked up his staff. Yang Xiong put the dagger in his waist sash and took his balberd. As they started to leave the ancient tomb, a man stepped out from behind a pine.

"So you kill people neath a clear blue sky and then go off to join the band in Liangshan Marsh," he cried. "I've been listening for a long time!" He dropped to his knees and kowtowed.

Yang knew him. The man's name was Shi Qian. He came from Gaotang Prefecture before settling in Qizhou. He could fly from roof to roof, climb walls, scale fences and steal horses. He had been brought before a magistrate in Qizhou, but Yang had intervened and saved him. He was known as Flea on a Drum.

"What are you doing here?" Yang demanded.

"I haven't had any business for several days, brother Warden, and I came to poke around in some ancient tombs to see whether I could dig up anything of value. I didn't venture to disturb you. Then I heard you say you were going to join the band in Liangshan Marsh. Around here all I can do is steal chickens and swipe dogs. I'll never amount to anything. How fine it would be if I could go with you two brothers up the mountain. Will you take me?"

"Since you're one of the bold fellows, and since they're looking for recruits in the fortress, they wouldn't object to one more," said Shi Xiu. "Come along."

"I know a good path," said Flea on a Drum.

With him in the lead, the three followed a trail to the rear of the mountain and set out for Liangshan Marsh.

To return to the two sedan-chair carriers who had been waiting at the halfway point. The sun was already in the west, but Yang and the two women still hadn't come down. Their orders were to remain where they were, but they could stick it out no longer, and they plodded up the path. They saw a flock of crows around an ancient tomb. The men drew nearer. The raucously cawing birds were fighting over a piece of human intestine.

Frightened, the porters hurried back to town and told Master Pan, who took them to the prefect. The county sheriff and coroners were dispatched to the scene, where they found and inspected the bodies. They returned and gave their report.

"We discovered beside a pine tree the dismembered corpse of Pan's daughter Clever Cloud. The maidservant Ying'er lies dead before an ancient tomb. Nearby, the clothes of a woman, a monk and a friar are heaped."

The prefect, recalling the killings of the friar and the monk Hai a few days before, carefully questioned Master Pan. The old man told how he got drunk in the monk's quarters and related the events leading to Shi Xiu's departure.

"It looks as if the girl and the monk were committing adultery, and the maid and the friar were acting as accomplices," said the prefect. "Shi Xiu probably was outraged and killed the friar and the monk. Today, Yang doubtlessly slaughtered his wife and the maidservant. That's what must have happened. We'll capture Yang Xiong and Shi Xiu and get positive proof."

He issued notices calling for the arrest of the fugitives and offering rewards for their apprehension. The porters were allowed to go home, pending further notification by the court. Master Pan bought coffins and had the bodies buried. Of that we'll say no more.

On leaving Qizhou, Yang Xiong and Shi Xiu and the Flea travelled steadily, resting at night and continuing the next morning. In a few days they reached the prefecture of Yunzhou. After crossing Fragrant Woods Hollow, they saw before them a high mountain. It was growing dark, and they made for an inn beside a stream. A waiter was in the process of locking up as they reached the gate.

"You must have come a long way to arrive here so late," he said.

"More than a hundred *li*," Flea on a Drum replied.

The waiter let them in and gave them a room. "Would you like a fire?" he asked.

"We'll attend to it ourselves," said the Flea.

"We've got no other guests and there are two pots of boiled water on the stove. You're welcome to use them if you wish."

"Have you any meat and wine?"

"We had some meat this morning, but people from neighboring villages bought it all. There's a jug of wine left, but nothing to go with it."

"That'll do. And bring us five measures of rice. We'll cook it here."

The waiter brought the rice to the Flea, who cleaned it and put it on to boil. Shi Xiu laid out his baggage. Yang gave the waiter one of the hairpins in payment for the wine and promised to settle the full account the next day. The waiter fetched the jug and opened it, and placed a few hot vegetable dishes on the table. The Flea carried in a bucket of hot water for Yang and Shi Xiu to wash their hands and feet with.

The wine was poured, and the three asked the waiter to sit down and join them. They drank from four large bowls.

Shi Xiu noticed a dozen good halberds under the eaves.

"Why do you need weapons in this inn?" he asked.

"They belong to the master."

"What sort of person is he?"

"You've been around, sir. Haven't you heard of this place? That big mountain out there is called Lone Dragon Mountain. The high cliff before it is Lone Dragon Cliff. On top of it is my master's residence. All the land around here for thirty *li* belongs to the Zhu

Family Manor. Lord Zhu, my master, has three sons. They're known as the Three Zhu Warriors. This manor has five or six hundred families, all tenants, and two halberds have been issued to each family. You're staying in the Zhu Family Inn. Usually, there are several dozen of our men spending the night here. That's why we keep the halberds handy."

"What use are they in an inn?"

"We're not far from Liangshan Marsh. Those bandits might come to rob our grain. We have to be prepared."

"If I gave you some silver would you let me have one of the halberds?"

"Oh, no. Each halberd has its owner's mark. My master would beat me. He's very strict."

Shi Xiu laughed. "I was only kidding. Don't get excited. Have some more wine."

"I can't. I must go to bed. Enjoy yourselves, sir guests. Drink all you want."

The waiter retired. Yang and Shi Xiu had another round.

"Would you like some meat?" the Flea asked them.

"Didn't the waiter say they don't have any?" Yang replied. "Where would you get meat?"

The Flea chuckled. He walked over to the stove and lifted a cooked rooster out of a pot.

"Where does that come from?" asked Yang.

"I went out in back to relieve myself and saw this rooster in a cage. I thought it would go well with your wine, so I quietly killed it by the stream, brought out a bucket of boiling water, cleaned the bird and cooked it. And here it is, ready for you two brothers to eat."

"Still as light-fingered as ever, you villain," said Yang.

The Flea grinned. "I haven't changed my profession."

The three laughed. They tore the bird apart with their hands and ate it, together with the rice they had cooked.

The waiter slept only a little while. Uneasy in his mind, he got up and looked things over, front and back. On the kitchen table he saw feathers and bones. A pot on the stove was half filled with greasy water. He hurried out to the cage in the rear of the inn. It was empty. He hastened into the room where the three men were staying.

"Is that any way to behave?" he demanded. "Why did you steal our rooster and eat it?"

"You're seeing ghosts," scoffed the Flea. "I bought that bird on the road. Who's seen you rooster?"

"Where is it, then?"

"Dragged off by a wildcat, eaten by a weasel, pounced on by a hawk — who knows?"

"That bird was in a cage just a short while ago. If you didn't steal it, who did?"

"Don't wrangle," said Shi Xiu. "We'll pay you whatever it's worth."

"It heralds the dawn. Our inn can't do without it. Even ten ounces of silver wouldn't be money enough. Give me back our bird."

"Who are you trying to extort?" Shi Xiu said angrily. "Just for that I won't give you a penny. What are you going to do about it?"

The waiter laughed. "Regular fire-eaters, aren't you? Our inn is different. We'll drag you up to the manor and try you for being bandits from Liangshan Marsh!"

"Suppose we were? Do you think you could capture us and claim the reward?" Shi Xiu demanded.

Yang Xiong was also very irate. "With the best of intentions, we were going to give you some money. Now we won't," he said. "Let's see you take us!"

"Thieves, thieves," shouted the waiter.

Four or five big bruisers, stripped to the waist, charged into the room and made for Yang and Shi Xiu. With one blow of the fist each, Shi Xiu knocked them flat. The waiter opened his mouth to yell. The Flea slapped him so hard that his face swelled up and he couldn't utter a sound. The bruisers fled through the rear gate.

"Those louts must be going for help," said Yang. "let's finish eating, quickly, and get out of here."

The three ate their fill, shouldered their packs, put on comfortable hemp sandals, attached their daggers, and helped themselves to one halberd apiece from the weapons rack.

"A henchman is a henchman," said Shi Xiu. "We can't let any of them off."

He lit a bundle of straw in the stove and set fire to all sides of the inn. Fanned by the wind, the thatched roofs burst into blaze, great tongues of flame leaping into the sky. The three men struck out along the highway.

When they had marched for about two watches, they saw before and behind them innumerable torches. Nearly two hundred men, shouting and yelling, were closing in.

"Keep calm," said Shi Xiu. "We'll take to the small paths."

"No," said Yang Xiong, "let them come. We'll kill them singly or in pairs. At daybreak, we'll go on."

Before the words were out of his mouth, they were attacked from four sides. Yang was in the lead, Shi Xiu covered the rear, and Flea defended the middle. With halberds they fought the charging vassals, who came at them with staves and spears. The pursuers didn't know what they were letting themselves in for. Yang, wielding his halberd, promptly felled half a dozen. The assault group fled pell-mell. Shi Xiu gave chase and hacked down half a dozen more.

When the other vassals saw this carnage, they decided they wanted to live, and that this was not a very healthy atmosphere. They turned and ran, with the three in hot pursuit. More shouting rose, and two long hooked poles snaked out of the dry grass, fastened onto the Flea and dragged him into the underbrush. Shi Xiu whirled to go to his rescue. From behind, other two hooked poles shot out. The sharp-eyed Yang Xiong swiftly knocked them aside with his halberd and stabbed into the thicket. There were cries, and the ambushers hastily departed. The two saw them pulling away the Flea, but they had no heart to fight in the depths of the thicket, and could only let him go.

They finally found a path and went on. The glow of the distant torches provided them with illumination, since the path was bare of trees or shrubbery, they proceeded along it in an easterly direction. The vassals, after searching for them in vain, collected their wounded. They brought the Flea, his hands tied behind his back, to the Zhu Family Manor.

Yang and Shi Xiu were still walking at daylight. A village tavern lay ahead.

"Let's buy some wine and food, brother, and ask directions," Shi Xiu suggested.

They entered the tavern, leaned their halberds against the wall, sat down, and ordered food and drink. The waiter served a few vegetable dishes, and heated some wine. They were about to start, when a big man came in. His face was broad, his eyes bright, his ears large, his appearance rough and ugly. He wore a tea-brown robe, a head kerchief decorated with swastikas, a white silk waist sash, and oiled leather boots.

"His Excellency wants those loads delivered to the manor right away," he shouted.

The tavern host replied hastily: "Everything's ready. We'll send them very soon."

The man turned to go. "Hurry it up," he said. He was passing Yang Xiong's and Shi Xiu's table on the way to the door. Yang recognized him.

"Young man, what are you doing here?" Yang called. "Won't you take a look at me?"

The big fellow stared. Recognition grew in his eyes. "What are you doing here, benefactor?" he exclaimed. He dropped to his knees and kowtowed.

And because Yang knew this man, the pledge of alliance between the three villages became as naught, and the roar of assembled tigers brought down disaster.

Who was this man whom Yang and Shi Xiu had met? Read our next chapter if you would know.

WAR AND REVOLUTION

From the time the First Emperor consolidated the Warring States two millennia ago into the unified single nation which became known as China, there was never a Chinese who did not know at least one war in his or her lifetime. There were wars of imperial conquest abroad, wars to repel foreign invaders, civil wars to overthrow existing rulers and create new dynasties, and endless internal strife and local squabbles for power. Everyone was affected, if not by personally coming under fire and bombardment, then by marauding troops, commandeered property, conscription, increased taxes... With the people, always the people, bearing the burdens. Although they supported defensive battles against alien attackers, or struggles to topple tyrannical monarchs, over-all they hated war. No matter who won, the ordinary folk always lost out in the end.

In the twentieth century the Japanese invasion had an impact on persons in every walk of life. Three ironic stories by Mao Tun head our list of War and Revolution samples. *Epitome* gives a glimpse of a third-rate concubine caught up in the vicious battles between rival opium gangs. *Wartime* tells how a mild-mannered minor editor is enraged into action by the Japanese bombing of Shanghai's Commercial Press. *A True Chinese Patriot* twits the businessman who, from a safe haven far in the rear, sanctimoniously opposes a united front against the Japaneses.

Then an extract from *Annals of a Provincial Town*, by Kao Yunlan, a novel about a famous jailbreak of revolutionaries in the thirties in Fukien province, where the local Kuomintang were collaborating with the Japanese.

Those who hoped the years of warfare in China were at last ended when the Japanese surrendered in August 1945 were soon disillusioned. Chiang Kai-shek, lavishly funded and supported by the US, moved his troops into advance positions and launched all-out drives against the Communist-led

EPITOME

The story tells of a certain Miss Ling, a Shanghai shopgirl who had been purchased by a town gangster chieftain and brought home to be his concubine.

The girl's name was Ling, or maybe it was Lin. Who knows? That kind of person never has any definite family name. People call them whatever they like.

The day she arrived, she first walked softly into the room of the Lao Taitai (*literally "Old Madame", the matriarch of the household*) to pay her respects. The old lady was munching some water chestnuts her granddaughter's husband had sent, and didn't hear her enter. When she suddenly became aware of the girl kowtowing in front of her, Lao Taitai started with surprise. She considered being shocked like this, at first meeting, a bad omen. It made her feel ill. What's more, the girl's modern hair-do, with its mass of curls, hurt the old lady's eyes. And so, although her son's wife had died some years ago and there was no proper mistress of the house, she refused to recognize the girl as a "wife". Still chewing her water chestnuts, Lao Taitai addressed her contemptuously as "Miss" Ling.

So it was "Miss" Ling! The family matriarch had used the term herself. From then on, this teen-aged girl, Ling, or Lin or whatever her name was was permanently relegated to the status of concubine.

Miss Ling had a mother. The Master, her present husband, while in Shanghai on business, had told her mother, "In the future, we shall treat each other as relatives." This was after sleeping with Miss Ling, whom he had met in one of the big department stores. Miss Ling had no brothers; her mother relied on her entirely for support in her old age. All this was made plain to the Master before Miss Ling left Shanghai with him.

But now everything had changed. The Lao Taitai naturally wouldn't recognize such "relatives". The Master forgot his promises completely. Whenever there was an opportune moment, Miss Ling would remark to him that her mother back in Shanghai must be having a hard time. But usually, these hints found him deaf and dumb. At other times he would glare and snort impatiently:

"What expenses does an old woman have! It's only been a few months; she couldn't have spent the whole three hundred dollars I gave her!"

The Lao Taitai was very displeased about this gift. She berated the Master severely, right in front of a woman servant who had been with the family for years.

"You give three hundred dollars for a smelly piece of trash you pick up off the streets of Shanghai! You spend money like water! When your own daughter got married you spent less than three hundred dollars. The wardrobe trunk you bought her was imitation leather; its lid dropped off the same day. Her in-laws still sneer about it. Anyhow, it was a very unlucky thing to happen. Three times she's given birth, but not one baby has lived more than a hundred days! But you, you scrape together a little cash, running "black" goods (*opium*), and you throw it around any old way! *Omitofu*! (*roughly, "Buddha preserve us!"*) Carrying on with a slut like that! Heaven might strike you dead!"

The Lao Taitai was famous for her nasty disposition, and the Master was a little afraid of her. Besides, now that he thought of it, Miss Ling hardly seemed worth three hundred dollars. She actually wasn't much better than that certain lady he knew right here in town. Regretting the money and smarting from the Lao Taitai's sharp tongue, the Master took it out on Miss Ling. This was the first lesson she received from his fists and feet.... She had been "Miss" Ling for just two months then.

Of course she didn't look the same as when she first came. There was no hairdressing shop in the town, and there certainly was no place to get a permanent wave. Miss Ling's modern curly mop had long since been pressed straight by her pillow. Her hair was now tied together at the back in a bun like a duck's rump. She didn't look any different from any of the town's other girls. Her lipstick was finished, her eyebrow tweezers were broken. You couldn't buy these things in the town, and the Master wouldn't buy them in Shanghai, though he often made trips there. Miss Ling grew less attractive every day, at least she was no longer particularly alluring.

Then the Master discovered something about Miss Ling that made him even more dissatisfied. Two days after the Master beat Miss Ling for the first time, he drank heavily. Although the sun was shining brightly outside, he dallied with her endlessly in their bedroom. Suddenly he noticed faint silvery lines on her abdomen, a tell-tale sign that a woman has borne a child. The Master was just coming out of a drunken haze. Seeing this sobered him almost completely. He leaped up, flung Miss Ling to the floor and slapped her face twice, hard.

"Stinking whore!" he grated through clenched teeth. "And I thought I was getting the original package! You put on a great show that first night in Shanghai!"

Miss Ling was afraid to utter a word. She wept, muffling her sobs.

When news of this afternoon amorousness reached the Lao Taitai's religious ears, the lot of Miss Ling grew harder still. To revile Miss Ling directly or indirectly became Lao Taitai's daily task. At times, quite forgetting her Buddhist principles of simple placid living, the old lady would work herself into a fine rage, pounding the table and kicking over the chairs, cursing Miss Ling till the girl barely dared to breathe. When a weasel stole one of the hens, Lao Taitai blamed that on Miss Ling, too. Poking her finger in at the girl's face, she swore shrilly:

"Slut! Vixen! Doing those things in broad daylight is a sin! No wonder the weasel got away with the hen! You'll die a horrible death, sinning against the Sun Buddha like that! Shameless hussy!"

The Master's business took him to Shanghai at least once a month. Each trip required three days to a week; there was no telling. On those occasions Miss Ling was happier than a condemned man with a last minute reprieve from the axe. Although the Lao Taitai's steady stream of abuse was worse than when the Master was at home, at least Miss Ling was freed from those episodes she had grown to fear more and more every day.

The Young Master, about her own age, was as lecherous as his father. Apricot, the little slavery, shivered at the sight of the Young Master like a mouse when it sees a cat. If there was no one else around, the Young Master went after Miss Ling, too. He would scratch his finger against the palm of her hand, or pat her face, or feel her breasts. Miss Ling didn't have the courage to make a row. All she could do was flee, her face crimson. The Young Master would gaze after her, but made no attempt to pursue.

More difficult to cope with was the Master's son-in-law, husband of that daughter the Lao Taitai so often mentioned. Just looking at him, the young concubine could tell he was the same kind of rake as the Master. He too addressed her as "Miss" Ling. Even in the presence of an old shrew like the Lao Taitai, he had the temerity to pinch the girl's thigh under table. Miss Ling avoided him in much the same manner as Apricot tried to steer clear of the Young Master.

Son-in-law had a post of some sort in the local police department. When the Master was away, son-in-law would become especially diligent about paying his respects to his wife's family. He would call often, with a pistol holster strapped round his waist. Miss Ling knew that the holster contained a gun, and her heart beat fearfully. At times like this she felt that things were better when the Master was at home, and even looked forward to his return.

The town had a "Protection Corps" which the local gentry and landlords had organized, allegedly for protection against "marauding bandits". The Master was the "Director" of this Corps. Each time he returned with "merchandise" from Shanghai, his "Captains" came to report. There were two of them, and two pairs of shifty evil eyes would glide over Miss Ling's contours at every opportunity.

Back from his latest trip, the Master was conferring with these worthies in his parlour. Off to one side were two large packages, wrapped in matting fruits of the visit to Shanghai. The Captains had been conferring with him for some time when, abruptly, the Master became incensed.

"He gets twenty per cent for sitting around doing nothing, and he's still not satisfied!" he shouted. "So he wants to make trouble, does he? What kind of fight can his men put up those scabby-headed rats! If he wants to get tough we can get tough too! Tomorrow, a hundred catties (*about 110 lbs.*) of the stuff is coming on the river steamer. You fellows be down there and stand guard. We'll give them a battle if that's what they're after; they're the ones who are starting this thing!... Tomorrow morning, five o'clock! Get up early. This is our public duty. We shouldn't be afraid of a little trouble!'"

"Our men..." one of the Captains began hesitantly.

"After we've won," the Master interrupted, "There'll be two ounces of opium apiece for each and every one!" His tone was still angry.

Miss Ling, all ears outside the door, was taken completely unawares when someone came up and pinched her arm. She nearly cried out, but caught herself in time. The one who had pinched her was son-in-law! Lust gleamed in his eyes. He looked as if he wanted to swallow her in one gulp. And the Master was just on the other side of the door! Miss Ling's heart pounded.

Controlling himself with a visible effort, son-in-law turned and went into the next room. He conferred in low tones with the Master for several minutes.

"That son of a bitch!" Miss Ling heard the Master explode hoarsely. "We'll take care of him, then! Tomorrow morning, I'll be there too!"

Son-in-law hooted his weird-sounding laugh. It grated on Miss Ling's ears like the cry of an owl.

Until dusk that day, the Master's face was dark iron. He spoke very seldom. He took his pistol apart, inspected it carefully, put it together again and loaded it. Several times he practiced aiming. Miss Ling's legs trembled whenever she had to pass near him. Then, without waiting for dinner, the Master took his gun and went out.

There seemed to be a stone pressing in Miss Ling's bosom. She was growing very frightened.

The Lao Taitai sat before a small Buddhist shrine, counting her beads with remarkable rapidity while muttering her prayers. Burning sandalwood in a little bronze urn glowed in front of the shrine.

About eleven that night, the Master finally returned, his face pale and splotchy. His bloodshot eyes looked smaller than usual. His head was steaming with sweat and he reeked of drink. He took out his pistol and thumped it down on the table. With palsied fingers, Miss Ling helped him remove his clothes. Suddenly, laughing boisterously, he grabbed her, lifted her up and tossed her on the bed. This had often happened before, but this time it was unexpected. Miss Ling couldn't tell what kind of a mood he was in; she lay motionless, not daring to stir. The Master strode up to her and angrily yanked open her garments, the black gleaming pistol clutched in his right hand. Miss Ling went weak with terror. She stared at him, her eyes large and distended. He stripped her, and placed the icy muzzle of the pistol against her breast. Miss Ling was shivering so violently the whole bed creaked.

"I'll practise on you first," she heard the Master say. "Let's see how good my gun is."

There was a roaring in Miss Ling's ears. Tears coursed down her cheeks.

"Afraid to die, slut? Hah! Don't worry, I still want to play around with you for a while yet!"

Laughing cruelly, the Master flopped into bed, and instantly began to snore, deep in slumber.

Miss Ling huddled to one side of the bed. She was afraid to sleep; she was unable to sleep. If only he had pulled the trigger, she thought, my misery would have been ended, quick and clean. Stealthily she took the pistol, looked at it, then closed her eyes, her heart beating fast. But finally, she put it down again. Life was bitter, but death was too frightening.

Some time after three in the morning, people began beating on the compound gate. The Master raised his head and listened a moment. Picking up his pistol, he ran to the window and pushed it open.

"What are you making such a blasted racket about!" he yelled.

"The men are all here!" a voice replied.

The Master put on a fleece-lined gown, tightened a silk sash around his waist, shoved the pistol into the sash, and hurried out. Miss Ling heard him talking with the crowd outside the gate. He swore savagely, and they all departed.

Miss Ling gazed at the sky. A few scattered stars, one or two frozen grey clouds. She shivered and returned to bed, her mind a blur. I'd better not sleep, she thought as she slipped beneath the covers. But before long she began to doze; her head slid from the backboard down to her shoulder. She dreamed that the Master had shot her. She saw her mother, too. Her mother held her in her arms and cried distractedly.... Miss Ling woke with a start. Her mother wasn't there, but someone else was embracing her, murmuring passionately. Her eyes flew open. In the light of the oil lamp burning beside the bed, she saw his face. She blanched.

"Young Master, you!"

She tried to fight him off. "If you don't go, I'll scream!"

"Go ahead! The old man's gone out to fight the police for opium and the Lao Taitai wouldn't care!" He grappled with her. Although only seventeen, he was much stronger than she.

"You're ruining me..." Miss Ling wept. But finally she let him have his way.

The oil lamp on the table gradually burned out. The sky was turning a fish-belly white. A cock in the courtyard crowed once, twice. Next door, the neighbor's cock took up the cry. Soon, cocks were crowing for miles around...

Down the street a loud hubbub of men's voices could be heard coming closer. A moment later, and thunderous blows began to rain on the compound gate. Miss Ling, terrified, jumped up and ran to lock the bedroom door. The Young Master dashed past her.

"Have you lost your mind?" he demanded. "Wait till I get out of here!" He sped from the room.

Miss Ling hastily put something on, hopped back into bed and pulled the covers over her head. Trembling, she curled herself in to a tight ball. There was a tremendous racket going on downstairs. The noise mounted till it was outside the door of the bedroom. She leaped up, took a grip on herself, and opened the door. Five or six men were waiting there, including the Master and son-in-law.

Two men were carrying the Master. His gown was opened at the chest. The white fleece was stained with blood. After putting him on the bed, the others went away, leaving only son-in-law and one of the Captains. The Master was bellowing like an injured bull. The Captain looked at his wound, then said to son-in-law:

"I don't think that wound can be treated here in town. It's queer, him getting shot like that. They were all in front of us, but he was hit from the side. Very strange. And that was no stray bullet. Whoever shot him was aiming for him! Anyhow, we did a fine job on that dog of a police chief!"

From the edge of the bed, Miss Ling saw son-in-law standing behind the Captain. He was concealing a grin.

Downstairs, the Lao Taitai could be heard throwing things around and cursing.

"It's retribution! Offending against the Sun Buddha! All because of that stinking baggage! I knew she was bad luck the day she came in the door! He doesn't need any doctor; just kill that dirty bitch and he'll get well! Kill her!"

Before mid-morning the townspeople were animatedly discussing the ferocity of the robbers. The President of the Chamber of Commerce reported the affair by long-distance telephone to the county authorities. He stated that the chief of police had been killed while "apprehending the criminals" and that the Director of the Defence Corps in the course of "assisting with the arrest" had been severely wounded. Relaying the report to the provincial government, the county converted the robbers into bandits, "between two and three hundred, all heavily armed, who came without warning and quickly disappeared after commission of the offense." On the basis of this information, the provincial authorities sent a company of troops to "eradicate" the bandits.

The day the troops arrived, they marched down the main street. Miss Ling saw them. She didn't know whether they had come to help the Master or to help son-in-law. For somehow she was positive that it was son-in-law who had shot the Master. But she kept this conviction to herself, not even mentioning it to the Young Master.

The Master's wound gradually healed. A tiny piece of bullet was still embedded in his flesh, but the wound had closed.

She privately begged the Young Master to think of a way to rescue her. He said there wasn't anything he could do, and only laughed.

A few days later, the Master was able to get up and walk around. Miss Ling was so worried she couldn't eat.

But the Master seemed to have something on his mind. He didn't bother much with Miss Ling. One of the Captains came frequently to confer. They talked in low tones, the Master frowning continuously. Once, when Miss Ling was serving the Master some bird's-nest soup, she heard the Captain say:

"Every day the Chamber of Commerce has to provide banquet dinners for two hundred people. This has been going on for more than half a month now. It's cost the Chamber over two thousand silver dollars. The President of the Chamber wants them to leave right away, but the commander of the troops says he was sent here to wipe out the bandits; unless he has a battle with them he can't go back and report 'mission completed'."

"The hell with his 'mission completed'!" fumed the Master, but his frown deepened.

After a pause, the Captain whispered something in his ear. The Master bounded to his feet.

"What!" he yelled. "We gave them thirty ounces of opium yesterday and today they want more? The crooks!"

"That's not the worst of it, they're hijacking us! When our men go out to make deliveries to our big customers, they hold us up on the road and steal our stuff! They've only been here half a month, but they know all the ropes!"

"It's an outrage!" The Master pounded his fist on the table. Veins stood out on his forehead like little fingers.

Miss Ling was as terrified as if the Master again wanted to take his gun and shoot her.

"If they stay another half month, we'll be out of business! You've got to think of something, fast!"

The Captain heaved a sigh. The Master sighed too. Then they whispered together for a long time. Miss Ling could see a somewhat happier expression on the Master's face. He kept nodding his head.

"Don't worry about a thing, Your Worship. We'll disguise ourselves well," the Captain assured the Master as he was leaving. "There won't be any slip-ups! That village northwest of here will be best. The peasants there have still got a little grain and things left. We might as well subsidize the trip while we're at it."

"Tell our scouts to look sharp. The moment they report that the troops have set out from town, you all get out of there. We don't want a real clash with the troops. We'll be the joke of the town if we're exposed!"

After the Captain had departed, the Master sat wrapped in thought, looking very serious. Then he dispatched a servant to bring his son-in-law. When she heard the word "son-in-law", Miss Ling felt very uneasy. She was dying to tell her suspicions to the Master, but in the end she said nothing and concentrated on staying out of the way.

Son-in-law talked with the Master for a while, rose and left quickly. He bumped into Miss Ling at the door and smirked at her, revealing big teeth in a wolfish grin. Her hair stood on end. She recoiled from him as from a poisonous snake.

In the evening at dinner, the Master began drinking. Miss Ling's heart became more troubled with each cup she poured him. She had a feeling that tonight was going to be bad. But oddly enough, besides drinking, the Master displayed no other inclinations. He drank from a small cup, sipping slowly and gently, putting it down from time to time and listening. At about nine, there was the sound of running feet in the street outside; someone was shouting commands. Obviously very concerned, the Master stopped drinking and lay down on the bed. He directed Miss Ling to knead his legs.

After another interval, rifles began popping in the distance. The Master jumped up and ran to the window. A patch of fire was gleaming to the northwest. The Master watched for a few minutes, then filled himself a big bowl of liquor and drank it down. Wagging his head with satisfaction, he stretched forward his two arms. Miss Ling knew this was his signal to be undressed, and she trembled inwardly.

To her surprise, after having her knead his legs a little longer, the Master went to sleep.

The next morning in the kitchen, Miss Ling heard the water vendor say that bandits had attacked the village to the northwest the previous night. The troops had fought the raiders for hours and captured many peasants who were in league with them, as well as one wounded bandit. He was now locked up in the police station.

In the front room, the Lao Taitai was throwing another tantrum.

"That's what he gets for losing his head over a witch! Now he quarrels with his son-in-law! Anybody who sins against the Sun Buddha...."

Carrying a bowl of lotus-seed broth upstairs, Miss Ling could hear the angry voices of the Master and his son-in-law. Just as she reached the door of the room, she heard the Master snarl:

"You're crazy! You dare to talk to me like that!"

"Didn't you get enough the last time you were shot?" hissed son-in-law. He laughed coldly in a way that sent shivers up Miss Ling's spine.

Though her heart was jumping, she entered the room. There was a gleaming black pistol in son-in-law's hand and it was pointing at the Master. Miss Ling's legs turned to water. Her blood seemed to congeal in her veins.

"Kill me? Hah!" snorted the Master. "Just try, and"

Bang!

At the sound, Miss Ling collapsed beside the door, her eyes staring. She saw the distorted evil face of son-in-law as he stepped across her body and went out. Everything faded into darkness.

It was the Master who had been shot, not Miss Ling. But she became ill, delirious. For two days she ran a high temperature. Her face was brick-red as if she had been drinking heavily, her eyes glassy. She ate nothing. At times she raved unintelligible gibberish. On the third day she was somewhat better, but quite weak. She felt dizzy, and slept most of the afternoon. Near dark, she awoke with a start, very thirsty. She saw Apricot, the little slavery, leaning over the window sill, looking out. Miss Ling couldn't understand why she was lying in bed; of the recent incident, she remembered nothing. She tried to sit up, but she didn't have the strength.

"Apricot," she said weakly, "what are you looking at? If the Master catches you there, he'll beat you!" She was feeling rather hungry.

The little slavery turned around and grinned at her.

"The Master's dead!" Apricot said with a ghoulish laugh. "See he was lying right there, blood all over the place!"

Miss Ling shivered. She remembered now. Again her heart beat fast, again her eyes blurred, again she drifted into a vague dream world. She saw the Master poking her breast with the pistol muzzle, she saw son-in-law take murderous aim at the Master. Last of all, she saw a face with cruelly twisting brows looking at her avidly. It was son-in-law! She thought she screamed, but the sound she heard seemed to be coming from the other side of a thick wall. A heavy weight was crushing her bosom. Again she sank into unconsciousness....

When she awoke this time, Miss Ling was sure she was dead. The lamp had already been lit and a man's shadow fell across the bed. Miss Ling recognized the Young Master, standing at her bedside, his back to the lamp. He was leaning very close.

"Am I dead?" she moaned.

"It isn't that easy to die!"

"I ache all over. I think...son-in-law..."

"He just left. I used a trick to get him out."

"You're a smart little imp!" She let the Young Master kiss her cheek. A smile played at the corners of her mouth. She was quite hungry.

The Young Master said that son-in-law had taken over the post of Director of the Defence Corps. He was running everything at home too. Miss Ling was stunned. She asked hesitantly:

"Do you know how the Master died?"

"The old man was careless and shot himself while cleaning his pistol."

"Who says so?"

"Son-in-law says so, and so does the Lao Taitai. She says the old man sinned against the Sun Buddha, so the spirits made his mind wander and he shot himself. She says you sinned against the Sun Buddha too, and after he died, the old man called you before the King of the Underworld to testify. That's why you've been dead for the past couple of days."

Abstractedly, Miss Ling considered this for several minutes, then she shook her head. She put her mouth close to the Young Master's ear.

"It's not like that. The Master didn't kill himself. Now don't tell this to anybody. I saw it with my own eyes; son-in-law shot him dead!"

The Young Master gazed at her, only half convinced. "Who cares how he died," he said indifferently. "He's dead, and that's the end of it!"

"Ah, I know son-in-law, sooner or later, is going to kill you too! And my turn will also come."

The Young Master said nothing. With a slight frown, he gazed at her searchingly.

"Some day he'll kill us both. If he ever finds out that you and I..." Miss Ling sighed.

Unable to think of any reply, the Young Master hung his head. She gave him a little shove.

"Don't hang around here. He'll be coming back soon!"

"That's what you think! He took office today. Tonight they're giving him a big feed at the house of that fancy lady in town. A fat chance of him coming back!"

"Bite your tongue smarty!" Miss Ling giggled. She didn't urge the Young Master to leave again.

But actually he was a little afraid. After fooling around for a short time, he got up and went away. Miss Ling fell into a deep slumber. She had no idea of how long she had been sleeping when someone shook her awake. Voices clamoured on the street; close by, rifles were popping like fire crackers on New Year's Eve. The Young Master, very frightened, was pulling Miss Ling out of bed.

"Real bandits have come!" he cried hysterically. "You hear? They're shooting! They're fighting at the West Gate!"

Miss Ling was too terrified to speak. Through the window she could see the slanting rays of the setting sun shining golden in a corner of the courtyard. While the Young Master was hastening her into her clothes, he reported breathlessly:

"That day the old man sent his men to the village to the northwest, they robbed and set houses on fire. Then the troops grabbed a lot of the villagers and said they were bandits. Well, now real bandits had come, and the villagers who were falsely accused have joined them! They want to kill our whole family."

Fierce yells from the street drowned out the rest of his words. Shops which had not yet boarded up their windows for the night were being broken into. The Young Master left Miss Ling and ran downstairs. Her legs shaking, she stood by the window that looked on to the street. The troops were running in disorder, looting the unboarded shops as they retreated. Bang! Bang! They fired crazily against the boards of the closed shops.

Miss Ling's legs collapsed under her. She sat down weakly on the floor. Just then, the Young Master came running back and pulled her to her feet.

"Bandits ... fought their way into the town!" he panted. "Son-in-law ... killed!"

They hurried down the stairs. The Lao Taitai was on her knees, kowtowing before the small shrine. Ignoring her completely, the Young Master dragged Miss Ling through the back door as fast as she could travel. Where are we going? Miss Ling kept wondering. She thought of her mother in Shanghai, and tears ran down her ashen cheeks.

Suddenly, there were many short whistling sounds. The Young Master was hit by a stray bullet; he fell like a log, pulling Miss Ling down with him. As she sat up and held him in her arms, another wild shot went through her chest. Her face twitched, then, without a sound, she sprawled on her back and moved no more. The corners of her lips seemed to curl with laughter and with hatred.

Black smoke rose from the house they had just left. There was a burst of flame. Sparks flew in all directions.

WARTIME

In January 1932 the Japanese attacked Shanghai, major seaport and important commercial and industrial center.

Ignoring the "Generalissimo's" flabby policy, the Kuomintang's 19th Route Army, then garrisoning the city, courageously fought back. Sixty thousand Chinese workers in Japanese-owned factories walked out. Chinese employees in all Japanese stores and establishments also quit their jobs. Students and young workers created corps of anti-Japanese volunteers which fought at the front, gave medical care to wounded soldiers, and collected food and supplies in the rear.

Mao Dun tells here about a few ordinary citizens caught up in the conflict — Mr. Li a minor editor and Hsiang a typesetter in Shanghai's large Commercial Press.

After four in the morning, the rifle and artillery fire ceased. Slowly getting up from the floor, Mr. Li put his right hand behind his back and lightly punched his stiff spine. He groped his way to a chair and sat down. With his head cocked to one side, he fell into a bemused trance.

Following his example, his seven-year-old son got up too, his small behind rising first, then the rest of him. The child's very first step brought him tripping over his little sister's fat leg. He thumped to the floor, emitting so lusty a howl that Mr. and Mrs. Li jumped with fright.

"This place is pitch dark! I don't suppose it would matter if I turned on the light now," Mr. Li said half to himself. Without waiting for his wife's consent, he flipped the switch.

At the sudden flood of light, the little five-year-old girl, who was only partly awake, rubbed her eyes with the backs of her chubby hands and began to cry. Mrs. Li glanced at the two-year-old little boy sleeping in her bosom, then reached out a hand and patted her small daughter.

"Don't cry, little sister. We won't let the Japanese soldiers get you!"

The seven-year-old stood before his father, intending to play their old game of riding papa's knee. But seeing how solemn and preoccupied his father looked, the child only leaned lazily against him, and imitated the way he cocked his head to one side. The parents were conversing in low tones.

"We can't hear them any more. Does that mean they've stopped fighting?" asked the mother.

"Who knows? I think I'll go out and take a look. It won't hurt to have a little look. I won't go far."

"Don't go, I tell you! Why don't you ever listen to me? All during the daylight hours people were leaving this part of the city; the foreign concession districts shut their big iron gates. On top of all that, the maid kept insisting she had to get away from here too — I was nearly frantic by the time you came home from the office. But you — free and easy — guaranteed nothing was going to happen! If the maid wants to go, you said, let her go!"

"We should have kept her. Then you wouldn't be afraid of the Japanese."

"Aya! Do you have to try and be funny? You see how nervous I am! Three little tots; somebody has to help carry them. If the maid were here she could carry at least one. Of course we won't be able to take our things — "

"So you still haven't given up the idea of moving away."

"And you only want to go out and take a look! What good is just looking going to do?"

Mrs. Li was a little angry. The heaving of her breast woke the two-year-old and he cried. She patted him, crooning, "Mama's here, precious, Mama's here." She shot her husband an aggrieved glance.

Mr. Li hung his head. Frowning, he rubbed his hand on his knee.

"What a mess! If we don't move, we won't feel safe. If we do move, we'll have to spend a lot of money. I never thought they'd really fight..."

"I'm afraid to spend the money too. That's why, even though it was still daylight, I agreed we should stay. We can just count ourselves lucky some shell hasn't hit us!"

Seeing her husband's mournful expression, Mrs. Li regretted she had spoken so sharply. Forcing a smile, she continued, "There hasn't been a sound in a long time now. There probably won't be any big battle. You'd better get some sleep. In a while, you still have to go to the office."

Mr. Li looked at his wife, and he too managed a smile, which he followed with a large yawn. He felt his wife was right. The Japanese soldiers were very fierce and cruel. When they were attacking Shenyang in the Northeast provinces, even though they hadn't met with any resistance, reports said they laid down a huge machine-gun and artillery barrage. Very likely all that firing just now was the same sort of thing. In that case, everything would be peaceful as usual. There wouldn't be any serious clash. The office would be open for business and he would go. Staying home he'd lose two silver dollars and fifty cents a day. What for!

Mr. Li's wife agreed, and he walked up the stairs, patting his stiff thighs. The seven-year-old boy wanted to follow, but Mrs. Li called him back. She kept the child beside her on the quilts they had spread on the floor, covering him with a blanket.

At the top of the stairs, Mr. Li again became worried. In front of him was a short ladder leading to a small open porch a few feet higher than the level of the upper storey but lower than the roof. He decided he'd better go and see how things really stood.

No sooner had he opened the porch door than — ping! ping! two sharp reports. Mr. Li shrank back and peered through the door crack. Frigid clouds filled the sky; here and there a few cold winter stars glimmered. The wind blowing through the crack was icy. Someone seemed to be standing on the porch of the house next door, surveying the darkened city. Mr. Li took a grip on himself and pulled the folds of his felt hat down over his face until only his eyes were visible. Thus fortified, he eased himself out of the door, crouching and sticking close to the wall. Once outside, he immediately squatted, his ears listening intently.

He thought he heard shouts in the distance but perhaps it was only the wind. The sky was free of any red glow or black smoke. It was just like any other winter night in the last month of the year. Mr. Li slowly rose to his feet and walked to the low cement railing of the porch to get a better view.

"Is that you, Mr. Li? A little while ago you could see lots of red flashes from up here. Must have been the Japanese artillery, the bastards!"

Mr. Li turned a startled face in the direction of the voice. Only when the man finished speaking did Mr. Li identify him as the fellow who lived in a cramped little room in the house next door. His name was Xiang and he was a typesetter in the publishing company where Mr. Li was employed. They were both in the same line, so to speak.

"Been up here long?" Mr. Li asked casually, frowning slightly. He strained his eyes, looking in all directions for any sign of a red flash. Although Xiang was a neighbor and they both worked for the same firm, since one was a "gentleman" in the editorial department and the other only a worker in the printing press, the two seldom met. When they did, an exchange of glances substituted for hailing each other by name. Mr. Li was replying now only out of common politeness; he was not intending to enter into conversation. To his surprise, Xiang responded with enthusiasm.

"We beat the Japanese!" Xiang replied joyfully.

Mr. Li was electrified. What? Were the Japanese actually beaten? That was rather hard to believe. He turn to face Xiang. The worker's white teeth flashed in a grin; he was swinging a clenched fist high.

"We licked 'em. They all ran back to the Japanese concession in the Hongkew district!"

It sounded convincing, but Mr. Li had to ask, "How do you know?"

"The cop on the corner outside our lane said so. Besides, I saw — "

"You saw what? What did you see?"

"I saw lots of 19th Route Army men going north. People said they were going to help the soldiers holding the railway station at Tiantongan. The Japanese attacked Baoshan Road, and they were knocked back there too. They had to retreat to Fuxing Road and take cover."

"Oh? Well...." Mr. Li was still a little sceptical. But he finally knew why the artillery had seemed to be coming from all sides a few hours ago. He and his wife and kids had tumbled out of bed and rushed downstairs to the parlor to sleep on the floor. Their house was directly between two lines of fire! Controlling himself with an effort, Mr. Li sighed.

"It's turned into a big affair. The Japanese certainly won't be willing to quit..."

"Then we'll fight the sons of bitches!!"

The words had just left Xiang's mouth when two sharp reports split the air, followed by the crack of other rifles returning the compliment. Mr. Li froze for an instant, then quickly squatted low, his legs trembling.

"Hah! They've started again," he heard Xiang shout. "Let 'em have it! Kill the Japanese dogs!"

After a brief exchange, silence again reigned in the night. To Mr. Li the quiet was like an iron slab pressing down on his heart. Still squatting, he shifted his feet uneasily and rose a little. The best thing to do, he thought, was to hurry back down the stairs and talk to his wife about getting out in the morning. Just then, a gust of wind struck his face. Over-wrought, he stifled a cry and dropped back to his squatting position. A machine-gun began chattering to the north. Even though Mr. Li's ears were covered by the thick felt of his pulled down hat, the sound nearly deafened him. He was sure the machine-gun was very near. And the porch had to face north, of course! In a cold sweat, Mr. Li squatted motionless. He didn't dare move, but he was afraid that if he didn't move he'd be killed on his own porch. Rat-ta-ta-ta, boom! boom! Wrapping his arms around his head, Mr. Li leaped up, but immediately fell forward like a log. Frantically, he crawled through the porch door and tumbled down the small ladder. He uttered one loud squawk, then seemed to lose consciousness.

"Ayo, my poor husband! Ayo, ayo!. . .

The wails from downstairs shocked Mr. Li's numbed senses back to life. The machine-gun was silent now; there was only occasional scattered rifle fire. Feeling his head, Mr. Li found it intact. He clutched the banister and staggered down the stairs. Sobbing tragically, his wife threw herself on his bosom. He held her for a moment, then sat down gingerly on the lowest step.

"My dear, what happened to you? Where were you wounded? Where were you wounded?"

"I'm alright," Mr. Li replied in a shaking voice.

A single question was nipping at his heart like a bedbug — How can we get away from here in the morning?

It was almost daybreak. The five-year-old and the seven-year-old were curled up under the blanket sleeping peacefully. The two-year-old baby, lying in his mother's arms, began to gurgle and sing. He obviously enjoyed the whole family sleeping on the floor together. It made such a nice big bed!

Outside in the compound, the cockerel they were keeping for their New Year's Day dinner, crowed loudly.

Mr. Li lay on his back, staring with red-rimmed eyes he hadn't closed all night. He frowned but did not speak.

The tramping of footsteps on the street beyond the lane's high solid iron gate didn't stop for a single second. The floor beneath Mr. Li's head vibrated with their tread. Noisy conversations drew abreast of the big gate, drifted past it.

Mrs. Li sat up, holding the two-year-old. Too listless to respond to his chortles, she automatically rocked back and forth. After a minute, she turned to Mr. Li.

"Have you figured out how we'll travel?"

"Wait till it's light and I'll ask. There's bound to be at least one road open from this part of the city to the foreign concessions."

Mr. Li's voice was hoarse. He rolled over and faced his wife. "There hasn't been any shooting for an hour. Maybe they'll talk peace today," he said with a wry smile. "If the British or the American Consul comes out and mediates, there's a a good chance the fighting'll end."

"Weren't you saying all day yesterday there wouldn't be any fighting? Then last night it started!"

"Well, alright. As soon as it's daylight, we'll move to the foreign concessions for a few days."

Mr. Li was already calculating how much it would cost to live in a hotel. Two adults and three children — one small room at a dollar or so a day would be enough. They'd probably spend another dollar a day on meals. He had over sixty dollar on hand; they could easily get by for nine or ten days. Anyhow, Mr. Li was sure the fighting would be over long before then. Shanghai was a big cosmopolitan city, and the eyes of the whole world were on it now. Would a battle be allowed to go on in a place like this for as long as nine or ten days? Mr. Li just couldn't believe it.

He kept his conviction to himself, however. Yesterday's prediction had discredited him badly. This "new" hope he retained as a private consolation.

Having reached this point in his rationalization, Mr. Li felt somewhat better. Exhausted by his sleepless night, he groggily closed his eyes.

Less than ten minutes later, he awoke with a start. Voices were clamoring in the lane; a deep powerful sound droned almost directly overhead. Mr. Li and his wife exchanged a frightened glance, unable to imagine what new disaster had struck. They heard people running and shouting in the street, right outside the gate of their lane.

"Japanese bombers are coming! Go home and take shelter!"

"Take shelter! Scatter! Bunching together you're sure to be hit!" Wildly running footsteps, followed by several loud bangs, very close by. People were slamming their doors and gates shut, and Mr. and Mrs. Li mistook the sound for exploding bombs. Their faces turned green. Nearer and nearer came the planes, engines throbbing. Now they were right overhead. Except for the roaring engines, alternately increasing and fading in volume, the lane was deathly quiet. Mr. Li and his wife sat back to back on the bedding spread on the floor. Stretching his neck, the two-year-old baby was listening too, his eyes frightened and staring. The two older children slept peacefully beneath the blanket. Mr. Li's whole family was here before him, all in one tight little group. If a bomb should drop now —

His blood froze in his veins. He didn't dare think any further.

It was already quite light, though there was no sun. Rain had fallen the night before and a pale grey curtain was stretched across the sky. The planes had gone, apparently. Only their faint droning could still be heard in the distance. After a while, that was gone too. Mr. Li heaved a sigh, again listened carefully. Those machine-guns and artillery pieces that nearly scared the life out of him the previous night were completely at rest. A babel of voices again rose in the lane, and on the street beyond the big gate footsteps resumed once more.

"What shall we do? I wonder what it's like, travelling on the streets?..." Mrs. Li said to herself, but aloud. She looked at the baby in her arms and the two children sleeping beneath the blanket.

Mr. Li stood up. "The only thing to do is go out and see. Nobody'll come and tell you, just sticking in the house!" His eyes seemed to pleading for his wife's consent. He patted the long fleece-lined gown he was wearing and got ready to leave.

Mrs. Li could think of no better alternative. Her only answer was a sigh. She shut her eyes to hold back the tears.

Afraid to wander too far, Mr. Li made a brief tour of the lane. Last night his neighbors, like himself, had not intended to run away either. Now many of them, carrying children and bundles, were moving out. Some said the Taiyang Temple Road was still open, and Mr. Li felt much better. He walked to the lane's entrance. The big iron gate was already closed, but the small door through it remained open. Two policemen standing in the street raised their faces from time to time to peer at the sky. Many residents were leaving the lane; practically none were coming in. People walked along the street in twos and threes. From the looks of them, all were on their way to the "foreign concessions". (In these enclaves foreigners, and some wealthy Chinese, lived in virtual autonomy.) Standing in the doorway of the iron gate, Mr. Li called to the policeman.

"Are the streets from here passable?"

"Sure!"

"Not dangerous, is it?"

"Hard to say."

"Have they stopped fighting?"

"Just listen!"

Mr. Li's heart leaped. He strained his ears. There were a few faint rifle shots. He listened again. Only silence. He looked up at the sky. High to the north were three tiny planes, chasing each other in a circle like mating dragonflies. Then they formed a straight line and slowly grew larger. He could hear the sound of their engines now. Soon he could see the red dot on each of their silver wings; their ominous droning was terrifying. A detachment of marching soldiers immediately scattered and pressed themselves close to thee walls of the houses lining the street. Mr. Li turned and ran. Just as he reached his own front door, he heard the first distant explosion.

"Boom!"

"Go, go, go!" Mr. Li chattered to the frightened wife rushing to meet him. He was very pale. His legs suddenly went soft and he sank to the floor in a heap, panting hard.

Mrs. Li could no longer restrain her tears. Picking up the baby, she burst into muffled helpless sobs.

In the distance, they heard it again.

Boom! Boom!

Mr. Li jumped up, his face as white as a sheet. Silently he picked up the older boy and the little boy. Mrs. Li carried the girl. They ran into the lane. When they reached the entrance-way, it was jammed with people. Both the big iron gate and the small door were shut tight. Outside, the policeman was shouting:

"Don't get excited! Stay in your houses! Running around in the open is just asking for it!"

At the gate, men were yelling, women screaming. A plane, its engine thrumming, appeared over the rear end of the lane and flew toward two rising columns of black smoke in the north. After circling the smoke, the plane suddenly plummeted downwards. The crowd inside the gate set up a cheer. But in another instant the plane came out of the smoke in a steep climb and turned east. And immediately following — Boom!

Mr. Li was panicky, irresolute. His children cried and complained they were hungry. Putting them down, he conferred with his wife. Better go back to the house and wait a while. If they were killed it would be because Fate intended it that way! He asked people about the Taiyang Temple Road and was told it was blocked. The only route open to the foreign concessions was a wide detour via Zaojiadu, a ten-mile trip. Steeling himself, Mr. Li decided to risk it.

Bringing the three children into the house, Mr. Li told his wife to feed them. He himself went upstairs to pack some of his books and clothing. He was thinking more clearly now. With no means of transport but his own two legs, he would have to cover ten miles, carrying three kids besides. He decided he had better leave the books behind and just pick out a few changes of clothing. At first he packed all his better clothes in a large bundle, but after weighing it in his hands, came to the conclusion that it was too heavy. With a sigh, he selected only enough to tide him over a few days and made a parcel of it. Even so, it still seemed heavier than his five-year-old daughter. There were ten miles of difficult road ahead. For the third time, he sorted his clothing. In the end, he picked only a few shirts and sets of underwear and the gown his wife liked best. The bundle now was no bigger than a pillow.

Wiping the sweat from his face, Mr. Li went to close the window. The sun shone weakly through the pall of black smoke that covered the sky. He was sure there must be a big fire somewhere, but his mind was too dull to give it much thought. Taking his small bundle, he went downstairs.

The three children had already eaten their fill. Holding on to a chair for support, the youngest was chattering animatedly in a language all his own. The two older children were out playing in the courtyard, chasing things that flew like small black butterflies. As Mr. Li watched his three lively little youngsters, he was oppressed by the thought that this happy home which he had spent ten difficult years building might be blotted out in an instant by a shell or a bomb. Tears came to his eyes.

Suddenly, Mrs. Li came running out of the kitchen, a dishcloth in her hand.

"Do you know what happened? Do you know?" she cried, distraught. "The Commercial Press was bombed! The whole plant is in flames!"

"What! Then that big fire is at the Press? Who says so?"

"Xiang's wife, next door!"

The seven-year-old boy bounded into the parlor with the little black things he had caught in the courtyard, his little sister right behind him. Mr. Li's eyes opened wide. Those black butterflies were bits of burnt paper! It was all clear to him now. His heart beat fast. The Japanese had mashed his livelihood, they had broken his rice bowl! Destroying China's biggest publishing house, they had broken the rice bowls of thousands of workers and employees! A savage laugh burst from Mr. Li's lips, his pale face became tinged with an angry purple.

"Those Japanese have gone too far!" he cried.

He forgot all about the danger of bombs. His "rice bowl" was broken. What more was there to fear! He rushed out of the door, why or where he had no idea, nor did he care.

Mrs. Li ran after him, "Don't go out!" she wailed. "Where are you going?" But the howls of all three kids bawling in unison pulled her back into the house.

Mr. Li ran to the entrance of the lane in one breath. Xiang and another printing-press worker were just coming in. Mr. Li greeted Xiang like a long-lost friend.

"What's the fire like at the Press?"

"Dozens of big blazes!" Xiang retorted angrily. He was in the uniform of the plant's fire-fighters. His clothing was half drenched, his face brick-red. On his head was a bright brass helmet. Wiping his mouth with the back of his hand, he said hotly:

"Japanese bombs fell like rain. Wherever they burst, fires started. There were fires all over the place. Our fire-fighting squad couldn't handle them all. And the Japanese wouldn't let fire-engines through from the concessions. The dirty bastards! I'm going to show those dogs a thing or two!"

"Plant Five is the only one left now," put in Xiang's workmate, "but sooner or later the Japanese'll bomb that too!"

Mr. Li didn't know the man's name but recognized him as another typesetter. Mr. Li's heart was pounding hard. It seemed to grow bigger with each beat. Standing with these two valiants, Mr. Li felt like a new man.

"The Japanese planes take off from Hongkew Park," he grated. "We ought to smash into there. Then we'd fix 'em!"

Xiang was confident. "That's just what we're going to do! Today, the 19th Route Army'll drive the Japanese back to their ships!" His big teeth flashed in a laugh.

"And the Army doesn't have to worry about men," said Xiang's friend, whose name was Chun-sheng. "We'll all join! The plant's burned down and we're out of work. But we're not leaving Shanghai. We're going to fight the Japanese!"

Mr. Li's thumping heart grew larger still; the blood rushed to his face. At that moment his wife arrived, leading two children by the hand. Hsiang's wife was carrying the baby. Mr. Li frowned, then he sighed. He looked at the muscular physique of Xiang and his workmate, then at his own white hands. The difference was too great. "Each must go his own way in life." Recalling the old axiom, Mr. Li felt less ashamed.

His only problem now was how to travel down Zhongshan Road and get across Zaojiadu. Plane engines, now near, now far, could still be heard overhead.

Although the second and third Japanese assaults were defeated, it became more obvious daily that the enemy would not be driven back to their ships as Xiang predicted. The Chinese troops held only the Chinese section of the city, while enemy soldiers swaggered about Hongkou — the Japanese concession, and awaited reinforcements from Japan.

One day, the Japanese planes bombed the Zhabei district. A dozen fires sprang up in the neighborhood of Baoshan Road; by nightfall, they still crimsoned half the sky. This bombing enraged Xiang much more than the destruction of the Commercial Press. He and his workmate Chun-sheng felt like throwing themselves into the fires and beating them out with their bare hands. They had no hose, no pump, no water. Flames spread to the most densely populated section of Baoshan Road and consumed the hovels of the workers. None of them had that essential qualification for finding shelter in the foreign concessions — money! Countless refugees had to sleep in the streets on the perimeter of the blaze. The Japanese planes bombed every place that was thickly congregated. Zhabei was turned into a field of rubble, Zhabei was turned into a hell on earth!

Though the section where Xiang lived did not catch fire, it was without water or electricity. His wife had run out of food. None of these problems disturbed him, however. He and Chun-sheng were busy loading trucks with ammunition and gifts from the people for the 19th Route Army. Xiang almost forgot that he had a wife waiting at home with nothing to eat.

Every day there was news of ships arriving with fresh Japanese reinforcements. But no reinforcements came for the Chinese troops. When a man was killed they were just short one more soldier. Hsiang and the other workers nearly went mad with rage. They realized it was a pure daydream to think the Chinese forces could drive the Japanese back to their ships. Now it would be a miracle if the defenders could even hold on to Zhabei.

But the workers were not downhearted. Though their bellies were half-empty, they put everything they had into their jobs.

The day of the four-hour armistice, early in the morning, Xiang went running to find Chun-sheng.

"I'm sending my wife away," Xiang announced resolutely.

"She'll starve to death, you nitwit! Out by herself like that, she'll be helpless."

"I've asked a friend from my old village to take her back there," said Xiang. He spat angrily.

Chun-sheng silently looked up at the sky. The men were sitting by the wall of the flame-blackened shell of a house. A truck heavily laden with furniture and household goods rolled past them down the street. The wealthy took refuge in the foreign concessions in proper style! Xiang spat again.

A soldier on leave from the front had wandered over while the two workers were talking. Munching a large wheatcake, he joined in the conversation.

"Got any relatives in your village?" he asked Xiang.

"Not a one."

"Hah! Then you're practically telling your wife to shift for herself."

"I can't help it. Zhabei's been burned to the ground, tens of thousands of poor people have been killed — didn't they all have mothers and fathers who loved them? I hate those rotten Japanese! I'll fight them to the death — it's them or me!"

The soldier nodded solemnly.

"Do you think we can get into your outfit?" Xiang asked. "We can fight the Japanese together!"

The question had been on Xiang's mind for several days. He and Chun-sheng had discussed it a number of times and had asked the man in charge of their work brigade about joining the army. He told them it wasn't as simple as all that; you couldn't just join whenever you felt like it. They then barged in and made application at a branch of the Shanghai Volunteers, but were rejected because they hadn't brought any letters of identification from their factory or union. They hadn't followed up on this, however, because they learned the Volunteers were not to be sent to the front. It came as a surprise to them that men who were willing to risk their lives fighting the Japanese needed to go to so much trouble, and even required a special introduction.

"We were a couple of months in the workers' detachment in '27," Chun-sheng replied excitedly, "when we fought off the warlord army of Zhang Zong-chang!" Beside him, Xiang was grinning with satisfaction.

"I'll speak to my platoon leader," said the soldier.

That afternoon, Xiang and a few dozen other workers were sent to the town of Miaohong, a few miles out of Shanghai, to dig trenches. This hardly satisfied Xiang's thirst for action, but he worked hard, ripping out great shovefuls of earth. Pausing to wipe the sweat from his face, he noticed something in the sky.

"Planes!" he said to Chun-sheng. "Are they Japanese or ours?"

Five black dots circled buzzing overhead. As they flew lower, the red suns on their silver wings became visible. Japanese, of course. They were directly above the workers now. The men glanced up, then went on with their digging.

Working vigorously, Xiang was soon dripping sweat. He rested the shovel against his leg and spat on his hands.

"Son of a bitch!" he swore. "Why did we wait till they got all their troops in position before starting to dig trenches out here?"

"The idea now is to hit 'em so hard they'll never come back!" a worker beside him laughed, giving Xiang a wink.

"If we'd pushed on through Hongkou that day and driven them to their ships, we could've saved ourselves a lot of grief," Chun-sheng put in. "Zhabei wouldn't have been burned down and thousands of people's still be alive today!" Angrily, he tossed a shovelful of earth out of the trench.

"Zhabei's in ashes now and all those people are dead," said Xiang bitterly. "The rest of us'll be dead too if we don't kill the Japanese!" He picked up his shovel.

"Stop your blasted gabbing!"

It was the overseer of the labor gang, carrying a long bamboo switch. He glared at them a few seconds, then stamped away. The workers continued digging, digging, digging. Sweat rained from their foreheads, soaking into the grey-brown clay, but their arms never stopped.

When the battle at Miaohong started, Xiang and Chun-sheng at last had an opportunity to go to the front. But there they were ordered to carry the wounded, not guns. Artillery shells whistled over their heads, they could see the flame spat by coughing machine-guns. They made trip after trip, carrying wounded soldiers to the rear and loading them on to trucks.

"What does it all add up to, Xiang?" Chun-sheng asked during an enemy artillery barrage. "A shell lands and bang! — a man is finished!"

"As long as you help beat the Japanese, and stop them from getting through, it adds up to your being a blinking hero!"

Xiang had become friendly with the soldiers. He saw that they had no thought of retreat, and weren't afraid to die. The Japanese would never pierce our lines! Feeling quite assured, Xiang was even a little less angry about not having a chance to shoulder a gun.

In several days of fierce fighting, Japanese artillery virtually levelled the town of Miaohong. But the Chinese soldiers stuck to their posts. Their lines seemed to be made of iron. Xiang and Chun-sheng were especially happy because their sweat had watered the digging of those trenches. Their efforts had not been in vain. What's more, they were almost certain they would be called to take direct part in the fight; for casualties were mounting by the day and our ranks had thinned out considerably.

In their dreams the two workers saw murderous Japanese tanks come rumbling toward them, and themselves, leaping out of the trench, throwing hand grenades. The tanks were blown to smithereens, and they would wake up smiling.

But the fighting around Miaohong gradually died down. The Japanese, having been knocked back with heavy losses each time they attacked the town, changed their tactics. Xiang and Chun-sheng were happy, but a little disappointed that their dreams about the grenade throwing couldn't come true for the time being. They were transferred to another sector — Bazeqiao. The situation was tense there and a great many workers were needed. Xiang and his mates were put to toting food and ammunition.

The battle grew fiercer every day. It was rumored that a Japanese general, Shirakawa, had arrived with three full divisions, supported by a fleet of over a dozen war vessels. The Japanese attacked on all fronts, laying down a heavy artillery barrage against the Chinese lines. The Chinese stuck to their positions, their casualties mounting by the hour. Taking ammunition to the front and carrying the wounded back, Hsiang and his mates hadn't slept for several nights. They didn't even have time to think. They worked mechanically with only one idea in mind — die but never retreat!

Xiang was in a labor detachment of fifty or sixty men. One night, laden with artillery shells, they followed the march of the army unit to which they were attached. They walked very quickly. A sickle moon hung in the the sky; there were a few stars and grey drifting clouds. Travel was difficult over the bumpy road. Following in the wake of the troops, the workers mechanically kept pace as usual. But gradually they began to feel that something different was in the air. The thunder of the big guns was growing fainter; it required a real effort to hear them at all.

Conscious of the peculiar atmosphere, Xiang was puzzled. After marching a little longer, he couldn't contain himself. He poked Chun-sheng, who was walking beside him.

"What's up?" Xiang asked in a whisper. "Have we taken the wrong road? I can't hear the artillery any more."

"I've just been wondering about that myself. We seem to be going toward the rear, not forward."

"They must be sending us to another front," a porter behind Xiang interjected.

Xiang wasn't so sure and only made an noncommital sound. A man in front of him laughed shortly. Turning his head, he said:

"You're all way off the track! I heard something, only I don't know whether it's true or not — the Japanese are too strong for us! We can't hold this line any more. We're retreating to our second line of defence!"

Xiang was shocked.

"Second line? Where's that?" Chun-sheng demanded.

"Not far, but not exactly near either. I heard it's Kunshan!"

Xiang snorted. He was speechless and his face was pale. His red-rimmed eyes looked ready to drip blood . Just then seven or eight mounted men came galloping up from behind and clattered past the work detachment. They were followed by rumbling artillery caissons and hundreds of foot soldiers, marching in close formation.

Xiang knew the score now. He flung his porter's pole to the ground. The whole detachment of workers halted to look at him. His eyes big with anger, Xiang shouted:

"Retreat? Zhabei's been gutted; Jiangwan and Wusong have been burned to the ground. Are we going to let the Japanese get away with that? We can't retreat! We have to hold on if it kills us! We're going to fight the Japanese, we're not going to run!"

Still yelling, he rushed after the retreating soldiers. Chun-sheng hadn't been able to restrain him, and now, also shouting, he started to follow. But before Chun-sheng had taken five paces, the labor detachment leader caught him and flung him to the ground.

"Are you tired of living!"

As Chun-sheng rose to his knees, he was struck a hard blow on the head. His ears rang and everything went black. He heard loud angry voices in the distance, then a few sharp reports of a pistol. Chun-sheng lost consciousness.

After all Chinese soldiers within a radius of twelve miles of Shanghai had withdrawn, the fighting stopped. Innumerable meetings were held to discuss terms for ending the war; finally a draft agreement was signed. Zhabei lay in ruins; from all over the city came cries, varying in degree of enthusiasm, calling for the restoration of Shanghai. China's losses had been severe. Reams of statistics were published in the local newspapers. The Commercial Press alone had been damaged to the extent of sixteen million dollars.

In any event a large institution like the Commercial Press — a publishing enterprise, a cultural institution — simply had to be put back into operation. It ran an announcement in the newspapers. The Press was discharging all its old employees; it would begin hiring, on a new basis, after repairs were completed. As to "retirement bonuses" for those being discharged, because of the "heavy losses the Press had suffered in the nation's time of trial", it would not be able to pay on the originally agreed terms.

This brought an immediate response from the more than five thousand former employees of the Press, including Mr. Li, who was now living in a small rented room in the French Concession. Mr. Li became very busy. His fellow employees formed an organization to demand payment of the retirement bonus in full. Mr. Li naturally took part. They inserted an announcement in the press denouncing their employer's unilateral action, they sent representatives to confer with officers of the company, they tried to enlist public support, they gave press conferences, they petitioned the Social Bureau of the municipal government... In all of this, Mr. Li participated. He had been with the Press for over ten years and had a retirement bonus of more than a thousand dollars due to him. He was so busy running around that he didn't have even a moment to help his wife with their two-year-old.

After two months of wrangling the Press offered what it described as a magnanimous concession. It knocked a tiny fraction off the huge cut it had already decided to make in the bonuses; beyond this it positively would not go. Now, even if Mr. Li wanted to be busy, he had nothing to occupy him. He could only sit in the dark damp of his narrow little room and sigh. His wife berated him for having wasted his time and money on missions for the discharged employees' organization.

Mr. Li stamped. "What do women know anyway!" His temper wasn't too good lately.

Again the company published an announcement. On a certain date, at a certain address on Sichuan Road, it would begin paying the retirement bonuses. The money would be waiting.

The union countered with its own announcement, stating that the dispute had not yet been settled and warning its members not to draw the money at Sichuan Road. Moreover, it decided to post a few men near the place to stop any of its members who might weaken, and persuade them to change their minds.

Mr. Li was sure he was not one of those who would need persuasion. But when asked to serve as a persuader of others, he was afraid he couldn't measure up to the job. He spent his time, therefore, sitting in the cramped little room, waiting for news of the outcome.

Mrs. Li was fully occupied with cooking and washing, and the three children tumbled riotously on the room's only bed. Too dispirited to bother about them, Mr. Li borrowed a newspaper from his next-door neighbor to read the advertisements. Blurbs about new books and magazines put out by the small publishing houses spread over a page and a half. The publishing world had made a lively come-back once the fighting stopped — or so it seemed to Mr. Li. The thought comforted him. But his hand instinctively moved to his much flattened wallet, and Mr. Li frowned. He skimmed idly though the pages of the newspaper, then turned back to the company's "money waiting" announcement...

Three days later, the company inserted another announcement in the press. It said it had already paid out many thousands of dollars, and gave the figure; it hoped that the few who had not yet drawn their money would do so immediately; it was extending its offer one final week...

When he read this, Mr. Li's heart leaped; the newspaper fell to the floor. It seemed to him that he was only one holding out so stubbornly. What for? He had five mouths to feed, the landlord wanted his rent, and here he was, flat broke! Raising his head, he looked at his wife, cleaning vegetables in the family washbasin.

"I suppose I'd better go and pick up that money. What do you say?"

"I'm a woman. What do I know, anyway!" She hadn't forgotten the remark he had made a few days before. Lately, her temper hadn't been too good either!

Mr. Li smiled a lonely smile, then took their last twenty cents and went out.

An hour later, he was at Sichuan Road, furtively entering the company's temporary office.

When he came out, there was a little over a hundred dollars in his wallet. His hand pressing his pocket, he stepped briskly, his backbone a bit straighter. He could see that Sichuan Road was still the gay colorful street it had always been.

Suddenly, from behind, a tragic voice assailed his ears.

"Give my back my Xiang!"

Mr. Li automatically stopped and turned around. There stood a woman, oddly dressed, her hair wildly awry, ashen-faced, the whites of her rolled-up eyes gleaming. It was the wife of his former neighbor Xiang! The events of those two frightening days of the bombardment flooded back to him.

"Give me my Xiang," the woman cried piercingly. "You know where he is!"

"But I don't —"

The woman bared her teeth in a terrifying laugh that made Mr. Li's heart race. Staring straight ahead, she began to wail.

"You do know! You're in the gang that schemed against him! You got your share, don't deny it! You know! Ha-ha, I know you do!... Xiang, they all want to suck up to the Japanese, they made a fool of you, you died for nothing!... I know you all ganged up on Xiang, don't deny it! You're in it too. Today I've found you out, don't deny it!"

Mr. Li shuddered, his heart pounding. Hastily he turned and walked away, not daring to look back.

"You all plotted against him! You can't deny it!..."

"A TRUE CHINESE PATRIOT"

Most of the big merchants and industrialists fled to Chongqing in the mid-thirties as the Japanese armies took over major cities like Beijing, Tianjin, Hankow, Shanghai and Nanjing. There was strong sentiment among them against the united front with the Communists to which the Chiang Kaishek's Kuomintang was nominally committed. They were hoping, though it was not considered diplomatic to say so openly, that the invaders would destroy the Communist-led military forces, which were actively fighting the Japanese, and which the conservatives deemed a far greater menace to their own interests.

This little cameo neatly reflects the devious soul of one of the more mealy-mouthed "patriots".

He started the day with hot milk, at seven a.m., as per schedule. Madam personally put in the two and a half lumps of sugar, and delivered the cup to his bedside. On the gilded Fujian lacquer tray also lay the morning newspaper.

Madam sat on the edge of the bed — according to schedule — and smilingly watched her husband sip the milk as he skimmed through the paper. According to schedule, he first read the advertisements, then the local news, and finally the important national and international news. By this time the cup of milk was empty and the Master put down the newspaper and looked at Madam with a smile also according to schedule.

After stretching lazily, or massaging his temples with his index fingers, he usually sank his head back into the down-filled pillow and closed his eyes. This was in order to think over the things he had to do that day. Then Madam would ring the bell, and the maid, who had been waiting for the signal, would glide in like a shadow, and remove the cup, the tray and the newspaper. Madam would follow her out, softly shutting the door behind her.

All this was the result of the scientific orderliness which the Master had been introducing into their daily routine over the past two years. These household rules didn't exist when the Master first began "serving society" through his activities in the commercial world. He drank milk then too, but not necessarily in bed. Nor did Madam have to put the sugar in herself and deliver it to him personally. Even less did she have to sit on the edge of the bed and watch him drink it. In those days the Master usually got up first and opened the window himself. Then the maid timidly came in and with quick light steps began tidying up the room while Madam, lying on her side, watched through half-closed eyes.

The innovations began with the expansion of the Master's commercial enterprises, when he changed from merely "serving society" to "serving the nation". In order to sacrifice his personal pleasures for the nation's sake, he decided to put his family life "on a scientific basis." The busier he became the more rules he brought into their home, so that every precious minute might be fruitfully utilized. Among other things, he asked Madam to go "back to the kitchen". In the course of a year the Master ate lunch at home only two or three times; only one day in ten did he return home for dinner. But every morning he did have breakfast at home, and it was then, with the hot milk, that Madam could demonstrate her respect for the "back to the kitchen" decree. Her personal attention to the sugar and the delivery of the milk became an impressive ceremony.

But why did she have to sit on the edge of the bed and watch him drink it? The reason is that in addition to having a "scientific" side, the Master was possessed of "tenderness"; he was a careerist with a "poetic" nature. His every nerve fibre was devoted to the service of the nation. "I have long since cast aside any thought of personal enjoyment," he was fond of saying. The morning milk time, however, was a bit of private life he felt he ought to retain. He explained that this was in keeping with the romantic-poet side of his nature.

"Of the twenty-four hours a day, we have only these few moments to partake of a little sweet intimacy, and it is only right that we should do so. Our connubial bliss, the union of our souls, when expressed in that wordless exchange of glances, attains life's rarest and truest flavor!"

"But why do you want to read the newspaper at the same time?" Madam asked him jokingly when he first offered the romantic-poet rationalization.

The Master's answer was extremely reasonable. "Ah, my dear wife," he exclaimed. "That's because my time is so precious. But though my eyes are on the paper, I am looking at you with my heart!" He squeezed Madam's hand affectionately.

Madam couldn't fail to be satisfied with this explanation. But as time went on she found it difficult to concentrate on blissfully gazing at him in silence. At times she drifted off into a reverie, at times she watched his facial expressions reflect what he was reading in the newspaper. She was even reminded occasionally of their eldest child — how bad tempered he had been as a one-year-old. He refused to sleep unless she lay beside him where he could nestle against her bosom. But whenever this thought occurred to her, Madam quickly drove it from her mind. Looking at her husband with an apologetic smile, she would say to herself: He's so busy all day — for the nation. Why shouldn't I indulge him in this one little quirk if it gives him comfort?

Today all the scheduled matters were performed according to schedule, except for one deviation — the Master opened his newspaper directly to the national news section.

Seated beside him, Madam was involved in her own thoughts. Although she continued to smile at him out of habit, she did not observe the change of expressions on his face. It was only when he noisily flung the newspaper aside that she was startled into attentiveness.

"Ah..." All of Madam's unreserved humility was expressed in the single syllable. Her eyes, though still tender, were a bit frightened.

"Aw!" said the Master, as if in answer. But Madam, who understood every one of the Master's "Aws" and "Ohs", knew that it was not an answer; what's more, he was frowning.

Caressingly, almost lying against him, Madam placed her lovely hand on the Master's forehead. It seemed a little hot. Her eyes went wide and she opened her lips in exaggerated alarm. Before she could speak the Master pushed her hand aside and took up the glass of milk.

"Ai!" exclaimed the Master, rather impatiently. He drank a sip of milk. "I'm alright. Perhaps it's because you put too much sugar in the milk?"

"I only used the usual amount!" Startled, she stared at him and assumed a hurt expression. Then she laughed gaily. "Don't try to fool me. Something's troubling you. It isn't that the milk's too sweet. I'm afraid you've found something in the paper too bitter!"

The Master smiled wryly and took another sip.

Madam wanted to look at the newspaper, but the Master stayed her hand. He drained the glass, put it down and leaned wearily back against the pillows.

"Why take it so hard? After all, what does it matter if affairs of state — " Madam cut herself short with a hasty laugh. She had almost forgotten that the Master had dedicated every one of his nerve fibres to the nation.

Fortunately he hadn't noticed. His gaze remained calm — an unmistakable sign of the profundity of his meditation.

With no regard to the schedule, Madam personally carried the glass and the Fujian lacquer tray to a table before the window, then stood looking irresolutely at her reflection in the mirror of her dressing table.

"Then yesterday's rumor was true!" muttered the Master. "Settle with the Communists peacefully! Goddam nonsense!" Catching himself, he shot an awkward glance at his wife. He never swore in the presence of ladies of her calibre, though he was free enough with his language at the factory. He rubbed his face and said fretfully:

"You don't understand. National principles are what count. Losing ten thousand men in battle — what does that matter? Yet there are some among us who insist on coming to terms with the Communists. Even our friend Chien the banker wants peace. It's enough to make anyone furious!"

"Yes, yes, of course," said Madam soothingly, walking back to the bed. She remembered her husband often saying that to lose one's temper right after eating was bad for the digestion, and she felt he ought to preserve his strength for the nation. Tenderly seating herself on the edge of the bed, she said, "Of course, you're right. But if it's already been decided to make a peaceful settlement, there's no use your getting excited. We have a woollen factory. No one needs wool to fight a war and you're not a munitions broker, so why get all upset over peace? When the Japanese attacked Shanghai in 1932 didn't you keep hoping for peace —"

"Bah!" The Master's impatient exclamation frightened his spouse into silence. Hesitantly, she again stretched her hand toward his forehead, but he brushed it aside.

"I have no fever. For heaven's sake stop mothering me. My dear wife, how can you be so addle-pated? 'Nothing is more precious than peace among those living together — true. But that doesn't apply to everyone. Suppose our cook or our maid started getting cheeky? Would you make peace, or would you put them in their place?"

Madam nodded. The mention of the cook made her a bit sad. Ever since the Master sent her "back to the kitchen" the cook always consulted her before going out to buy food. He offered it for her inspection on his return from the market and requested her supervision when it was ready for the pot. All this was in accordance with the Master's "rules". Out of respect for her husband's will, Madam could not say to the cook, as she wished — "Don't bother me. Do as you think best." The whole thing gave her a headache.

Now, smiling her agreement, she nodded again.

But the Master had just got into stride. Taking Madam for one of the proponents of peace, he drove ahead relentlessly.

"And another thing — Isn't there a proverb which says that one who fails to see far will court immediate danger? The question has to be considered from all sides. Our Japanese neighbors have offered to form an anti-communist front with us, to help clean out the rebels. How can we make peace with the communists at a time like this? If the Japanese decide to crack down on us, if they send a couple of divisions and a few hundred planes — what will we do then? Do we dare go to war with such a powerful enemy? Ha, my dear wife, if that day ever comes, not only will our woollen factory be smashed to dust, but you and I won't be here any longer, chatting in our comfortable bed!"

Round-eyed, Madam admitted complete defeat, but it gave the Master no joy. While blasting Madam as a peace proponent, he had frightened and depressed himself by his own eloquence. Sinking his head deeper back into the pillow, he wearily shut his eyes.

Madam heard a noise outside the door. She tiptoed from the bed and called softly:

"Who's there?"

"It's me," answered the maid. "I've been waiting for the bell a long time. I came to see. I was afraid it's broken."

Madam was reminded of the daily schedule. "It's not broken," she replied, automatically pressing the button.

When the maid left with the empty milk glass and the tray, Madam followed and gently closed the door behind her. But she forgot to take the newspaper; it was still lying on the bed.

At eight-thirty the Young Master and the Elder Young Mistress left for school in the car. The car returned at nine, and the Master departed for the office. After that, Madam and the Little Young Master took over as guardians of the mansion. At four in the afternoon Madam telephoned the Master to ask whether the car should pick up the children at school. If the Master needed the car, Madam notified the school, then sent the maid to call for the children in a taxi. This was also in accordance with the Master's rules.

After the children returned they were served an afternoon snack which the cook had already prepared. Madam had to go to the kitchen to examine it first because, as the Master often said, people like the cook had "no conscience". Unless you watched them carefully they served you food that was dirty and unsanitary. Five o'clock was Madam's busiest time of the day. While listening to the children tell what happened in school that day (she later had to report this to the Master), Madam kept at the telephone, trying to locate the Master and ask him if he was coming home for dinner. This procedure too had been fixed by the Master.

Only during the period when she and the Little Young Mistress

satisfactory answer.

"Fine woollen yarn is two-strand wool."

"Aiya, wife!" The Master was disappointed. "Fine woollen yarn is a semi-finished product — a semi-finished product! It's quite different from sweaters. When a country imports more semi-finished products that's a very good sign!"

Madam hurriedly nodded and rose to go "back to the kitchen". "I'll buy your wool tomorrow," she said.

As a well-educated person quick to grasp a lofty principle, Madam decided that for the sake of helping the Master serve the nation she would have to be more patient even in matters which tried her patience sorely.

Any pastime which is converted into an obligation loses its taste. That was how Madam had felt about mahjong in the days before her life was put on a scientific basis. And if you top off the obligation with a pompous high-sounding title, it becomes not just tasteless but downright obnoxious. Although Madam respected her husband, she was a woman of delicate sensibilities.

One day while she was forcing herself to carry out his latest edict, the madam of another family came to call on her. On learning why she was knitting, the aristocratic visitor laughed heartily.

"You are patient, my dear, and so thrifty. But really, for the sake of a few dollars, why work yourself to the bone?"

Madam blushed. As hostess, she couldn't very well trot out the Master's theories on the matter. She mumbled something about it being a pastime; it wasn't that they were trying to save money.

The next day she took the bit of sweater she had started and hired someone to finish it for her. Of course she didn't tell the Master.

And so when Madam kept vigil with the Little Young Mistress, she had to find some other way to occupy her time.

Every morning after the Master left for the office she telephoned to various friends and relatives. Nothing was sacred in their conversations, there was no matter they didn't discuss. With these useless amenities Madam was able to spend half the day. If, on any given day, there was no little boy's head cold to chatter about , or no quarrel between the Young Master and Young Mistress of another family to discuss, Madam found it extremely difficult not to become bored.

Occasionally, while still desperately struggling to keep busy, Madam would discover that the children had already returned from school. Then she would heave a deep sigh, as if she had just been relieved of a heavy burden.

Fortunately, this sort of thing seldom happened more than once or twice a month.

The day the Master broke with precedent to expound upon a political theme during the morning milk also turned out to be one of those days when Madam could find nothing to do. None of the ladies she tried to reach on the telephone were at home. She decided to see what was new in the department stores and instructed the cook to serve lunch half an hour earlier.

After lunch she dressed and leisurely put on her make-up. The Little Young Mistress, having learned that a trip was in the offing, had long since persuaded the maid to dress her for the street. She sat waiting for her mother.

Just as Madam was about to summon a taxi, the Master's car was heard pulling up to the door. Madam hurried downstairs and found the Master reclining on the sofa, a half-smoked cigar between his fingers. Remembering how he had excited himself that morning she approached quickly to feel his brow.

He caught her hand in mid-air and with studied casualness pushed it aside.

"I'm alright," he drawled. "I was having lunch with a few friends at Maury's when I felt a kind of pressure on my heart. It's nothing. It'll pass."

Madam sat down beside him on a small stool. "Shall I ask Dr. Huang to come and have a look at you?" she inquired hesitantly.

"It's not necessary." The Master closed his eyes. After a moment, he laughed coldly. "Damned peculiar. Even a big businessman like Lu is opposed to fighting the Reds! At lunch today all four of them were against me..."

Madam's plucked brows drew together. But seeing that the Master's forehead was smooth, she immediately erased her frown and forced a laugh.

"You haven't heard the worst!" the Master continued. "They quoted an editorial in the British North China Daily News. I have it here." He patted his pocket. "Wait till you see. Damned strange!"

The Little Young Mistress tugged Madam's hand and looked up with bright black eyes which obviously were asking why Madam was delaying the visit to the department store. Unconsciously, Madam pulled the little girl close, then called to the maid:

"You take her. If she likes any toys buy a few of each kind, but don't let her eat any candy."

"Oh, were you going shopping?" asked the Master. It was only then he noticed that they were dressed to go out. "Go ahead, then. I need a little quiet for my letter to the North China Daily News..."

"Aiya! What do you want to write a letter for? You're not feeling well. Why should you tax your brain now?"

"I'll feel better when I get it off my chest. Writing won't do me any harm. You just run along."

Madam's eyes were large. She couldn't understand how it was that the Master, who had always despised "scribblers", should have such a change of character. It also occurred to her that if the letter were not published — or worse still, if it was, along with some satirical comment by the editor — the Master would be greatly embarrassed. After all, the paper was run by very influential foreigners. She couldn't let him risk it.

"Better not write," she pleaded. "You're a man of position. Why should you lower yourself to quarrel with a lot of ink slingers? It's not worth it!"

"Don't interfere!" the Master retorted sharply. "Just run along to your department store!" Then he added in a softer tone, "Don't worry. I won't use my real name."

"Then what will you use?"

"Go ahead. And bring me two boxes of cigars." The Master stood up. "I've already thought of a pen name. I'll sign myself: 'A True Chinese Patriot'!"

Gao Yunlan (1910-1956)

Gao Yunlan, the author of Annals of a Provincial Town *and a native of the city of Amoy, was there when the jailbreak of revolutionaries happened in 1930.*

On the coast of Fujian province, Amoy, today called "Xiamen", is opposite Taiwan. It was typical of what Mao Zedong described as "semi-feudal, semi-colonial" China. Amoy had all of the attributes. It was full of prostitutes, thieves, and beggars, and was crawling with contagious diseases.

In the thirties, foreign goods flooded the Amoy market, foreigners controlled the Customs Office. British companies like Asiatic Petroleum, Butterfield & Swire, Hongkong and Shanghai Banking Corp., and British-American Tobacco Co., controlled the oil, transport, banking and cigarette trade. American gasoline and auto imports became more profitable than the opium smuggling and trafficking in human labor of an earlier period.

The Japanese were the strongest foreign interests in the city; some of the most powerful business firms were theirs. They ran newspapers and schools. Chinese rascals who acquired Japanese citizenship got away with all sorts of outrageous conduct and crimes.

The foreigners kept a tight grip on the people through subservient Chinese officials, gangsters and feudal clan leaders. Every street, every section of town had its local bullies, grafting and extorting. On the sea and on the docks, three big foreign-backed clans ruled. They waged bloody battles at the least provocation, costing many lives.

At the same time, Amoy was the center of secret Communist operations in Fujian province. It was an enemy-occupied island in a sea of revolutionary bases. In 1930 the reactionary government caught and imprisoned dozens of underground Communists, and was preparing to execute several of their leaders. A jailbreak was planned by the underground and successfully carried out.

Gao was then only 20, and it stirred him deeply. Under a pen name, he wrote a short story about it entitled "The Night Before", which was published in Shanghai in 1931. (In his fictional presentation, he stages the break in 1935). But Gao was not satisfied. He felt a heroic event of such proportions deserved the full treatment of a novel. He was working on this, after having moved to Malaya, when the Japanese invaded that country in 1937, and the unfinished manuscript was destroyed in the flames of war.

After the Japanese were defeated Gao returned to new China in 1949. He started the novel again in 1953 and was putting the finishing touches to it when he died of cancer in 1956 at the age of forty-six. Annals of a Provincial Town *was a best-seller in China, and was adapted for stage and screen.*

Our brief extract details preparations immediately prior to the break. Involved are contenders on opposite sides of the political spectrum, and lovers caught up in the clash.

ANNALS OF A PROVINCIAL TOWN

Zhao Xiong, head of Amoy's Public Security Bureau, sat in his office going over some documents. His secretary, Shuyin, entered quietly.

"Did you send for me?" she asked.

"Yes. Sit down, sit down, I want to talk to you." Zhao Xiong rose, smiling courteously. He brought a chair forward for her. Shuyin sat, neat and prim, rather like her own meticulous handwriting. But the faint smile on her face seemed to indicate that she was no longer the same severe, cold girl she had been previously. It was also obvious that because of her warmth, Zhao Xiong had become fairly well-mannered. He was even careful not to open his mouth too wide when he laughed.

As if seeking her sympathetic understanding, he told of his recent meetings with Wu Jian. His voice was gentle, moving. Zhao Xiong posed as the most benevolent of gentlemen, using the utmost patience to rescue an errant friend. He related how Wu Jian, years ago, had saved him from drowning. He had never forgotten. He had long cherished the wish to repay him.

Shuyin appeared convinced and touched. She said that as a little girl she had seen him and Wu Jian act together on the stage; people still talked of what a great team they had been. She said that Wu Jian had once been her teacher; she hated to see him destroyed. She realized that Zhao Xiong's feelings and motives were entirely those of a friend.

"If Wu Jian should be killed," she concluded, "not only would it be a serious reflection on his close friends for not having prevented it, but public opinion would be sure to condemn — "

Zhao Xiong cut her short with a wave of his hand. He was afraid of "public opinion".

"I know, I know," he said. "Some of those silly literati would like nothing better than something like this to embroider upon; they'd write all sorts of articles. But let's not talk about that now."

Then he asked whether Shuyin would be willing to talk with Wu Jian on his behalf.

Shuyin was stunned. Her heart beat wildly. Heavens! Will I really be able to see him? she wondered.

"What's wrong? Are you afraid to speak to him?" Zhao Xiong was amused. "Just look at you. Your face is absolutely white."

"Why should I speak to him? Is it really necessary?" Shuyin countered, trying hard to conceal her tenseness.

"Every lock has its key. Perhaps you are the key who can open the lock that is Wu Jian."

"No. I don't know anything about this sort of thing."

"You'll be able to get closer to him than I. In the first place, you were his student; secondly, you're old friends; thirdly, because you're so beautiful — "

"What are you talking about!"

"Why blush? I'm speaking quite seriously. No man could ever resist a lovely young girl. It's human nature; no one is an exception."

Holding her chin with one hand, Shuyin lowered her head and thought for several minutes. Her mind was in a turmoil.

"Alright," she finally said. Her voice was calm. "If it will be of any help to the office, I can try. But I'm very inexperienced. You'll have to tell me what to do."

"Naturally. He's a big shot in the Communist Party. He's no fool. You've got to have a plan before you talk to him. When necessary, a trick or two won't be amiss."

Lowering his voice and leaning close, Zhao Xiong outlined his strategy to Shuyin.

About three o'clock that afternoon, the car and guards again brought Wu Jian from the prison to the Political Security Bureau office. As he entered the room, Wu Jian saw a figure in a pale grey dress standing by the window with her back to him. At the sound of his footsteps she turned around quickly and looked directly at him with her deep, dark eyes. Wu Jian was speechless.

Shuyin was dressed simply, almost severely, and she wore no make-up. It was three years since Wu Jian had seen her last. She still possessed that cool, sombre beauty.

Lovely — and deadly — like an opium poppy... Wu Jian thought with instinctive revulsion.

"Surprised?..." Her voice was so low she seemed to be talking to herself.

Shuyin's face was expressionless. When she observed Wu Jian's cold, contemptuous glance, she dropped her eyes. A chill ran up her spine.

"Where's Zhao Xiong?" Wu Jian queried, as he took a seat.

"He's gone across the strait. He'll be back soon." Shuyin's voice trembled slightly. "I never thought I'd meet you today...and in a place like this..."

"I knew that you were working here."

She looked out of the window for a moment. She said she had been intending to quit, but that when she heard he had been arrested, she decided to stay on... Shuying spoke breathlessly, as if under great stress. Her pale slim fingers suddenly brought out a small folded paper from the hem of her dress. She handed it to Wu Jian, then quickly and apprehensively again looked out of the window.

Wu Jian read the note. It was brief:

We are working to save you. Anxious to establish contact with underground. Please give necessary information to Shuyin. Don't delay.

Hong San

Wu Jian returned the note to her indifferently.

"I don't know the writer of this."

"You don't know her?" The note shook in Shuyin's hand. "Look again. Hong San wrote it herself."

"I don't have to," he said hostilely. "I told you. I don't know her."

"Didn't she shelter you when you went inland? You posed as her school's cook — "

"Nonsense. I never even heard her name before."

Shuyin turned pale. Her lips trembled. She couldn't speak. Abruptly she turned away, tears gushing from her eyes. But she dried them at once, and brushed from her cheeks a few tear-dampened strands of hair.

Wu Jian said nothing. Extracting a crumpled cigarette from his pocket, he lit it and slowly inhaled. Although his face was icy, his heart was burning like fire. He had no reason to trust a girl working in the Public Security Bureau, even though he had once been in love with her. The damnedest part was that he couldn't tell whether the note was true or false; he didn't remember Hong San's handwriting. Hong San was a good friend of the Party, and she had indeed let him pose as her school's cook after he went inland. But suppose Shuyin was only using this information to trick him? He'd injure Hong San if he wasn't careful, and implicate others as well.

"I know you don't trust me," Shuyin said, lowering her moist eyelashes. Her tear-washed face was icy as winter moonlight. "You think I'm helping Zhao Xiong to trap you. What do you take me for? Even if you don't consider me fit to be your friend, you should at least remember that I was your student."

"You're forgetting, miss," Wu Jian said. "I'm not your teacher any more. I'm your boss's prisoner."

Shuyin's pale cheeks flushed pink, then turned white again.

"It's easy enough for you to talk like that," she said with a bitter smile. "But did you ever think that in the three years you were away you never wrote me a single letter? If you had taken me with you, I wouldn't be in this place today!"

"What's past is past. There's no use talking about it."

"I want to talk about it! I'm full of grievances. Who can I tell them to if not to you? After you left, you don't know how I waited for you!"

Tears again glistened on her eyelashes.

Zhao Xiong's puppet! Wu Jian cursed her mentally. You play your role well!... From his heart he hated those pleading, reproachful eyes.

"Fortunately you didn't wait for me very long," he said. "Otherwise you wouldn't have got this fine job."

"Don't be sarcastic. Let's say I made a mistake. I ought to have a chance to make up for it. I was all ready to leave Amoy with Hong San. But I stayed, because of you. We want to save you!"

Wu Jian shivered.

"How fortunate I am," he said with a cold laugh. "So many people want to save me. There's your boss, who says I'm his saviour. And there's you — my student and friend. I really don't know how to thank you all!"

"You're truly cruel! I never thought you'd repay my sincerity with ridicule!'

"I'm speaking the truth, miss."

"Maybe I'm wrong, but as I remember you weren't like this before," Shuyin said miserably. "Why are you so different from that day on Mount Malong? Have you forgotten everything?"

"Let me remind you, Shuyin. I'm a man whose head is liable to be cut from his shoulders at any moment. I hardly think it worthwhile to spend my last few days dreaming of Mount Malong!"

He brought out another crushed cigarette and lit it. Through the haze of smoke he carefully observed Shuyin's face.

"I may not have another chance to meet you like this," she said in an anguished voice. "Don't think I'm trying to fool you, I beg you. This may be our only chance. If you don't want to tell me how to make contact, send someone you can trust to see Hong San. She lives at the foot of Bijia Hill, number 301. Please send someone right away, the quicker the better. Remember — 301!"

Wu Jian shrugged. "This has nothing to do with me."

In the next room there was a sound of someone opening a drawer. Shuyin listened, cast another quick glance out of the window, then struck a match and burned the note in the ash tray.

"Whether you believe me or not, I must tell you this," she said. "Don't they often call for you in a car and bring you here? That's our chance. We're planning to stop the car somewhere along the road and get you out! Be prepared. We're looking for men to do the job right now."

It was all Wu Jian could do to keep from seizing her and shouting, "That's not the way to do it!" But he controlled himself.

"Hong San says you have a relative called Wu the Seventh. She wants me to ask you — can we go to him directly?"

This upset Wu Jian even more. But just then footsteps were heard outside. Giving him a significant look, Shuyin whispered:

"He's come back. Talk about something else." Raising her voice, she said, "Yes, it's a shame. Of all the girls graduating with me, only one was able to to go on to the university — Xiuyun, do you remember her? That round-faced girl..."

"Waiting long?" Zhao Xiong entered, smiling. He nodded to Wu Jian.

Shuyin demurely rose to her feet. Pointing at her, Zhao Xiong said with the ease of an accomplished socialite:

"Remember her? When we acted together, she was our most loyal fan. Wore her hair in two short braids. She was just a little girl then."

Shuyin glanced at Wu Jian, then at Zhao Xiong, and smiled embarrassedly. Wu Jian didn't know which one of them she was trying to fool.

"Yes. She used to come to the theatre with her older sister," Wu Jian said, to break the strained silence. "Time certainly flies. Ten years gone in the flash of an eye."

Shuyin again smiled, and lowered her head. She evidently didn't like this kind of talk.

"I must be going," she said to Zhao Xiong. "I've got some work to do that must be finished by four-thirty, and it's four already."

Zhao Xiong didn't detain her. As he watched her going through the door, a lascivious gleam came to his eye.

Wu Jian caught the look, and to his mind it brought a new question, one to which he had no answer.

When he returned to Cell Three, Wu Jian told his comrades what Shuyin had said.

"What do you think of her?" asked Simin. "Can she be trusted?"

"If you ask me," said Jianping, "it's a trap. No question about it."

"I think it probably is, too." Chongjian looked at his cellmates indecisively and pushed back the glasses which had slid down to the tip of his nose. "Maybe she's a plant."

"Why all the 'probably' and 'maybes'? She is — for sure!" said

Jianping.

Chongjian blushed. Embarrassed, he again adjusted his glasses.

"She's a spy alright," Peixun interjected. "It's another one of Zhao Xiong's tricks. The beautiful woman angle is a favorite with that type of organization."

"I agree — one hundred percent!" cried Jianping.

"Keep your voice down." Chongjian peered apprehensively at the corridor beyond the bars. He turned to Simin. "Why don't you say anything?"

"I haven't quite made up my mind."

"Let's hear what you're thinking anyway."

"I look at it a little differently. I'm not so sure the girl's a plant. Judging by the way Zhao Xiong has been operating in the past, this doesn't seem to be his method."

"Don't be naive,"" said Peixun. "He's not as stupid as you think."

"It's just because he's not stupid that I say he wouldn't pull anything so obvious as forging a note with Hong San's signature."

"You think he's clever, then?" Peixun interrupted.

Wu Jian pulled at his sleeve. "Let Simin finish."

Simin continued. "In view of Shuyin's former relationship with Wu Jian, what she told him today is not necessarily false. If she were trying to attract him, why should she weep?"

"So you think she's on the level?" Peixun exploded.

"Probably."

"Ai-ya-ya-ya," cried Peixun impatiently. "You're relapsing again. Only a few tears and you go completely soft!"

Simin flushed slightly. But he only smiled and rubbed the month-old stubble on his chin.

"No matter what you say, I'm still convinced the note is genuine."

"It's positively a fake!" said Jianping. He plainly sided with Peixun. "To say anything in the hands of a spy is genuine, is sheer illusion. Shuyin couldn't have met Wu Jian without Zhao Xiong's permission. That alone proves they're plotting together."

"I agree with Jianping," said Peixun.

"Me too," echoed Chongjian.

Simin felt he was standing alone.

"I still can't see it your way," he said softly but stubbornly. "I agree that Wu Jian's action was correct. He acted with caution because he was suspicious. That's not the same as what you're doing. You're insisting your suspicions are facts, without any proof. You're frightening yourselves with shadows of your own creation. That's not going to get us anywhere. If she's on the level, we're not only misjudging her, but we're hurting ourselves as well."

"Do people who are on the level work in the Public Security Bureau?" demanded Jianping, red in the face.

Peixun, Chongjian and Jianping all attacked Simin for his "softness", his "blindness". Simin didn't argue; his eyes were still crinkled up in a friendly smile. Finally he turned to Wu Jian.

"Why not give us your ideas? You're the one who's involved."

"I can't be too sure," replied Wu Jian. "My first worry is — what about Hong San? Is she still free, or has she been arrested? Is she or isn't she being watched? Is she still inland, or has she really come back to Amoy? I don't know the answer to any of these question. I couldn't ask Shuyin because I can't tell whether the note is genuine in the first place. I couldn't risk the safety of Hong San and other comrades. It seems to me we have to investigate; only then can we judge. This thing affects the fate of all of us."

That night, prison guard Yao Mu dropped by Cell Three. He was a secret member of the Communist underground. Wu Jian told him what had happened. He instructed Yao to check up immediately.

One evening, half a month prior to Wu Jian's transfer to the Amoy Jail, Shuyin had gone to call on her former teacher, Hong San. The older woman had just returned from the interior of the province, where she was the principal of a primary school. Shuyin was hoping Hong San would take her on as a teacher there, so that she could leave her job in the Public Security Bureau.

Hong San was about forty. She had taught school in Amoy for over ten years. Though married, she had no children, and Shuyin was like a daughter to her. Hong San's husband — an old Kuomintang Party member — had been caught and buried alive by Kuomintang agents because he opposed Chiang Kai-shek. It was a terrible blow to Hong San. She threw herself into school work and educating children. Recently, in the interior, she had applied to join the Communist Party, but the application had not yet been approved. It was now the summer vacation period, and she had come to Amoy to buy books for the school.

Shuyin hadn't seen her for five years. Hong San was older and thinner, but her spirits were high. She still wore her old-fashioned spectacles and spoke in the same loud voice. When she walked, the floor shook beneath her tread. She was the very picture of an "irritable old lady".

Shuyin promptly told her all about her family misfortunes and how she had taken a job with the Public Security Bureau.

Before Shuyin had finished, the teacher, red to the ears, seethed:

"How could you sink so low! Don't you know that Bureau is a den of incendiaries and murderers?

"I didn't — when I first started there —"

"Don't lie to me! You're a high school graduate, not a three-year-old child!"

"Really, I didn't know." Shuying felt very sorry for herself. Tears ran from her eyes.

"Quit sniveling!" snapped Hong San. "Now listen here. I don't propose to help anyone who's an accomplice to those assassins!"

"Me? An accomplice?" Shuyin couldn't believe her ears.

"Of course!"

"But I never killed anyone; I never joined any of their organizations. How can you say I'm an accomplice? I'm absolutely clean!"

"Clean, eh? You don't get white cloth out of a dyeing vat!"

"Who do you think I am? I'm just a little thirty-dollar-a-month clerk. I only took the job to keep the family alive — "

"That's no excuse, miss. We may starve to death, but we never sell our souls!"

Hong San angrily paced the floor, her heels stamping sharply.

Shuyin set her lips firm, wiped her tears and stood up.

"I never thought you'd be so mean, Hong San," she said hotly. "So you're going to abandon me to that pack of wolves! Very well, goodbye."

"Sit down," roared Hong San, She took off her glasses. "How dare you lose your temper? I've scolded you; so what? Don't you deserve it? Little nitwit! Can't take it, eh? Sit down. I'm not through with you yet."

The teacher strode fiercely to the door and locked it. Shuyin waited, a bit frightened, for the storm. But Hong San, while continuing to berate her, showed a visible softening. Shuyin stood with her head bowed, not daring to sit down. Behind the hard words of the "irritable old lady" she could sense the strong loves and hates of a direct, righteous woman.

From then on, Shuyin went to Hong San's every day after work. The two women often talked far into the night. Shuyin told her teacher all that had happened to her in recent years, even her deepest secrets — including her feelings toward Wu Jian. Finally, she said if only she could get away from the Public Security Bureau she would willingly put up with any hardships.

"We've got all the teachers we need this term," said Hong San slowly. "The only thing open is a servant's job."

"I'll take it," cried Shuyin, jumping up delightedly and seizing Hong San's hand.

"Now, now, miss, it's too hard. You have to cook and wash clothes —"

"What's so hard about that?"

" — and sweep the dorms and clean the toilets — "

"Easy! I can do it!"

" — and carry water from the stream for fifteen teachers, with no one to help you — "

"Fifteen, or double fifteen, I can do it!"

"Don't exaggerate, miss. Let me see your hands... Humph, expect to do hard manual labor with those slim fingers? Forget it. It's out of the question."

"Then what am I going to do?" Shuyin dropped her hands to her sides. Her eyes grew damp.

Hong San had only been testing Shuyin. Now she told her the truth — she could take her along to the interior. As long as Shuyin was not afraid of difficulties, Hong San would do her best.

Overjoyed, Shuyin threw her arms around her teacher and hugged her.

Hong San would finish buying her books in a few days. Then Shuyin would ask the Bureau for a day off, and the two women would leave immediately for the interior. Once there, Shuyin would assume a new name to prevent Zhao Xiong from tracing her.

But before the day of departure arrived, Zhao Xiong told Shuyin a bit of news that nearly frightened her out of her wits. Wu Jian had been arrested! He had just been transferred to the Amoy Municipal Jail.

"I arranged to bring him here," Zhao Xiong boasted. "Our old friend. I had to do something to try and save him."

Shuyin shivered. She knew what Zhao Xiong meant by "save".

That night, she passed on the information to Hong San. The teacher was very upset. Only now she revealed that she knew Wu Jian. During the two years he had been operating in the interior she had often provided cover for him. Once, they had fooled the local police by having Wu Jian pose as the school's cook.

"It's a very serious situation, Shuyin," said Hong San gravely. "We can't just walk away from it."

"I know. That's exactly what I wanted to talk to you about. Isn't there some way — "

"We must rescue him. An important man like that. And he's our friend. From whatever angle you look at it, we cannot avoid our responsibility."

"I'll do whatever you say, Hong San. Just tell me what to do, and I'll do it."

They put off going to the interior. Shuyin remained in the Public Security Bureau. All with the aim of saving Wu Jian.

Hong San went to the editor of the paper where Wu Jian had been working as literary editor. The man was a friend of hers of fifteen years standing; he knew Wu Jian quite well too. Hong San urged him to write articles to arouse public opinion in favor of Wu Jian being set free. But the editor didn't have the courage. He admitted that he was afraid the authorities would close his paper down.

She then called on a distant relative who was a cook in the jail. When she asked him whether he could bribe a few keepers to help her rescue a friend, the old man nearly had a stroke. He begged her to keep her nose out of such affairs.

Next, Hong San and Shuyin hit upon the plan of holding up the car that brought Wu Jian nearly every day to the Public Security Bureau. Where could they find people bold enough to do the job? Hong San immediately thought of the Communist Party. She could plainly see that the thing was impossible without the aid of the Party and the masses. But how could she get in touch with the underground? The only Party member she knew in Amoy was Wu Jian, and he was in jail.

"For Wu Jian's sake," she advised Shuyin, "you'd better be a little more friendly to Zhao Xiong."

Shuyin complied. The result was that Zhao Xiong proposed that she "work on" Wu Jian. When the girl breathlessly reported this to Hong San, the teacher seized upon it as a good chance to make direct contact with Wu Jian. She never dreamed he would be unable to recognize her handwriting, and therefore not dare to accept the note.

That night, after Shuyin left, Hong San sat alone, worried and perplexed. The bell rang, and she opened the door. A thin, somewhat hunchbacked young man stood before her.

"Does Hong San live here?" he asked.

"I am Hong San."

"Which Hong San, please?"

"My name is Hong San," said the teacher. She wondered whether the young man could be someone sent by Wu Jian. "What do you want to see me about?"

"Sorry, I'm afraid you're the wrong Hong San. I'm looking for Hong Yuren, who also calls herself Hong San. Sorry to have disturbed you." The hunchback walked away.

Puzzled, Hong San went back into the house. A few minutes later, the bell rang again. When she opened the door this time, there wasn't a soul in sight. Something that had been stuck in the door fluttered to the ground. Hong San picked it up. It was a note. The teacher opened it and read:

Hong San,

Please come immediately to the foot of Riguang Cliff. I must talk with you.

Rain

"Rain"? Who could that be? Half suspicious, half hopeful, the teacher set out for the designated place. The road, which was near the seacoast, was very still. She had the feeling someone was following her, and her heart beat fast. She was about to turn back, when a slim figure came striding toward her, then halted beside a lamp-post.

"Hong San?" he asked in a low voice.

Peering at him, she recognized him as a man she had met inland a few years before. He called himself Zheng Yu.

Another man hurried up from behind. It was the hunchback who had pretended to be looking for "Hong Yuren".

Zheng Yu introduced him as Yao Mu.

Mutual suspicions dispelled, they all returned to Hong San's house. She told them of the plan she and Shuyin had to stop the Public Security Bureau car and rescue Wu Jian. She asked Zheng Yu whether he could introduce her to Wu the Seventh, a stalwart fisherman who was related to Wu Jian and was brash, fearless and bold.

"Stopping that car wouldn't be so easy," said Zheng Yu slowly. "Let's ask Wu Jian whether he agrees first, then we can talk to Wu the Seventh."

The three discussed in detail their future cooperation. When they parted, the sun had already risen.

Yao Mu went back to the prison. Through the bars of Cell Three, he softly related what had happened at his meeting with Hong San. Jianping, Chongjian and Peixun were delighted, but also rather embarrassed. The night before they had all berated Simin for his "gullibility". Simin apparently had forgotten the previous night's debate. He only smiled and rubbed his bristly beard with his big thick hand, while pondering this latest news.

After talking it over, the inmates of Cell Three informed Yao Mu of their decision: First, Zheng Yu should immediately notify Hong San and Shuyin to drop their plan to stop the car, which would serve only one person, and start working on a general jailbreak which would bring freedom to all the political prisoners.

Second, contact should be made with higher Communist Party authorities, and these should be consulted regarding the manner in

Wu Jian reported what he had learned about the watch-tower. It had three iron doors, an alarm bell, an observation platform, and a machine-gun. Day and night, six guards were on duty in shifts. It had been built after the jailbreak twenty years before. None had ever been attempted since.

"There are a lot of other things we have to know, too," said Simin. "How many buildings are there in the jailyard? How many guards? How many weapons do they have?..."

Jianping, Peixun, and Zhongjian were struck dumb. Then Zhongjian said: "That's right. How can we try a jailbreak if we don't know all the details?"

"Perhaps the information I've gathered will help," said Wu Jian. "There are forty-two guards in this prison, five keepers, one head keeper, one warden, one corridor door guard, three cooks, two masons, fifty-three rifles, nine pistols, two machine-guns. There are a total of 243 prisoners, of whom 86 are political prisoners. All the buildings together have 41 rooms, and there are 16 cells, big and small. Of the political prisoners, 5 are in Cell Three, 7 in Four, 39 in Six, 35 in Seven — plus 5 ordinary prisoners. The prison wall is 20 feet high, with electrically charged barbed wire on top. The watch-tower is in the corner of the yard on the left side. There is a telephone in the warden's office. The head keeper has a dog that barks but doesn't bite..."

The men listened in amazed silence as Wu Jian, in a simple, matter-of-fact tone, poured out the figures. This was something they needed as desperately as a ship's captain needs navigation charts and a sextant.

Now Jianping understood why Wu Jian had been asking Yao Mu so many questions the last few days, and why he had been striking up conversations with guards and keepers. Because Wu Jian was favored by Zhao Xiong, those dogs were always very polite to him.

Cell Three's inmates continued their discussion.

Shuyin passed the word to Zheng Yu: the turncoat Zhou Shen didn't know Li Yue and couldn't identify him as a Communist. As a result, Zhao Xiong's suspicions of Li Yue were diminishing.

Sure enough, a few days later, Li Yue was freed.

The day before, he and Wu Jian had a brief talk while washing their clothes at the faucet in the jail yard. Li Yue said he already had roughed out a preliminary plan for the jailbreak. The major problems that had to be solved were: first — men, second — weapons, third — transport. He said they would have to work fast because the situation was changing constantly. It could take a turn for the worse at any time.

Back in the cell, Wu Jian found Jianping and Zhongjian fiercely arguing in whispers over how long Li Yue would need to arrange help from the outside.

"How many more days it will take to prepare isn't a matter for debate," Wu Jian went on. "We have to wait for Li Yue to leave the prison and size up the situation outside, then decide. There's no use getting all worked up. I'm confident that once Li Yue starts moving, things will happen very quickly."

An hour after Li Yue returned home, he left to hide out in a relative's home in a small hamlet on the mountrainside. The same day he consulted with higher Party authorities and made contact with Zheng Yu, Hong San and several other comrades. Lastly he sent a man for Wu the Seventh.

The big man was delighted to find Li Yue out of prison. Though he asked many questions about Jianping, he said nothing of Wu Jian, for he didn't know that he had been arrested. When Li Yue told him, he was thunderstruck. He rose swiftly to his feet, a murderous light in his eyes.

"I'm going to see Zhao Xiong," he said coldly. "Goodbye."

He turned and strode from the house. Li Yue ran after him and tried to pull him back. But he couldn't hold him. Wu the Seventh was ploughing forward like a locomotive.

"Listen to me," Li Yue ordered sharply. "Come back. I've got something to discuss with you!"

That stopped him. Breathing hard, he went back into the house with Li Yue. The weather was hot and his face was beaded with perspiration.

"Sit down. Acting this way won't do Wu Jian any good. Sit down." Li Yue pushed him into a chair. "How can I talk to you if you don't cool off!"

After the big man had calmed down a bit, Li Yue told him of the jailbreak they were planning. Before Li was half finished, Wu leaped to his feet.

"Give the job to me. I've got men — as many as you need. They'll do whatever I tell them. I'm not boasting — at one word from me, if they don't crack open the Amoy prison my name's not Wu!"

"That's not the way —"

"Why not? You want men — I've got 'em. You want guns — I've got 'em. We charge right in with forty or fifty men. Isn't that enough? There's nothing to it! You'll see. I'll get that Zhao Xiong and wring his neck..."

It's not so easy —"

"Who says it's easy? Do you think I'm a fool? Don't worry. I know you need strategy as well as force. I've had plenty of battle experience in my thirty-five years..."

"We've got to do this differently. It has to be organized according to plan —"

"Of course we need a plan. Don't I know that? Didn't I do street fighting with Wu Jian? I may be an amateur at giving out political handbills and marching in demonstrations, but if it's fighting you want, I'm your man! If I don't rescue Wu Jian and Jianping you can cut my head off!..."

It was simply impossible to halt his flow of words. Li Yue let him talk himself out. Then he asked: "Have you finished?"

"I'm finished," Wu the Seventh said, a trifle embarrassed.

"Good. Now it's my turn. I've one request. While I'm talking, don't interrupt. After I'm through you can have your say again."

In a calm, even tone, Li Yue outlined the plan. On a piece of paper he sketched the layout of the jail, indicating the physical set-up in and outside the yard, and related the relative strengths of the prisoners and guards. Then he revealed the planned break, step by step.

Wu the Seventh listened quietly, impressed and somewhat humbled by Li Yue's intelligence and reasoning.

"What does Wu Jian think of this plan?" he asked.

"We worked on it together."

Wu the Seventh smiled. He was very fond of Wu Jian.

"We've got to beat them with our brains. Our four ounces must beat their thousand pounds," said Li Yue. "The idea is to rescue everybody without losing a single man. If we use out heads now, it will save the blood of our comrades when the time comes. Our plan mustn't have any loop-holes."

"What do you want me to do?"

"Get hold of a large motorboat that can carry about a hundred men. After they break out, you will be responsible for getting them across to the mainland. We'll work out the details tomorrow."

Wu the Seventh thought a moment. Then he said unhappily, "Why don't you let me take part in charging the jail ? I'm at my best with a gun."

"You can take your gun along. What if the enemy tries to stop you while you're at sea? None of our comrades know how to make the crossing. If you don't handle it, who will? When can you have the boat ready?"

"In three days."

"For sure?"

"For sure," Wu the Seventh said solemnly. "If I don't produce the boat in three days, dispose of me in accordance with military law!"

"Good," Li Yue smiled. "There's another thing. Can you get us twenty pistols and ten hand-grenades?"

"So 'many?' Those guards are a bunch of punks. Do we need that much force?"

"We want to take care of the watch-tower. We've got to knock that out first."

"Mm..." Wu the Seventh pondered. "I can get you all the pistols you want, but grenades... We only have two at the moment."

"Two's not enough."

"I'll see what I can do."

"When can you let me know?"

"Tomorrow. I'll come tomorrow at noon."

"Right. I'll meet you here at twelve o'clock."

Three days later Zhao Xiong received a telephone call from his superiors on the mainland informing him that Li Yue was a leader of Communist underground in Amoy. Fuming, Zhao Xiong ordered his immediate re-arrest. But Li Yue was nowhere to be found.

The men in Cell Three were very worried about him. Wu Jian only smiled. He said Li Yue could "predict the weather with one look at the sky!"

That night, through Yao Mu, Li Yue transmitted his plan for the jailbreak to Cell Three. He set the time at six forty p.m. on the eighteenth of October.

The following day — the thirteenth — Yao Mu informed the political prisoners in Cells Four, Six and Seven of the plan, and told them to get ready.

But that night, just before the bell for bedtime rang, Yao Mu hurriedly brought news to Cell Three that stunned the five inmates. He had got the information from Shuyin:

A secret order had come down from provincial headquarters in Foochow directing that Wu Jian, Simin, Chongjian, Peixun, and two political prisoners in Cell Six, be transferred to the provincial penitentiary. There was a steamer leaving Amoy for the mainland on the eighteenth, and Zhao Xiong had decided to send them on that. Shuyin thought he would probably use the imminence of this transfer to press Wu Jian for the last time to "see reason."

The steamer would sail from Amoy the morning of the eighteenth at nine. At six forty in the evening, the hour the jailbreak was supposed to take place, the ship would be halfway to Foochow!

It was now 10 p.m., October thirteenth. From this moment to the morning of the eighteenth at nine o'clock there were only 108 hours. Time was short. Outside, Li Yue was busy making all kinds of complicated arrangements. If they wanted to advance the date, could he make the necessary changes in time?

"Does Li Yue know?" Wu Jian asked Yao Mu in a low voice.

"Not yet. I went to his place as soon as I heard. But he was out, so I came right back."

Wu Jian hastily penned a note and handed it to Yao Mu.

"Go there again and wait for him. Give him this personally. We'll wait for your report!"

Yao Mu quickly left.

The five men kept a tense vigil. At one in the morning, like a shadow, Yao Mu slipped to the bars of their cell.

"The date's changed," he whispered.

"When?" Chongjian asked softly.

"It's advanced one day. The seventeenth. Everything else is the same."

Yao Mu stole away and disappeared down the corridor.

All was still. From the street outside, the cry of a food vendor drifted through the quiet summer night.

Du Pengcheng (1921-1991)

Born in 1921 in a poor peasant family in Shaanxi province, where Yan'an is located, Du Pengcheng joined the PLA and served at the front as a war correspondent for the Xinhua News Agency. Almost all of the PLA soldiers involved in the battle around Yan'an had been peasants originally, and they were actively supported by the bulk of the predominantly peasant population. Du Pengcheng was the ideal man to write Defend Yanan. *As a peasant native of the area, and as an intimate of the PLA officers and men, he knew and shared their feelings and those of the local villagers. He conveyed these so trenchantly that Mao Tun was moved to say: "The people in Du's works are bold and vigorous as if sculpted by a huge axe. Through the conflicts in which his characters are involved, he creates a tense, heated atmosphere."*

Like many of China's authors, Du Pengcheng was persecuted during the "Cultural Revolution". He survived and managed to continue writing, but suffered from a bad heart. He died only recently, in 1991.

Yan'an had a special significance to the millions of Chinese struggling for liberation from the combined tyrannies of domestic feudal oppression and foreign incursion. For it was Yan'an in the arid mountains of western China which the decimated Red Army finally reached in 1936 after surviving repeated Kuomintang "annihilation campaigns" during the 8,000 mile Long March. It was Yan'an where the Communist Party, under the leadership of Mao Zedong and the Central Committee, rebuilt the army, strengthened political and administrative organizations, and established a unified command of the revolutionary bases spreading throughout China. Yan'an was the fountainhead of progressive literature and art, it was the heart and soul of the Chinese revolution, the place where stubborn dedication conquered adversity, cheerfully, almost light-heartedly.

Everyone was stricken, therefore, when it was announced that beloved Yan'an had to be evacuated. In March of 1947, Chiang Kai-shek's warlord ally Hu Zongnan launched a massive attack on Yan'an, and Mao decided to withdraw his heavily outnumbered forces. The PLA soldiers couldn't understand it, they wanted to stay and fight. Mao explained that it was only a strategic tem-

porary move, and the city was reluctantly abandoned.

This extract describes the pull-out and one of the clashes which immediately followed. (Yan'an was retaken in April of 1948, a year and one month later.) It reflects the highly charged idealism of the period, and the deep emotional loyalty to what Yan'an symbolized, a feeling which persists in the Chinese psyche to this day.

DEFEND YANAN

The Luliang Mountains were still a mass of snow and ice in early March 1947. A howling north-west wind swirled in across the white misty peaks. The dull yellow rays of the sun shining through the bare branches of the trees cast mottled reflections on the snow. In the frigid ravines, big icicles hung like curtains from the sides of the cliffs.

Long lines of soldiers, mounted men, animals laden with small cannon, moved across the mountain tops and through the valleys, directly into the cutting gale. Men stuffed handfuls of snow into their mouths as they marched. Some sucked small icicles chopped from the cliffsides with their bayonets. The soldiers had slept out in the snow the previous night. Their grey cotton-padded uniforms, frozen stiff, crackled with every step they took.

This was a column (*equivalent to an army*) of the PLA — the People's Liberation Army. It had left central Shanxi Province under orders and was pushing west as fast as it could travel. Like the people's soldiers on every front, from the day the War of Liberation began, these men had been fighting steadily for over eight months without a let-up. The battle they were hurrying to commence was going to prove much crueler than any they had previously taken part in, and would be fought in much more desolate surroundings.

Rifles seldom leaving the men's shoulders, the horses never unsaddled, the column had been proceeding at a forced march for ten days. Now it had reached the east bank of the Yellow River.

On either side of the river rose towering cliffs. To the men who gazed up from the river's edge, the sky seemed a long stretch of fluttering ribbon. Perhaps if you stood on one of the cliff tops the clouds would sail past you face; if you put out your hand you could touch the frozen blue heavens. In the chasm, the turbid yellow water churned huge chunks of ice and pounded them thunderously against the precipitous crags lining both banks. The river emitted a chill that was stifling as a fog. It crept into the marrow of your bones; it penetrated your very blood vessels. No wonder the old boatmen in these parts said you had to wear fleece-lined coats here even in summer!

The advance units of the column had assembled at the mouth of the gorge where it met the river, and began preparing to cross. Five or six American-made fighter planes, marked with the insignia of Chiang Kai-shek's KMT (*Kuomintang*) Army, wheeled overhead, diving and strafing. Rifle fire and the smell of powder, added to the roar of the river, gave the impression that the battlefield was just ahead. The men were quiet, tense.

Chen Xingyun, brigade commander, rode his horse at a fast trot out of the mouth of the gorge. He reined in sharply when he found the Yellow River in front of him. The big, sleek chestnut stallion shook the sweat from its body, pricked up its ears, and whinnied at the sight of the tumbling water. Flicking its tail, the horse swayed its head and pawed the ground, as if it would clear the river in one leap the moment Chen slackened his reins.

Brigadier Chen jumped from his mount and handed the animal over to the messenger who had been following. Walking forward a few paces, Chen cast a practiced eye at the surrounding mountains. He folded his hands across his abdomen and gazed at the turbulent waves.

Regimental chief of staff Wei Yi and battalion political instructor Zhang Pei walked out of the gorge to stand beside him.

(*From their earliest inception as the Red Army, and then when they were renamed the Eighth Route Army, to their present designation the People's Liberation Army, China's revolutionary military forces have always had political officers on every unit level from company right on up. These officers were members of the Communist Party. Their duty was to analyze the domestic and international situation, to explain to the men national goals and ideals, present tactics and long range policies, and even help soldiers solve personal problems. Although theoretically political officers had no part in planning and conducting battles, they almost invariably took part in combat.*)

The two made an interesting contrast. Square-faced and bushy-browed, the dignified Wei Yi was a credit to the big men of Shandong province with his height, solidity and broad shoulders. Zhang Pei was a head shorter, frail, his face thin and pallid. He had been wounded in eight different engagements and had lost a lot of blood. He was not very strong. From the look of him it was hard to believe he had been through ten years of battles.

"The number of times we've crossed this river, in one direction or the other! The Yellow River is our old friend." Chen spoke in the cheerful direct tone of voice that Wei Yi and Zhang Pei were accustomed to hearing from him.

Wei Yi shrugged slightly. "The fact that we've had many meetings with the Yellow River is nothing to get annoyed about."

Chen laughed. "Who said it was?" He turned to Zhang Pei. "You're still the same. Never have much to say."

"My habits are hard to change," replied Zhang Pei, "and my

progress is slow."

"Nonsense! You've got a fine disposition. The men in your battalion probably consider you a sort of mother. Right?"

Zhang Pei smiled. "I'd be happy if that's how they really feel."

"We've been driving ahead, day and night," said Chen. "Can you take it?"

"I've got no kick coming. I have a horse to ride. It's the men who have it tough."

The brigadier knew the answer very well, but he asked anyhow: "Wei Yi, does Zhang Pei ride that horse during the marches?"

Wei Yi was embarrassed. He hunched his shoulders. "He always gives it to one of the men with bad legs."

Chen frowned. "I'm tired of having to keep talking about this!"

Zhang Pei knew the reason for Chen's dissatisfaction. Half a month before, he had still been lying in a hospital bed. His chest wound had healed, but his health was very poor. When he heard that the army was going to fight on the west side of the Yellow River, he pleaded that he be allowed to return to his unit ahead of time. The day before the column set out, he arrived back at the battalion. During the past few days of forced march, every time Brigadier Chen met him he had scolded: "You're in rotten shape. Why were you in such a hurry to return?"

Now, the five or six enemy planes, circling above the river dropped a few clusters of small bombs and took a strafing run. Then they screamed up into the clouds, out of sight.

"Every minute counts," said Chen grimly. "The situation is serious here in the north-west. Extremely serious."

He said that in other places the enemy had been forced to go on defensive. In Shandong and the north-west provinces they were trying to retaliate with what they called "concentrated assaults on important points". They were attacking in Shandong with several hundred thousand men.

"Here in the north-west," Chen said, "the enemy has mustered over 300,000 troops, and is using two-thirds of them on the front lines. Warlord Hu Zongnan is marching north up the Xianyang-Yulin Highway and to its east with 150,000 men, with Yan'an as their objective. In the west, Ma Hongkui and Ma Bufang, warlord allies of Chiang Kai-shek, are driving on our East Gansu Area and our Sanbian Area. In the north, Kuomintang troops in and around the city of Yulin are getting ready to attempt to take Suide and Mizhi — both country seats held by us."

Wei Yi and Zhang Pei observed the granite cast of Chen's features. That was how he always looked then they were about to go into battle.

"Defend the Central Committee!"
"Defend Chairman Mao!"
"Defend Yan'an!"

The shouted slogans blended with the boom of the Yellow River waves into a mighty roar. A roar like a sudden storm in the middle of the night — with thunder and lightning and wind and rain.

Brigadier Chen, Wei Yi and Zhang Pei looked back. In the mouth of the gorge the troops were holding battle rallies.

Standing in front of one of the companies was the man who was obviously its commander. His chest distended, waving his fist in the air, he was shouting, "We're going to cross the river right away, comrades. This very minute. The enemy is attacking Yan'an. Yan'an, where our Party's Central Committee and Chairman Mao have been living for more than ten years..."

The eyes of the men fastened on the mountains west of the river. Several soldiers stood up angrily, then sat down again. They seemed to want to say something.

"Who is that?" asked Chen, pointing at the speaker. "Ah, of course, Zhou Dayong." He looked at Wei Yi and Zhang Pei. "Yes, we must keep explaining the significance of this Shaanxi-Gansu-Ningxia Border Region campaign whenever there's a chance." He thought a moment. "The road ahead is hard. We must make it clear to the men that the Central Committee and Chairmen Mao are here with us in the north-west directing our battle personally. That is the surest guarantee of victory! Alright, then. Start organizing the men for the crossing immediately. I'm going to see whether the general has arrived yet."

The wind blowing in from the desert beyond the Great Wall filled the air with particles of yellow sand. It billowed the clothing of the soldiers moving up into the mouth of the gorge and struck their faces with stinging force.

Waves whipped up by the gale pounded against the cliffs, flinging a drenching spray.

The river bank became crowded with men, horses and pack animals preparing for the crossing. There was a clamor of men shouting, animals whinnying.

Unit commanders rushed about getting things ready. Liu Yuanxing, First Battalion CO, waving his cap, yelled to his messenger:

"I want the commander of First Company. Bring him here on

the double!"

The messenger was off like a streak. Two or three minutes later, he came trotting back with Zhou Dayong, whose Mauser pistol bounced on his hip as he ran. The young commander steadied it with his left hand. Reaching Liu, Dayong drew his heels together, saluted, and stood calmly waiting for orders. Well-proportioned, with broad shoulders, a bit over medium height, Dayong had a square face and a pair of stubborn eyes flashing beneath black brows.

"These Luliang Mountains are cold," said Liu, rubbing his hands together. "And the banks of the Yellow River are even colder."

"Jump up and down a few times, commander," said Dayong. "That'll put fire into your veins."

"Too old for tricks like that. Now if I were your age, and had your iron constitution, I could jump into an icy pit and never fear the cold!"

Dayong laughed. "You're only thirty-four."

"I've still been eating ten years longer than you, comrade."

Liu looked across the tumbling waves at the enemy planes savagely diving and strafing beyond the opposite bank.

"Sons of bitches. Do they think that will stop us? Dayong, your First Company will lead the crossing."

"That's the order we've been hoping for." Dayong's eyes gleamed.

The battalion commander glanced at his watch. "It's now two p.m. Brigade wants everyone over by dusk. Alright. Get your company up here."

"Right." Dayong saluted and turned to go.

"Not so fast. After you're across, set up anti-aircraft positions on that mountain top opposite." Liu pointed at the planes. "Those wretches are scared of their own shadows. Give 'em a couple of bursts from your machine-guns and they'll really fly high. Ah, see there? The boats have come. Load your men, quickly."

After the column crossed the Yellow River it travelled in the direction of Yan'an.

The troops continued marching all night. The next day, the 18th of March, they were pushing through Yanchuan County. Although sixty miles from Yan'an, the place had the atmosphere of battle. Officials of the local people's government were shipping the contents of the public granary to safer places so that nothing would be left for the enemy. Women and old men were caching all useful household utensils and farming equipment. Children stood as lookouts at cross-roads and entrances to the villages. Armed with rifles and red-tasseled spears, squad after squad of local self-defence units marched down the road — evidently on the way to put themselves into position.

The PLA men hurried on. Messages on walls of little temples, on the sides of cliffs, caught their eye. Said one:

> Commanders, soldiers, and service personnel of the border region armies: You are about to take a glorious stand. The eyes of all China, of the people of the whole world, are upon you. The Chinese people entrust you with their most important hopes. Now is the time to put into practice all that Chairman Mao and Commander-in-Chief Zhu De have taught you!

The flames of war are beginning to burn in the Shaanxi-Gansu-Ningxia Border Region, Dayong thought agitatedly. The Region was about 250 miles from east to west, and 300 from north to south. Dayong had seen almost every city and town, every valley and stream, in this mountainous area. He and the local peasants had been through hard days together. He had helped them spread fertilizer and gather crops in the Wuding River valley. On the banks of the Yanshui, they had told him tales of the Land Revolution in north Shaanxi.

Yan'an and north Shaanxi were as dear to him as his native village. When he was a child no taller than a rifle, he had followed the Workers and Peasants Red Army on its famous 8,000 mile Long March that ended in north Shaanxi. Later, the Red Army was re-organized into the Eighth Route Army, Dayong, like many other Red Army fighters, weeping, had put his beloved cap with its red star into his knapsack, and went off to fight the Japanese invaders. In the past ten years, he and many of his battle companions had been in and out of north Shaanxi and the city of Yan'an several times.

Today, he was again heading for Yan'an. But this time was different, for now the flames of war were burning here, and they were licking close to the home of the Central Committee of the Chinese Communist Party. The thought was painful, infuriating, unbearable. Though he had faced death often and had seen many tragic things in battle, nothing had ever shaken and angered him so intensely. It was like coming home to his ancestral village and finding bandits murdering his own mother!

On the morning of the 19th as the sun was rising behind the eastern hills, the column entered a long valley and headed toward Yan'an, 35 miles due west. A thick pall of dust hung in the valley, for it was crowded with peasants, coming in the opposite direction, travelling slowly away from endangered Yan'an. They were walking, riding in carts, astride little donkeys. Women carried children on their backs, old ladies bore bundles and live chickens, old men shouldered farm implements, bedding, clothing... No one spoke, no one looked at anyone else. It was as if they were all strangers. Once in a while, some turned their dust-covered faces to look back at the sky above Yan'an. Everyone was plainly exhausted and distressed.

The peasants were all very upset, but the moment they saw their own army marching past them toward Yan'an, they became calm and sat down by the roadside. They were confident the PLA would finish off the enemy quick as a flash, and that the fighting would end and peaceful days would return once more.

Mothers carrying children beamed. The peasants broke into excited conversation.

"Ah, just look. So many of our men and horses! There's nothing to fear any more. Those White army soldiers — may they be struck by five thunderbolts! — can't come here now."

"Everything's alright. You see — several hundred thousand of our troops have come from east of the river."

Several hundred thousand? Dayong thought. There are only about eight thousand of us altogether!

He had run across this sort of thing often in wartime. People invented good news or believed reports, even if contradictory or ridiculous, as long as they were optimistic.

"Is the enemy far from here, neighbors?" he called as he marched.

"Far? Some folks say they've already reached our Yan'an City. The way I figure, the're probably about seven miles to the south."

"Huh! Blind talk! Comrade, the enemy are at least 10 or 15 miles from Yan'an."

"Yan'an...it looks bad, very bad."

This divergence of opinions among the peasants showed how confused the situation was. Dayong felt depressed.

"Neighbors," he said, "we heard you left the danger zone long ago. How come you've travelled only this far?"

A dozen voices answered at once.

"No one likes to leave his home and bit of land, however humble..."

"The poor treasure their shacks more than the rich love their gold and silver mansions..."

"It's hard to say. The head of our township government has been urging us to move every day, to settle some place far away where it's safe. But we thought: our army will never let the Whites take Yan'an. They'll finish them off in a couple of days, and we'll be able to come back. But today everything is so mixed up. It's hard to say..."

"When will the fighting end? How are we going to live?"

Dayong's face was dark. He tried, as he walked long past the peasants, to make them understand why it was necessary to wage a long campaign.

The road was so jammed with refugees, the column was unable to move forward. At the order of the brigade commander, the troops in the lead swung off the road to the right to march along the river. The rest of the column prepared to follow.

Dayong halted beside a big cart on which a boy of eleven or twelve, who had been wounded by enemy strafing, lay groaning. A woman stretched out beside him had stopped breathing. Peasants said she had also been hit by the strafing, a few miles back.

Dayong stood rigid, his right hand clutching his leather belt, his left hand tightly grasping the wooden holster of his Mauser. His face was stony, expressionless. The blood seemed frozen in his veins. His heart felt like it was being twisted by a pair of pliers. Several paces away, Wang Chengdu, First Company's political instructor, noisily expelled an angry breath.

Dayong's eyes shifted from the cart to the faces of the PLA men. All the men were looking straight ahead, as if they couldn't bear the tragic scene on the cart.

An old lady stood beside it. The dead woman was her daughter-in-law, the boy her grandson. She stared at them dazedly. Everything was blurred, like in a dream. Her gaze drifted to the stern-visaged soldiers, then back to her loved ones. The merciless flames had already crept to Yan'an, they were burning about her head! War had destroyed the home she had struggled so hard to build, with sweat and blood, drop by drop.

Tears rolled from her eyes.

"Son," she said bitterly to Dayong, "you must rip the dirty hearts out of those murdering White bandits!"

"Don't you worry, old mama," said a PLA man. "We're not going to let them take Yan'an, no matter what."

Dozens of children trooped among the soldiers, taking their hands, asking all sorts of questions. One little boy about seven, standing on a mound, wrapped his arms around Dayong's neck and said:

"Uncle, I brought my schoolbag along. Our teacher said we could have races again in a couple of days, uncle."

Dayong turned around and took the child's face in his hands. He gazed into the little boy's eyes a long, long time.

Suddenly, from the head of the column a bugle blared an

air-raid warning. Other buglers passed the call down the line, an agitating call that sent shivers through a man's heart.

Three enemy fighter planes, without even pausing to circle, flew low along the valley and strafed the packed refugees. A woman threw up her hands and dropped in a pool of blood. The child she had been suckling at her breast was flung far to the side of the road. Disregarding the rain of bullets, Dayong rushed to the baby and clutched him close to his chest, using his broad back as a shield. Actually, the child was already dead.

Dayong — who had endured much in life, who had marched thousands of miles through the flames of battle — had tears in his eyes. His every nerve was painfully taut, his every corpuscle ready to burst!

When the planes had gone, peasants from villages along the road came hurrying to offer their help, bringing wooden doors to serve as stretchers. As they dressed the wounded and buried the dead, their eyes were dry. They neither wept nor wailed. They did not speak, or even sigh. A solemn hush hung over the valley. Dust and the smell of powder filled the air.

From the head of the valley, a dozen district and township officials came running, all with rifles slung across their backs. They had been working day and night without rest, and their eyes were bloodshot. They spoke to the milling peasants, telling them where to find safety.

The refugees — thousands of old folks, women, children — moved off toward the big gorge in the mountains to the east. Miserable with the pain of having lost dear ones, they walked on, their heavy steps raising a cloud of dust that obscured the heavens.

Dayong's face was black with fury. He couldn't erase from his mind the old lady's tragic expression and the lively eyes of the little schoolboy. Cheng De, the company political instructor, appeared beside him, shouting in a cracked voice:

"Comrades, remember them! They were killed by America's running dogs, with American planes and American bullets!"

But Dayong didn't hear a word. Like the other PLA men, his blood was boiling. He had only one thought, one desire — to move on immediately, get hold of those savages invading the Shanxi-Gansu-Ningxia Border Region, and shove his bayonet through them!

The column flew forward. And as he marched, Dayong fixed his hawk-like eyes on the sky above Yan'an. Only a few lazy clouds floated above the city, clouds ringed red as fire by the rising sun.

Noon of the 19th of March, 1947, found the column at Ganguyi,

With the Central Committee and Chairman Mao firmly in Yan'an, the Shaanxi-Gansu-Ningxia Border Region became a joyful place. People had enough to eat and wear. Every year after the autumn harvest peasant representatives, bearing melons and fruit and vegetables, came to Yan'an to report the size of their bumper crops to Chairman Mao. He often strolled with his worker and peasant visitors through the lovely hills, chatting with them about factory production methods, or how to get good yields on their farms.

At dawn and at dusk, flocks of sheep and herds of cattle on their way to and from grazing grounds, crossed the mountain slope opposite the cave in which Chairman Mao had his home. Herdsmen, their eyes on the windows of his cave house, sang ballads in his praise.

The best weather in north Shaanxi comes at the end of summer and the beginning of autumn. In the early morning heavy mist covers Yan'an and all the surrounding hills and streams. It is difficult to see more than a few dozen paces. The bells around the necks of the pack animals can be heard with particular clarity, heralding the beginning of another day. From the far mist-shrouded peaks come the strains of a folk song. The gorgeous red rays of the rising sun strike the tip of Baota Hill, and the mist parts like a curtain. Yan'an emerges into the sunlight.

When Yan'an was the headquarters of the revolution, groups of people on the slopes and in the ravines at that hour conducted classes and discussion groups. Fat sheep and goats gambolled on the mountain-sides. A child tending them lolled on a hillock of wild flowers and played a tune on a flute. The wind swayed the millet and sorghum covering the slopes. Old men sat beneath the fruit trees in the valleys, humming to themselves as they twisted strings of yarn. A girl, leading an ox or some woolly sheep to the river for a drink, drifted into a reverie as she stared at the rippled reflections of the Precious Pagoda.

Yan'an at sunset was a symphony of song. Near the city a chorus of young voices rose: Some of China's best youth had gathered on the shores of the Yellow River... People meandered at the foot of the mountain where the Central Committee and Chairman Mao had their offices.

When swarms of fireflies glowed in the dusk along the banks of the Yanshui, Yan'an sank into profound thought.

At night, orange lamplight shone in the windows of the row upon row of cave-dwellings that lined the sides of the mountains surrounding the city. From Yan'an the mountains gave the impression of huge skyscrapers. Behind those mystical myriad of windows, thousands of people concentrated on their work, their reading, their discussion.

Stars like crystals in the heavens; on earth, the gurgle of flowing water. Democratic, sacred Yan'an — how beautiful in the night!

But today, the 18th of March, 1947, the vast city of Yan'an sprawled in frigid darkness. In the northern and southern ends, houses bombed by enemy planes had burned for several days. Their wooden frames were charred and blackened, emitting only an occasional spark that flew into the night sky. Except for the security patrols, which would be the last to leave, the streets were deserted. Administrative personnel, students, local residents...every single one had departed. There was no singing, no laughter, no thousands of lamps gleaming in the mountain cave dwellings. Only the waters of the Yanshui, flowing endlessly to the east, were still the same.

Very late on the night of the 18th a large detachment of the Northwest Field Army entered the south gate. They were withdrawing from the southern front. Their flashlights pierced the darkness, revealing the big whitewash letters on the city wall:

DEMOCRATIC SACRED YANAN BELONGS TO US.
WE SHALL RETURN!

The men marched in silence, their steps heavy and slow, as if they were deliberately trying to prolong their stay in Yan'an. At times an angry explosive breath could be heard. One soldier, his head swathed in bloody bandages, still smelling of gunpowder, caressed the sides of buildings as he walked. A wounded man begged his stretcher bearers to set him down and remove the quilt covering his face so that he could see Yan'an. From the sound of his his voice, he had just recovered consciousness.

Emerging through the north gate of the city, the detachment split into two columns. One followed the ravine leading west; the other took the ravine leading east.

Stern-looking sentries ringed the hamlet to Wangjiaping, beyond Yan'an's north gate. In the ravine leading to the hamlet, near a grove of peach trees, many military and administrative personnel were waiting for the order to depart. Some stood by their horses, and the pack animals laden with documents. A few paced among the trees. Some sat around small tables in the grove, talking in low tones.

A lamp was burning in the window of a cave-dwelling half-way up the slope. The men waiting in the ravine kept looking toward the window.

Heavy explosions and machine-gun fire were audible in the distance.

Six horsemen, galloping up from the north, sped through Yan'an

City and out of the north gate, wheeled right and splashed across a shallow ford in the Yanshui River. They dismounted, and two of them turned their horses over to their companions and strode up the slope to Wangjiaping.

The two cavalry messengers who had taken the horses walked them along the river bank. One of the other two — apparently officers — lit a cigarette. He and his companion paced back and forth beside the Yanshui. They cast frequent glances at the shining window on the slope.

"It will soon be dark," said one. "At dawn the enemy will be able to take Yan'an. But Deputy Commander-in-Chief Peng Dehuai still hasn't left." He turned to his companion. "Now that our brigade commander and political director have gone to see him, I suppose he won't stay much longer."

"How can he — at a time like this."

The officers fell silent, each seeming to concentrate on the glowing tip of the other's cigarette. One heaved an exasperated sigh.

"We've given the enemy a bellyful these past few days, in spite of their heavy attacks in the south and southwest."

"Our troops have plenty of courage. Hu Zongnan is throwing 150,000 regulars against us. We've got only about 5,000 men here, but we've put more than that number of the enemy out of action in the past week alone, and killed He Qi, the general of their 48th Brigade. Most important of all, we've won time — time for the Central Committee and our various organizations and schools and the people of Yan'an to leave safely. We've spiked the enemy's scheme to charge into Yan'an and take our Central Committee by surprise."

"We fought very well, but we have to withdraw. Still, what else can we do? That's the way war is sometimes. In another two or three hours Yan'an will fall into the hands of the enemy. Losing Yan'an hurts no matter how you look at it."

Their eyes drifted to a hilltop ahead of them to the left, where lay the two small villages in which the Central Committee and Chairman Mao lived and worked — Date Orchard Village and Yangjia Ridge.

"They must have gone north somewhere."

"This is our last look at those little villages."

"Wait a minute. Aren't those lights over there?"

At the foot of the mountain to their left a lantern appeared, then a second, and a third.

The dark mountains on either side of the river loomed against a pitch black sky. Muffled explosions rolled in from the distance.

There was a smell of cordite in the air. Silent Yan'an seemed to be brooding on the impending disaster. How strange seeing lights in this sombre setting — and such bright lights. They were like the mast lights of a ship on a vast and stormy sea, riding out a night of gale and rain, never leaving her charted course, sailing straight on toward her destination.

The lights passed within twenty yards of where the officers were standing. They could clearly see the long military column. At the head of it were several people carrying large lanterns. Behind came animals laden with radio equipment, documents and baggage. Bringing up the rear were what appeared to be combat troops.

As the column marched by — very slowly, in neat formation — quiet footfalls blended with the sound of the flowing waters of the Yanshui. There was the light clink of metal weapon fittings, the soft tread of shod hoofs.

The lantern lights and the column filed by the foot of Qingliang Mountain, then turned and proceeded slowly toward the valley leading east from Yan'an.

The two officers who had been reporting to General Peng Dehuai came down the slope to the bank of the river. The other two officers hurried up to them.

"You saw him, Brigadier? What did he say?"

"He said if we hold on to Yan'an at this time it will be a burden on our backs; if we give it up, it will be a weight on the enemy. He said we shouldn't fly off the handle. The enemy will never get the best of us. They're heading for a fall. That's how it was in the past, that's how it is now, and that's how it's going to be in the future."

"Was he very angry, Brigadier?"

The political director standing behind the brigadier answered for him.

"Not that we could notice. In fact he advised us to be calm and methodical, to capture the enemy's positions one by one, and bit by bit build up our own strength. He said it was wrong to throw yourself blindly against objectives without regard to your striking power."

The brigadier sat down on a rock and looked at the dark city of Yan'an. "General Peng has ordered our main force to assemble in the neighborhood of Qinghua Gorge, twenty miles northeast of Yan'an, and wait for orders. He's also sending a small detachment northwest, in the direction of Ansai, to retreat slowly and draw the enemy after it, until our main force is ready to attack. General Peng apparently has everything nicely arranged for Hu Zongnan. He said the enemy will make a big grab at Yan'an and catch nothing but the empty air. They won't gain anything politically, and they'll get even less militarily.

"But, General Peng said, once they take Yan'an they'll go crazy with conceit; they'll sneer at our army. Except for a small garrison to hold the city and protect their lines of communication, they're sure to send their main force out to finish us off. Our detachment luring them toward the northwest will play on this psychology of theirs. A wild dash against another mirage in Ansai County will take some of the starch out of them."

"Not only that," added the political director, "but they'll be forced to make mistakes which our army, at its leisure, will be able to take advantage of." He swung his left hand. "What happens after that, depends on us." The director looked at the lighted window halfway up the slope. "General Peng is going to leave here immediately."

The sound of artillery fire came closer, shaking the air with its vibrations. It would soon be dawn, and the night momentarily became deeper.

The messengers led the horses forward. With his hand on the saddle, the brigadier said:

"Let's go, comrades. The advance guard of the enemy's left wing is only seven miles south of Yan'an."

They all mounted.

The brigadier looked around at Yan'an. It was dark and he couldn't see anything clearly, but he had to take one more look. Who knew how long it would be before they returned?

"Did a column just pass here a few minutes ago?" he asked in a hoarse voice. "It did? That was Chairman Mao and the Central Committee."

"What do you mean, Brigadier?" the two officers demanded. "They're leaving Yan'an only now? Impossible. Why is Chairman Mao leaving so late?"

"Don't ask me, comrades," replied the brigade commander, anger and bitterness welling up in his throat. "I don't know. Let's go."

He dug his heels into his horse's sides and the animal broke into a run. The other five riders raced after him. They followed the path just taken by Chairman Mao and the Central Committee — toward the east. In the dark night, the drumming hoofbeats intensified the warlike atmosphere hanging over Yan'an.

Two hours after the horsemen had departed, enemy artillery shells raised black pillars of smoke from the city's streets. Yan'an was in flames. The glow of the disastrous fires reddened half the sky.

The army which was speeding from Shanxi on the east side of

the Yellow River assembled in a gorge west of Ganguyi and awaited orders. Shortly before dark in the evening of March 19, 1947, Wang Shaoxin, a young mounted messenger from the regiment, came cantering up the gorge. As he passed the encampment of First battalion, a few of the soldiers who knew him hailed:

"Where to, Shaoxin?"

The young messenger checked his horse. "Brigade political department to pick up the news bulletin."

"Anything happening?"

"I hear the enemy has taken ... Yan'an ... and ... and — anyhow I'm not sure."

The faces of the soldiers drained of color. All crowded around Shaoxin.

"What's the real story about Yan'an, you blasted imp!"

"You can't get blood from a stone," retorted the boy, worried and a little angry. "I'm not the commander-in-chief. How would I know so much?"

He jerked his reins and slammed his heels into his horse's flanks. The animal flew down the gorge like mad, the drumming of its hoofs on the icy ground pounding fiercely against the soldiers' hearts. A pall of misery descended on the lonely gorge.

"Yan'an abandoned?" The shocking news spread like the wind from one unit to the next. The men discussed it anxiously. Some said it was just a rumor; the Party's Central Committee and Chairman Mao were both in Yan'an; would we let the enemy take it so easily? Others said we've come to defend Yan'an; how could it be given up without even giving us a chance to get into action? Impossible. Not in a million years!

It didn't take long before the original news had changed completely. A few soldiers said yes, the enemy had reached Yan'an's walls, but that they still hadn't entered the city. Some claimed that an enemy detachment had broken in but that we had thrown them out again. Others alleged that the abandonment of Yan'an was a story invented by an enemy agent; that he had been caught and was under heavy guard.

But no matter how each man embroidered the story to suit his personal fancy, no matter how staunchly the soldiers asserted they didn't believe a word of it, foreboding hung in every breast like a stone. In First Company half the food at dinner was left over.

That night a big wind arose. It blew out the stars and spread a black curtain of clouds across the sky. The distant artillery fire often could be heard quite clearly; other times it was dim and muffled.

A meeting of First Company was called. The men assembled on

a small field beside the river and seated themselves tensely in a neat formation. Company meetings usually were preceded by a lot of friendly banter, joking, swearing. Men were called upon to recite topical jingles they had composed. This platoon or that was asked for a song. The men came from all over China, and a great variety of folk art could be heard in these pre-meeting intervals — happy, boisterous sessions ordinarily. Today, the men sat tense, solemn, gloomy. To break up the depressing atmosphere, the cultural instructor stepped out and led the company in a song. The men's voices were loud and angry:

As sure as China's mountains raise their heads high,
As sure as China's rivers surge rushing by,
So surely our country independent must be,
The people of China demand to be free.
Gladly we follow Mao into the fight,
We smashed the Japanese with our might.
Today we'll pound into a bloody wreck
America's running dog Chiang Kai-shek,
Fight on, fight on, wherever you may be,
From victory to victory to victory!

Over and over, the song rang out. Not until the officer of the day declared the meeting opened did the men still their voices.

Zhang Pei, political instructor of First Battalion, stood listening off to one side. Near him Zhou Dayong slouched with his back against a tree. Dayong's head was lowered. One hand gripped his belt; the other was pressed against his forehead.

"Our company political instructor has gone to a meeting at the regiment's political department," Dayong said to Zhang Pei. "He won't be back for some time. We'd better not wait for him. Go ahead and speak."

"No, you speak first. I may not want to say anything."

Dayong was a direct, cheerful young fellow. To tell the truth, he seldom knew what it was to brood. He usually addressed meetings in a clear strong voice. But now when he opened his mouth he only got as far as "Comrades..." and then something seemed to stick in his throat. He couldn't see the soldiers, he couldn't hear the wind; he hadn't the faintest idea of what he wanted to say. After a long pause, Zhang Pei nudged him. Only then did Dayong remember what he had to announce. He forced out the words:

"Our army has withdrawn from Yan'an."

As if in response to an order, every man in the company leaped to his feet.

For a full five or six minutes no one spoke. The only sound was the light quick breathing of the assembled men. You had the feeling that a single word, even a cough, would spark a tremendous explosion.

Gust after gust of wind, laden with sand, rolled in over the mountains and moaned through the ravines and gorges. Veils of blowing sand darkened the sky.

The silence was unbearable. Suddenly a soldier burst out:

"You mean Yan'an, where Chairman Mao and the Central committee are ... has actually.... Speak, commander!"

Except for the men's harsh breathing, the field was deathly still. Hearts thumped like drum beats, eyes dimmed, heads whirled. The ground underfoot seemed to melt away like spring snows.

Dayong stood woodenly, his mind in turmoil. A sledge-hammer seemed to be pounding against his burning heart. Hot tears began to roll down his cheeks.

A soldier wept quietly. In an instant the whole company was in tears. Men sobbed and stamped their feet. Tears dropped on hands, on chests, on the icy rifle butts.

Zhang Pei could see that Dayong was unable to go on. The political instructor stepped before the men. He wanted to speak, but he couldn't get the words out. Though he knew well the purpose and significance of the departure from Yan'an, at the moment he was in the same state as the men — his eyes were filled with tears.

"Comrades," he cried in a voice that trembled, "sit down. It's true that we've left Yan'an. Today is the nineteenth of March. We'll never forget this day."

"Report!" Soldier Ma Changsheng stepped forward. "Yan'an ... the Central Committee ... Chairman Mao..." He beat his chest with his fist as if there was something inside ready to burst.

Repressing his own turbulent emotions, Zhang Pei checked his tears. "Comrades," he said, "the Central Committee left Yan'an with complete safety. You don't have to worry. Our brigade commander tells us that Chairman Mao will remain in north Shaanxi directing the nationwide war of liberation. What's more, he will lead the forces here personally. Chairman Mao is with us, right now — "

Ma Quanyou, leader of Squad Two, jumped to his feet. "Report! Political Instructor," he shouted, "I have something to say. We Communists, we revolutionary soldiers, marched day and night from Shanxi, hurrying to defend Chairman Mao and the Central Committee, to defend Yan'an, and now.... What kind of Communists, what kind of revolutionary soldiers are we, any way!"

"Instructor!" cried a soldier. "For our Chairman Mao — give us an order! Fight! We want to fight!"

Like a clap of thunder the men roared in unison:

"Fight! Fight!"

"We'll fight to the finish!"

The weeping changed to shouts, the shouts became battle vows, vows that swept higher than the rising gale.

"Don't feel badly, comrades, don't cry," shouted Zhang Pei. "Listen to me, listen to me. It's not our strategy to cling to any one city or piece of ground. Once we wipe out the enemy's armed forces, we'll be able to take Yan'an back — and we'll liberate Xian, too. Chiang Kai-shek and his gang have taken Yan'an, but it's no victory for them. It only means they'll be going to their deaths that much faster. Comrades, don't take it to heart, don't cry. Sharpen your bayonets instead, sharpen your bayonets —"

Ma Quanyou thrust his rifle against the sky. "Instructor, we swear ... we'll fight to the last man to retake Yan'an! We swear it!"

Throughout the meeting Tiger Wang, leader of Squad One, had sat with his back against a mound, silently crading his rifle in his arms. Nor did he move when the meeting ended, not until Ma Quanyou tugged his arm and said: "Come on, Tiger. Let's go."

Then he rose, as silent as before. Quanyou want to question him, but he knew it would be useless. In the entire company, Tiger Wang was the man most able to keep hatred buried deep in his heart.

The following evening Wei Yi, regimental chief of staff, and Zhang Pei, the First Battalion's political instructor, made a tour of the companies. Leaving the row of caves in which Second Company was quartered and descending the slope, they entered a ravine and followed along the small stream flowing through it.

Someone hurried up behind them and cried: "Report!"

Zhang Pei looked around. Although he couldn't see the man's features in the dark, from his chunky outline Zhang recognized the veteran cook of First Company — Sun Quanhou.

"What's on your mind, old Sun?" he asked.

"Instructor," began Sun. He swallowed hard. "Instructor, am I only fit to wield a vegetable chopper? I... I can do combat duty. The instructor and the comrades all say I'm too old. Fifty-seven, well, instructor ... I ... anyhow I'm a Communist ... even if I were eighty. Now everyone has vowed to defend Chairman Mao and the Central Committee. I want to be transferred to a combat squad. Just let me kill a couple of the enemy with my own hands, and I'll die happy!"

For the moment Zhang Pei didn't know what to say. Clasping his hands behind his back, he lightly scuffed the ground with his right foot.

Wei Yi walked over to the cook. "You've a loyal heart, old Sun," he said. "The Party is well aware of that. But cooking is an indispensable job too."

Unhappy, Sun lowered his head. "There's a feeling inside me..."

Zhang Pei took his hand. "Your attitude is fine, old Sun. We all want to do something worthwhile in life and stand in the forefront of the struggle. But not everyone need carry a tommy gun, some must hold a cooking ladle. Do you see what I mean?"

"Yes, I suppose so. Instructor ... I..." Sun hesitated, then slowly turned and walked away.

Wei Yi and Zhang Pei proceeded side by side along the path through the mountain ravine. Neither of them spoke. Both had been quite moved by Sun's request.

They approached a cave-dwelling where they could hear the sound of lively conversation. Lamplight was shining in the open doorway. Dayong, deep in thought, stood outside beside the wall.

"Holding a meeting?" asked Zhang Pei.

"Party branch."

(Members of the Communist Party with each unit of the army had their own Party branch. They met frequently to discuss their particular duties in given situations — generally to demonstrate exemplary behavior, and to encourage the other men in their unit.)

Zhang Pei put his head in the door. Wang Chengde, the company political instructor, was speaking.

Zhang Pei turned to Dayong. "Why aren't you in there?"

Dayong didn't answer. He knew now it was true that the PLA had left Yan'an several days before, but he still couldn't bring himself to believe it.

His mind was fuzzy, as if he had just awakened from a bad dream.

"This war is going to be a long drawn-out affair," said Zhang Pei. "We'll have to put up with a great many trials and tribulations."

"I understand the reasoning alright, Instructor. But I just can't get it all down in one swallow." There was a slight tremor in Dayong's voice as he replied. "If the enemy had beaten us we'd have to admit defeat. But nothing like that has happened."

"Let me ask you, Dayong," said Wei Yi, "what do you think we ought to do? Throw ourselves at the enemy blindly? Here in the northwest the enemy has mobilized several hundred thousand troops. We have a total of only a little over twenty thousand. The enemy has American arms and equipment. And we? Let's take rifles. Japanese 38's and guns that Shanxi warlord Yan Xishan made in his Taiyuan arsenal — with only a few bullets for each. In other words, we have to rely on rifles, bayonets, explosives and hand grenades to beat an enemy equipped with the most modern weapons. And we have to get everything we use by pulling it out of the enemy's hands.

"If you take my advice, you'll do your work patiently and keep making this point clear to your men: Our job is to wipe out enemy troops. Once we do that, everything else will come easy. You men shouldn't waste a minute, Dayong. We're going into action very soon!

Dayong's spirits immediately rose. "On the level?" he asked quickly.

"On the level. Tomorrow afternoon, we move."

The main force of the Northwest Field Army was concealed behind mountains forming the east and west sides of the deep Qinghua Gorge.

All day officers surveyed the terrain from the tops of the mountains along the gorge. Near the summits some men were digging fortifications.

Zhao Jin, commander of the regiment, led a group of about thirty officers on a tour of the mountain tops. From time to time he peered through his field glasses, then he and the officers, gathering around a military map spread upon the ground, discussed deployment of forces, and methods of attack.

All nodded in agreement at something Wei Yi said. "Yes, it's perfect for an ambush."

"It certainly is," said Liu Yuanxing, commander of First Battalion. "You couldn't find an inch of cover in the Qinghua Gorge if you looked for it with a lantern. If we can get the enemy in here, we can finish off every one of them. It's a beautiful spot for an ambush."

Qinghua Gorge is about twenty miles northeast of Yan'an. The Xiangyang-Yulin Highway runs east from Yan'an about fifteen miles to a village called Guaimao, and there turns north to enter the Qinghua Gorge. Flanked by high mountains on the east and west, the gorge is traversed lengthwise by a small river; the highway parallels the river.

After inspecting several more mountain tops, the regimental CO and his party again laid out the military map. They leaned over it thoughtfully as the officers gathered in a circle around Zhao Jin.

With a twig, Zhao Jin pointed at positions on the map. "Our army is camped on these surrounding mountains," he said. "When the enemy enters the ambush region, Qinghua Gorge, our troops at the northern end will open fire. Other units will then attack from the heights on both sides. The mission of our regiment will be to cut off the enemy's retreat and guarantee our main force the opportunity to wipe out the enemy's Thirty-first Brigade." His eyes swept the faces of the officers around him. "That is how our units will be disposed."

The officers looked at the nearby summits as they considered his words. A few made notes.

"It's a sack, alright," said one in a low tone. "Once the enemy get in here, we'll take care of them nicely."

"But what if they don't come in?"

"None of us are fortune tellers," said Liu, First Battalion CO, "but it's very possible the enemy will come this way."

"Not just possible — absolutely positive," interjected Zhao Jin.

He told them that after Hu Zongnan's troops occupied Yan'an, the enemy became very arrogant. They charged wildly about the countryside, boasting that they were going to "exterminate" the main force of the PLA. A small detachment fooled them into believing that it was the main force and led them a merry chase all the way to Ansai Valley, northwest of Yan'an. Yesterday, over fifty thousand enemy troops charged into Ansi county to wipe out the "main force". At the same time, the enemy Thirty-first Brigade, which had been sent out as a right wing, moved up towards Qinghua Gorge. It had already reached the village of Guaimao, where the road from Yan'an turns north, and was now only nine or ten miles from the ambush position.

"So you see," the regimental commander concluded with a grin, "we've got the enemy taking orders from our General Peng Dehuai. Our job now is to put General Peng's plan into effect."

Zhao Jin's appearance showed his years of military service. His belt and puttees always fitted neatly; he held himself ramrod straight. Because he had been wounded about ten times and had lost a lot of blood, his face was thin and sallow.

"Look there," he cried suddenly, pointing to an officer on the eastern slope. "701 is coming."

Brigade commander Chen, accompanied by five or six officers, was seen climbing toward Zhao Jin's inspection party.

Chen's forehead was beaded with sweat. He had already visited several mountain positions. With the alert movements of a soldier, he took up his field glasses and examined the surrounding terrain. On the mountains west of Qinghua Gorge, Chen could see small groups of officers of other units also making surveys.

After a few minutes, Chen let the glasses hang by the strap around his neck and rest on his chest. "Don't forget concealment," he said sharply to the messengers standing near him. "What are you all crowding together for!"

Placing his hands behind his back, the brigadier faced Zhao Jin's inspection party. "Our first volley must go off with a bang that will take the starch out of the enemy." Handing his field glasses to his escort orderly, Chen patted the dust from his uniform. "Have you got a pretty good idea of the layout now?" he asked Zhao Jin.

The regimental CO stood stiffly at the brigadier's side. After a moment's thought he replied, "We've made a preliminary survey. We've also started some of our units on digging in."

Chen questioned him about the regiment's gun emplacements and deployment of troops, then turned to one of Zhao Jin's junior officers. "You're clear on your regiment's mission in this engagement, are you? Good. Let me hear it."

"After the enemy has entered the area of ambush and firing begins at the far end," said the officer, "we are to cut off their retreat at all costs and tie the mouth of the 'sack' tight." He pointed left to the entrance of the gorge. "That's the mouth we have to seal."

For five minutes or so Chen looked toward the gorge entrance in silence. "Where is your best line of attack?" he asked another officer.

"Jump that ridge in front of us and cut straight down."

Chen considered this. "Have you examined the other side of the ridge personally?"

"What for? It's a simple stretch of ground. Anyone can see it at a glance."

"As simple as all that, eh? Well, I'm going to have a look." Chen glanced at Zhao Jin. "Some of the things that appear to be the most simple, in battle often turn out to be the most complicated."

Zhao Jin stared straight ahead without batting an eye. He had a feeling that Chen's last remark was directed against him. He accompanied Chen as the brigadier toured the regiment's mortar and heavy machine-gun positions on another ridge. There, Chen personally checked the machine-gun sights.

"You haven't inspected here yet, Zhao Jin?"

"Not yet."

Chen turned to the officers commanding the position. "What is the mission of these weapons?"

"Our mission is to seal the mouth of the gorge," said one of the officers.

"I can't even see the mouth of the gorge through the sights of this machine-gun in its present position. How many heavy machine-guns does this regiment have? How many rounds of ammunition?"

"Four heavy machine-guns, with an average of 350 rounds each."

"Nonsense. One of those guns — the Maxim — can't be used. Right?"

"Right."

"A few hundred rounds won't last long, once the battle starts," Chen said to a machine-gunner. "What will you do when your ammo is gone?"

The soldier, standing at attention, made no reply.

"When the bullets are used up, Chiang Kai-shek will send us some more — is that what you are thinking? But you won't get him to send you any more with your gun in that position." Chen looked at the officers in charge of the emplacement. They were very embarrassed. Again he pointed at the machine-gun.

"You won't be joining the battle, you'll just be adding to the noise. Bullets move faster than men can run. But unless you use your fire power to break the enemy's legs, you'll never tie up the mouth of that 'sack'. Some comrades like to say, 'Three rounds of artillery, a burst from our machine-guns, a good grenade charge, and the battle is won. Well, just try it and see what happens. You'll get your head broken if you continue to wage warfare on that level. There's nothing polite about a battle."

After a pause, his eyes fixed on Zhao Jin, the brigadier continued, "This idea that everything is 'simple kills a lot of people. I consider it dangerous, and so should you." Without waiting for the regimental CO to reply, Chen turned and strode away.

Wei Yi, the regiment's chief of staff, took charge of correcting the machine-gun position himself.

Chen continued his tour, hailing the soldiers as he went, shaking hands with those nearest him, exhorting, "Comrades, let's make that first volley good and loud!" His cheerful voice rang through the trenches.

"We guarantee one that'll blast 'em, 701," the men shouted in response.

The brigadier questioned them about conditions in the companies — their battle preparations, the state of morale, whether they were cold sleeping at night, how the food was, whether they had tobacco...

Approaching a trench, Chen found Dayong discussing something with platoon leader Li Jiangguo. "How are the men's spirits, Jiangguo?" the brigadier asked.

Jiangguo snapped to attention and looked Chen straight in the eye. "High as a kite and still climbing."

Chen burst into laughter. He examined Jiangguo from head to foot and said, "You're a perky young fellow, but don't think you can get by just on verve." He pointed at the soldier's head. "You've got to put that thinking machine into action."

He turned his smiling eyes to Dayong. "Young Old Revolutionary, Jiangguo is a dashing, clever fighter, right?"

"Right."

Jiangguo concealed his delight behind an expression of the utmost sternness.

Suddenly the brigadier's face became grim. "Comrade Zhou Dayong, instruct every leader in your company that this battle must be fought well. No mistakes will be permitted."

After Chen left, Jiangguo jumped down into the trench to stand beside Dayong. "That nickname the brigadier's given you — 'Young Old Revolutionary — it's really got around. Everybody knows it now."

"When he calls me 'Young Old Revolutionary', that's not so bad," said Dayong. "But when he calls me 'Comrade Zhou Dayong, I know I'm in for it. Nine times out of ten it means he's going to tick me off. I've learned that alright."

All that night the men feverishly dug fortifications and built firing positions on the heights around Qinghua Gorge. Companies which finished first immediately began practice manoeuvres, making changes in their sector's fortifications wherever the manoeuvres proved them necessary. The mountain tops echoed with the sound of picks and shovels, rapid footsteps, brief orders. It was forbidden to speak loudly or smoke. But there was always someone on the far side of the mountain, his head buried inside his opened jacket, taking a few quiet puffs. Every veteran knew you could go a day or two without food and not feel too bad. But if you couldn't have a smoke once in a while, your throat itched like the devil.

The men worked through the night. When the sky was a murky grey, they had camouflaged their positions and artillery emplacements. During daytime, except for a small force which remained to keep watch for the enemy, most of the troops withdrew behind the mountains forming the eastern and western sides of the gorge.

They took their positions again at dawn the next day. It was said that the enemy's vanguard was approaching the ambush area. The PLA soldiers loaded their guns, opened the safeties on their hand grenades and lay them in readiness on the lip of the trench. Their eyes on the entrance to the gorge, the men waited — one hour, two hours... Late afternoon, and still no sign of the enemy. The heart of every man was in his throat with excitement; eyes ached from staring. To strike the first blow hard and accurately was vitally important.

Because no one was watching, the sun took advantage and plunged behind the western hills like a meteor in the night sky.

The experienced fighters — Jiangguo, Ma Quanyou, Ma Changsheng — fumed with exasperation. They knew the enemy never dared to move after sunset.

Tiger Wang, leader of Squad One, his long-stemmed pipe clamped in the corner of his mouth, squatted on his heels in the trench, silent, unperturbed. Through half-closed eyes, he gazed at the bowl of his pipe as if studying an object of rare beauty. His stolid appearance gave the impression that he wouldn't be upset if the sky fell.

One of the soldiers in his squad, Ning Jinshan, said to him uneasily: "We're not very far from Yan'an and there are several thousand of us. Is it possible the enemy doesn't know we're here?"

His eyes still on his pipe, Tiger drawled: "What are you worrying about? The impatient man always eats half-cooked rice. Understand this — our ears are sharp and our eyes are bright, but the enemy — they're deaf and blind."

"I came over to the PLA from the KMT army less than a month ago," Jinshan ventured timidly, "but I'm not exactly an amateur about battles."

He looked at Tiger Wang, calmly rapping the ashes out of his pipe. Jinshan didn't understand. What made Tiger and his mates so sure the enemy would walk into the ambush? He wasn't at all convinced. He thought the KMT fought very cleverly. Would they walk into the trap with their eyes wide open? Besides, their major actions were directed by the Americans and they were equipped with a lot of American heavy artillery — much stronger than the PLA guns.

Jinshan gazed up at the enemy scouting planes flying high overhead. It wasn't only this battle he wasn't very enthusiastic about. The PLA won't make much of a showing in future battles either, he thought.

For some reason, Ma Quanyou suddenly became enraged. Glaring, the short scar on his face flaming scarlet, he yelled, "What are you talking about? I'll pull your tongue out by the roots!"

Jinshan thought Quanyou's anger was directed against him, and his heart began clattering like a bucket-chain in a well.

But then a soldier beside Quanyou replied heatedly, "Oho, so you can't tell a man's honest heart from a donkey's liver? So that's how you take my good advice? Alright, we'll settle this at the Party branch meeting!"

Jinshan breathed a sigh of relief. The argument had nothing to do with him.

The sun was nearly down. Red fleecy clouds reflected their crimson hues on the undulating hills. Thousands of ravens, cawing, flew home to their nests.

Still not a shadow of the enemy!

At four a.m. the PLA soldiers headed for their positions in the dark. On slopes left and right of the gorge, troops were in motion. Except for their footsteps and the occasional clink of a bayonet against a hand grenade, all was silent.

By four thirty every man was at his post. Regimental CO Zhao Jin made telephone contact with brigade headquarters, then sat down in the small cave serving as the regiment's command post and had a smoke.

Regimental chief of staff Wei Yi came striding along the ledge. He was always in high spirits, with apparently limitless energy and enthusiasm. Stooping, he entered the cave, knelt down and telephoned each of his battalions, instructing them to check their preparedness for battle.

Putting down the phone, he said to Zhao Jing, "Brigade political director Yang says he's going to First Battalion."

He gave some instructions to a staff officer and a communications platoon leader, then again turned to the regimental CO. "I want to take a look at our ammo depot," he said. "I'll be back in ten minutes."

After Wei Yi had gone, Zhao Jin also left the dugout and walked north along the ledge. Men were digging air-raid shelters, camouflaging the trenches with branches, talking in low tones. A few sat snoring, with their backs against the bluff. Suddenly, Zhao Jin spotted the beam of a flashlight.

"Is he trying to tell the enemy where we are?" he fumed softly. "The dumb fool!" He walked rapidly toward the beam.

From darkness till dawn, from dawn to sun-up, the men waited in the damp trenches.

"Today's the day," they said to themselves hopefully. Their faces, worn from lack of sleep, were anxious.

The commanders judged the passage of time by the shortening shadows of the trees. But the damn things didn't seem to change. The hands of their watches evidently were asleep too. Time always seems to take root just when you want it to move quickly.

"Rat-tat-tat-tat ... boom! boom!" Rifles and hand grenades suddenly sounded near the mouth of the gorge where it met the long river valley leading east from Yan'an. The men were instantly alert, listening with every pore of their bodies. Startled, they looked at each other.

But it was only the nervous firing of KMT sentries well over a mile away. It quickly died down, and the area relapsed into a pre-dawn hush.

First Company, PLA, occupied the height nearest the mouth of the gorge. Battalion commander Liu telephoned them frequently from his command post to check on their observations.

Chengde, the political instructor of First Company, reminded the men behind the ridge to tighten their shoes. Dayong, company commander, stuck his pistol in the belt of his trousers. Crouching, he ran along behind the shelter of a low mound and gave his instructions:

"Hand grenades ready. Don't let any earth get in the muzzles of you rifles. Keep calm. No firing till I give the order."

A tense atmosphere spread across the battle area. It was silent as an old temple which no one has visited for hundreds of years.

Men talked in whispers. Some squatted behind the mound taking turns puffing a precious cigarette. A few huddled, cradling their rifles, breathing softly.

"I wish the shooting would start. I'm pins and needles all over."

"My heart is beating like mad. It won't go back to normal till we rip into the enemy."

"Listen. You hear those grenades clinking against each other? They're saying they want a chance to speak their piece."

Suddenly three enemy fighter planes streaked across the sky. They circled several times over the Qinghua Gorge area, made an exploratory strafing run along the gorge, then flew off.

The fighters eyes trailed the planes until they disappeared.

"Attention. Enemy troops."

Although the command was spoken very low, many of the men heard it. More of them sensed it. Tense and excited, their hearts seemed ready to burst through their throats. The weather was cold, but the majority of foreheads were damp with perspiration.

Most excited were the PLA soldiers at the furthest observation outpost. It was ten o'clock in the morning. They saw a long yellow column of enemy troops enter the gorge. Behind the advance guard came many KMT soldiers, marching down the road. Their pack animals were laden with mountain cannon, mortars and heavy machine-guns. Enemy officers sat astride their mounts, riding crops dangling from their wrists. How peaceful and idyllic. Like a tourist outing in mountains. Some of the enemy officers cast uneasy glances at the heights flanking the gorge, but most sat their plodding horses with folded arms, deep in thought.

Platoon after platoon of enemy infantry marched by. The KMT soldiers were weighted down with heavy packs in addition to their rifles, and they walked bent forward at the waist, heads drooping. They looked exhausted. Some were using their rifles as shoulder poles, and carried officers' luggage tied to each end. Some ported light machine-guns from which they had not even bothered to remove the covers. One soldier accidentally jabbed an officer's horse with his rifle, causing the animal to shy. The officer turned around and beat the soldier about the head with his riding crop.

From a concealed position above the gorge, Dayong and several of his men watched the enemy filing by. Dayong's chest was pressed against the low breastwork. His head propped by the fists supporting his chin, he glared down at the troops of KMT warlord Hu Zongnan. These were the dogs who had occupied our Yan'an, Chairman Mao and the Central Committee's Yan'an! Dayong ground his teeth, his face contorted with rage.

The cruelty of the enemy was hateful enough, but their pompous complacency was even harder to bear!

"Carve them into bits with our bayonets, and I'll feel a lot better!" said Ma Quanyou.

"Use our grenades, blast them into minced dog meat!" was Ma Changsheng's comment.

Li Jiangguo swore in an uncontrollable fury.

"Keep your voices down," ordered Tiger Wang.

"Squad leader..." began Ning Jinshan timidly.

Dayong quickly drew back into the position. "Don't make a sound — anyone."

The enemy had sent out detachments to cover both flanks, and they were proceeding along the heights on either side of the gorge. One of the detachments, with over a hundred men armed with tommy guns, was nearing First Company's position. The KMT soldiers were shooting wildly in all directions and yelling:

"Come out! Come out! Don't try to fool us. We know there aren't many of you!'

Dayong could see that some of his men were itching to open fire. But if that happened the enemy would draw in its head like a turtle. The victory they had been waiting for would fly away. All their painstaking preparations would be wasted.

The enemy kept coming closer and closer...

Every second seemed a year.

Dayong clutched the cloth of his shirt with both hands. His face was crimson. Great beads of perspiration dripped from his forehead.

What should they do? The enemy flanking guard was now only 300 yards from the PLA camouflaged heavy machine-gun position ... 250 yards.... Every man held his breath, his eyes fixed on the advancing enemy detachment. If only they had a magic hood, like the one in the folk tales the men sometimes told during their rest sessions, to put over the enemy's head and blind them! But wishing was no good. The enemy was still coming on. If we don't open fire in another thirty seconds, it will be too late!

Now, the KMT flank guard was only 180 yards from our heavy machine-guns. After firing a burst at random it turned and passed to the right of our concealed forces. The enemy detachment crossed the summit and followed along the ridge toward the north.

The PLA men blew out their breath. Soft laughter was heard. Everyone had been highly tense and excited. It was only now they realized that their perspiration had soaked through the backs of their cotton-padded uniforms.

The young soldiers jostled and poked one another jokingly. They felt happy, affectionate. The warm rays of the sun brightened the misty battlefield, the smiling faces. It shone on the ponderous, solemn big artillery pieces, on the agile mischievous machine-guns.

"My tunic is sticking to me like an icicle," said Tiger Wang with a grin. "I say that enemy detachment deserves a commendation."

Jiangguo immediately supported him. "We're always saying the KMT is rotten and useless. But you see, some of them are not so useless."

"Now what are you supposed to mean by that?" Quanyou demanded.

"How can you ask? Didn't that gang that just went blundering by help the Chinese revolution? Sometimes their uselessness is very useful. If they weren't so dumb and useless, they'd never have missed us."

The men stifled their laughter.

"The way I see it," drawled Tiger Wang, wiping the sweat from his brow, "even if old Truman gives the KMT his whole treasury, he can't make a human being out of Chiang Kai-shek."

Changsheng was observing his own chest. "A mangy dog can't support a crumbling wall," he quipped, without looking up.

Someone started an argument about "luck". A few insisted there was such a thing, citing as proof strange things that had happened to them on the battlefield. But most of the men maintained that anyone who believed in luck was a "superstitious melon-head".

"Look sharp!" company commander Dayong suddenly cried in

a low voice.

The men stared. Almost all of the enemy brigade was now inside the gorge. It must have been about ten minutes later, when a machine-gun began to chatter at the northern end of the gorge, five or six miles ahead.

Exploding hand grenades immediatly filled the air, belching black smoke. Rifles and artillery started to roar. Every weapon we had poured down its fire on the enemy. The KMT soldiers scattered in panic. A pall of smoke filled Qinghua Gorge.

"Charge!"

"Let's go! Charge!"

Like a mountain torrent, the PLA men flooded down into the valley.

Bugle calls echoed on the heights, blaring their stirring commands. A young bugler stood on the highest summit, head back, blowing with all his might, the bit of red silk tied to his trumpet streaming in the wind.

The mission of Zhao Jin's regiment was to block the enemy's rear. His men rushed toward the mouth of the gorge. Victory was in sight, and they let nothing stop them. They jumped ravines, they slid down cliffs.

First Company was running in the lead, the two platoons led by Dayong being the furthest out in front. A third platoon under company political instructor Chengde raced along Dayong's right flank. A man running beside Chengde shouted in a high voice:

"Cutting off the enemy's retreat means victory!"

The PLA soldiers turned their heads to look. It was Wei Yi, regimental chief of staff, his face wet with perspiration, leading a detachment to the right of First Company. Flying along First Company's left flank were Second and Third Companies under the command of battalion CO Liu. He was in shirt-sleeves rolled up to the elbow. For some reason he was swearing vigorously.

Thick clouds of dust covered the slopes. Rifle and artillery fire blended in a wild blur of noise that shook the mountains. From a rise, Zhao Jin directed the battalion's fire. A series of rifle volleys slashed the enemy's retreat route like a sabre. Artillery shells of many calibers burst in the mouth of the gorge, raising a mountain of dust and smoke that climbed to the heavens, a pall so dense that no bird could pierce it.

Although the gorge didn't appear very wide from the heights, the PLA men had to race two or three miles before they could reach a point narrow enough to seal off the entry.

For seven miles, the entire length of the gorge was packed with enemy troops, washing from side to side like a tide. First they rushed to the eastern side of the gorge, and were met by a crushing volley of rifle fire. Then they turned and made for the western side, only to be showered with grenades. Artillery shells bursting among them terrified their mules and horses. The animals reared and trampled in their frantic efforts to get away. Some KMT soldiers crawled along the sunken banks of the river, firing stubbornly. Some, with fixed bayonets, savagely met our charging men.

The battlefield rang with the calls of the PLA men — "Surrender and live!" and the clash of rifle butts on bayonets.

Zhao Jin, regimental CO, leading a battalion, came tearing down the mountain to reinforce the units fighting in the gorge. Plunging into the midst of the enemy, he and his troops encountered fierce resistance every step of the way. In some places only one man remained of an enemy squad, but that one fought desperately, refusing to give up his weapon except as a last resort.

Driving north, Zhao Jin came across a captured enemy officer — the commanding general of the KMT Thirty-first Brigade. The man was standing woodenly at the edge of the road with both hands hanging limply by his sides. His face twitching and running with cold sweat, his eyes lacklustre, the officer was angrily muttering, "Is this how it ends? Is it all over so quickly?" He seemed unwilling to accept what had happened to him. Abruptly, he squatted down on his heels and grasped his head in his hands. "I can't believe it. It's too quick," the general said furiously. "We didn't even have time to get into position. The whole brigade ... the whole brigade... It can't be. It's impossible!"

Pockets of enemy troops were hiding out in gullies, ravines, mountain clefts. East and west, rifles spat, grenades exploded. Enemy planes circled overhead, but they neither bombed nor strafed, for they couldn't distinguish friend from foe in Qinghua Gorge.

Zhao Jin's men had captured over three hundred enemy prisoners, and the regimental commander ordered that they be assembled together.

The PLA soldiers loaded themselves with as many captured belts of ammunition as they could carry. Some cradled brand-new American tommy-guns taken from the enemy. Addressing one of the shiny automatic weapons affectionately, a PLA man said, "You've come a long hard way from America, pal. Now you can help me serve the people."

Smiling broadly, Brigadier Chen approached. The men crowded around him.

"Short and sweet," he commended. "You finished off 4,000 of

the enemy in two hours; not one got away. That's what I call drawing the net tight."

The men were practically dancing for joy. Everyone talked of how many prisoners he had taken, how many arms he had seized. Men rode astride captured enemy big guns. Bearers piled their stretchers with KMT rifles and ammunition.

Then came the order — withdraw immediately. Escorting their prisoners, carrying their new arms and equipment, the PLA men sang as they marched:

Chiang Kai-shek, our chief of supply.
Has sent us more guns from his US ally.

When the KMT reinforcements arrived a few hours later, except for enemy corpses and the American-made helmets which littered the ground, Qinghua Gorge was empty.

The People's Liberation Army had vanished like a gust of wind, leaving no shadow or trace, gone to where no one knew.

News of the crushing enemy defeat at Qinghua Gorge spread with lightning speed throughout the Shaanxi-Gansu-Ningxia Border Region. People counted on their fingers — the victory had been won exactly six days after the main force of the PLA had evacuated Yan'an.

Qu Bo (1923-)

Qu Bo, author of the unusual novel "Tracks in the Snowy Forest", was born in 1923 in a poor peasant family in Shandong province. He joined the Eighth Route Army (the forerunner of the PLA) in 1939, and served successively in a number of military posts. Badly wounded in the campaign against the bandits in Northeast China, he was discharged from the army in 1950. He later was appointed Vice-Director of the Planning Division of the First Ministry of Machine Building. In recent years he has devoted most of his time to writing.

The novel tells of a period in the late forties after Chiang Kai-shek's armies had been driven out of what had been called "Manchuria". In the mountains and forests of the wilderness, puppet officials under the Japanese, KMT military police, hostile landlords, and bandit gangs remained, lurking in heavily fortified hide-outs. They raided villages, slaughtered the inhabitants, and sabotaged the land reform program the Communists had instituted.

The enemy had to be destroyed. To attack with a large military force would be futile. Only a small, flexible, strong unit could do the job.

In Tracks in the Snowy Forest *the leader of the PLA task force given the assignment is called Jianbo. He was in fact Qu Bo, who bases his novel on personal experience. Our sample describes the shrewd mix of psychological and actual warfare waged against the wily bandits by PLA scouts enveloped in a haze of local traditions and romantic myths.*

TRACKS IN THE SNOWY FOREST

The sky was dark and the earth was black. A howling wind slung stinging particles of sand against the men's faces. The severe northern winter was coming. Jianbo and his small unit set out for the Aristocratic Range, with its endless mountains and deep forests.

Craggy peaks pierced the heavens like great stone teeth; mountain gales roared over the tree-tops like tremendous angry seas. Dense trees blotted out the sky overhead; thick grass concealed the ground underneath.

The Aristocratic Range — who knew how high it soared into the sky? Or over how vast an area it sprawled? People said it had thirty-eight hundred peaks. After several days of marching, the little unit had crossed only a dozen mountains. The evening of the third day, they made camp in a cave in a huge overhanging cliff, halfway up Mount Peony. Compared with the entire mountain, the cliff was no bigger than a fingernail, and Jianbo and his thirty-five men took up only a small corner of the cave. It wasn't often you could find such a comfortable billet in the wilds.

In the fading daylight, the men looked out over the forest stretching below them. Not far off, in a crotch of a big tree, was a hole as big as a millstone. A large black bear laboriously climbed the tree and disappeared into the dark opening. Well, no one could say they had no neighbors.

On a bone-chilling morning, the unit arrived at Nine Dragon Confluence, a hamlet in the heart of the mountain range. They had travelled about two hundred *li* (*a* li *is roughly 1/3 of a mile*) after leaving the last village on the edge of the forest.

The hamlet got its name from the nine mountain streams joining together in a deep rocky pool. When the streams were dry, the pool was like a mirror reflecting the nine mountains crouched around it and the clear blue firmament above. At night, the pool was filled with stars, as if a piece of the sky lay beneath its waters. In the rainy season, the streams poured turbulently into the pool, throwing up a mushroom-shaped splash a hundred meters high.

The local peasants claimed the pool was enchanted. According to them, the second day of the second lunar month was when the dragons raised their heads. It was also the birthday of the God of the Mountains. On that day every family in the hamlet burned incense and paper gold or silver ingots at the edge of the pool and respectfully kowtowed.

There were thirty-six families in the hamlet, and they planted their grain and vegetables in the black soil beside the streams. They never knew drought and they suffered no floods; every year they gathered a rich harvest. Between seasons, they dug medicinal roots, hunted, and picked mushrooms. They lived either in log cabins or in cave-dwellings which they hollowed out of the mountainside. They had little in the way of crockery; most of their bowls and basins were made from gourds. In every household two spirit tablets were worshipped. One represented the God of the Mountains; the other, the King of the Dragons.

When the People's Liberation Army had made its large-scale search through this region before, scout Zerung had found a white sneaker about thirty *li* southeast of Nine Dragon Confluence. That was why Jianbo brought his men into this hamlet. But where were the bandits? The sneaker couldn't tell them, nor could they find any other clues in the vicinity.

The forest was so vast and the PLA fighters were so few; it was difficult to discover any trace of the bandits. When they questioned the local inhabitants, the only answer they got was, "We're all Chinese. Why do you have to fight?" Or, "We haven't seen any soldiers since the Japanese army passed through here three years ago."

Jianbo and his unit searched for eight days without finding a single clue. For the first time that the men could remember there was no smile on the face of the enthusiastic, cheerful Jianbo.

Now he sat alone in a cabin, wondering about Zerong and Dade — nicknamed "Longlegs". The night the unit had arrived in Nine Dragon Confluence, the two scouts disguised themselves as traders and went off in the direction of the sneaker. Eight days had passed without a word from them. Why had they adopted the garb of traders? Because traders were the only strangers who ever came to this region — and only one or two every couple of years, at that. Offering rough cloth and crude farm implements and household utensils, the unscrupulous merchants would obtain in return — at very low cost — commercially valuable furs, ginseng root (mandrake) and deer horn. The local people hated these adventurers heartily.

After reaching the place where the sneaker had been found, Zerong and Longlegs made a careful search for further clues. But in this deep overgrown forest it was like looking for a needle in a haystack. Though they combed the mountains and gullies for several days, they had no success. They were drenched with sweat in spite of the chilly early winter weather.

"It's hopeless. Let's try some other approach," Longlegs pleaded in an exhausted voice.

Zerong sat down on a boulder and stroked his beard. "There must be a story behind that sneaker. It couldn't have come here by itself. Someone had to be wearing it." To encourage the young scout, the older man pretended more confidence than he actually felt.

"Maybe some hunter threw it away. Or maybe he was eaten by a wild animal and the sneaker was all that was left. Otherwise, why can't we find any other traces of him?"

"That's hardly possible," Zerong smiled. He drew the sneaker out from his coat and examined it closely. "You see, there are no bloodstains. And there's no blood or human bones in the area where I found it. So the wearer couldn't have been eaten by a wild animal. Besides, as I understand it, hunters around here don't wear sneakers. There's even less chance that any of the local people could afford them. You're from the mountains yourself. Am I talking sense?"

"Yes, of course." The young scout stared off into the distance. "But sometimes there's something special..." Suddenly his eyes narrowed. Still muttering, "Special ... special...," he rose quickly and ran straight forward. Mystified, Zerong hurried after him.

Longlegs covered ground rapidly. In a moment, he reached a big tree. Leaping for joy, he smacked both hands against his thighs and crowed, "Zerong, ha-ha, special, special — I've found something special."

Turning, he pulled Zerong over to the tree and pointed to a white slash as wide as a man's hand in the bark of the trunk about head high. "Is that special or isn't it!"

The older scout peered at the cut intently. "It's a knife slash alright," he said. "No doubt about it." ...But what does it prove? he wondered. He thought a moment, then clapped the young fellow on the shoulder.

"Longlegs, this is our first discovery in three days. As the old saying goes, 'When a wild goose passes it trails its sound behind; when a man passes he leaves his footprints. The bandits couldn't have gone through here without leaving a trace. I don't believe it. Patience, boy, let's keep looking."

Zerong circled the tree several times. There were no other cuts in the bark. Had some hunter been testing the keenness of his blade? Or was the slash made with no motive at all? And what was its connection with the sneaker? Did it really have nothing to do with the bandits?... These questions ran through Zerong's mind.

Walking around to the back of the tree, he inspected every tree in line with the rear. He examined them one by one, from branches to trunk, from trunk to roots.

"Good. Another one," he suddenly shouted. "Longlegs, come over here. Here's another one." He ran to a tree that was forty odd paces beyond the first. Again, head high, a piece of bark had been cut off, revealing white wood beneath. Zerong hurried back to where he had found the sneaker, walked to the first tree, then went on to the second. His path, a total distance of about one hundred metres, had proceeded in a straight line from southeast to northwest. Continuing in the same northwesterly direction, they found a third slash, a fourth, a fifth....

Zerong stroked his beard and smiled. "We've got something this time, Longlegs. Those slashes must have been made by someone who was afraid of losing his way. What do you say?"

"Right." The young scout's spirits had fully revived. "Absolutely. But was it a hunter? Or someone out picking mushrooms? Or someone digging ginseng roots? Or was it a bandit? Hard to say."

"Never mind about that now. First we've got to track him down and get to the bottom of the matter."

"Right. Let's go." Bursting with energy, Longlegs swung into a ground-consuming stride. Together with Zerong, he pushed into the deep forest, following the trail of slashes.

Zerong was an experienced scout. Originally a hired farmhand, he had joined the army to fight the Japanese and had served in the battles on the east coast of Shandong province. Now, at the age of forty-one, he was the leader of the regiment's scout platoon.

Life had been hard for him. He had never been able to go to school, but he was very intelligent. He could recite from the famous classical novels by heart, engrossing his listeners with his fine dramatic talents. Before he left the farm, during the rainy weather or in the slack winter season he had always been surrounded by people listening to his stories. He was like a warm fire in winter, a shady spot in summer. Everyone liked him. It was his keen intelligence, plus his courage and painstaking attention to detail, that made him so successful a scout.

The two PLA men followed the trail for three days. Their dry rations were finished, but they couldn't kill any game for fear of revealing themselves. They had to live on plain boiled mushrooms.

That night they climbed to the top of a steep mountain. Pausing to catch their breaths, they observed smoke rising from a hollow below. Both men forgot their fatigue. Straining their eyes, they made out a dozen or so small log cabins. Zerong checked his compass and calculated their present position and the distance from their unit in Nine Dragon Confluence.

"Another discovery," he said. "This hamlet isn't on the map. When our troops searched these mountains the last time, I scouted through here. We didn't see any signs of bandits then. We're north of Nine Dragon Confluence, not more than thirty *li*, I'd say."

"I'll take your word for it." Longlegs was alertly watching the log cabins. "The bandits probably all ran away then, but came back later. What should we do? The hamlet may be a bandits' lair, at that."

"Not necessarily," Zerong replied with a smile. "We've only been searching for six or seven days. I'd be very surprised if we've discovered a bandits' hide-out this quickly."

From the hamlet came the sound of dogs barking and hens cackling. Zerong shook his head. "Did you ever hear of bandits who kept dogs and chickens?"

The young scout sighed. He despondently sat down on the grass.

Zerong forced a comforting laugh. "Let's go down and get something to eat. Don't relax your vigilance. Remember — I'm a trader and you're my helper. Be careful. Don't talk much and keep your eyes peeled. Understand?"

Longlegs nodded. They checked each other's disguises, and descended the slope towards the nameless hamlet.

It was dusk when they entered the settlement. Lights were gleaming in the windows of the handful of families living there. They burned resinous torches for illumination. Zerong pushed open the door of a small cabin at the west end of the hamlet. An old man and his wife were eating in the light of a torch. They were frightened speechless at the sight of the strangers.

"We're traders from Peony River City. Don't be afraid," said Zerong quickly, making a deep bow. "We've just arrived. Could we trouble you two old folks to let us spend the night here?"

Somewhat reassured, the old man queried, "Where are you coming from?"

"Nine Dragon Confluence."

The old man was startled. "Oh? I hear there are soldiers there. Is that so?"

It was Zerong's turn to be taken aback. The presence of the PLA unit in Nine Dragon Confluence was supposed to be a secret. How did they know about it here?

"We let the army attend to the soldiers. We're only interested in trading," he said casually, and he brought the conversation around to the business of buying local products.

There were two things he had to find out — how far the hamlet was from Nine Dragon Confluence, and how the old man had learned of the arrival of the unit. Fortunately, the old couple were simple, honest people, and Zerong soon got the information from them. Nine Dragon Confluence was only twenty *li* away, just on the other side of the ridge. They knew about the PLA men because hunters from the hamlet, when they went to the top of the mountain, had seen the soldiers practicing cliff-scaling.

Early the following morning, Zerong went from door to door, pricing ginseng roots, deer horn, raw furs. None of the local people would quote him a figure in money; they insisted on barter. Three years before, a couple of scoundrels had cheated them with counterfeit notes.

At noon, Zerong and Longlegs sat down beside the small street and rested. They were soon surrounded by dozens of people — adults and children — probably the hamlet's entire population. Zerong asked all manner of questions. He was interrupted by a cry from Longlegs.

"Hey, Zerong — I mean ... boss!"

He looked in the direction Longlegs pointed with pursed lips. His eyes fell on a small boy. The child was about ten. On his right foot was a wooden sandal, on his left a torn white sneaker which was much too large for him.

Questioning revealed that the child's family consisted of himself and his parents. His father had been ill for the past three months. A few days ago, an uncle had arrived. He was a man of about forty, a Tinker. He had come to see his sister and brother-in-law and little nephew. The Tinker wore none of the garb of the mountain folk except on his feet; these were clad in the high leather boots of the local hunters.

Late that night, Zerong ordered Longlegs to keep a close watch on the cabin where the Tinker was staying. He himself, in accordance with the information he had obtained from the old man and with the aid of his compass, stole away toward Nine Dragon Confluence.

Jianbo was making an entry in his diary in the lamplight when Zerong came in.

"Still not asleep, commander?"

At the sound of Zerong's voice Jianbo leaped from the *kang* (*a brick platform bed*), and grasped his hand.

"Zerong, Zerong, you must have had a hard time. Here, have some water."

The scout gulped the drink down, wiped his mouth, and gave a rapid recital of what had transpired with him and Longlegs. In conclusion, he said, "We've found the mate to that sneaker. We think they belonged to the Tinker. What do you say? Shall we bring him in for questioning?"

"Yes," replied Jianbo. He frowned. "No. Those bandits aren't the same as the average Kuomintang soldiers we capture. Besides, we can't prove anything yet. Arresting him now would be too early."

"But we can't keep waiting either." Zerong rubbed his chin. "The secret of our being here isn't a secret any more."

"We let the news leak out on purpose just to see what the people in the neighboring hamlets would do. My idea is that we drive him away and see where he goes. That will get us much better results than questioning him now. Right?"

Zerong grinned and nodded.

"The important thing is to watch where our suspect goes. If he heads for the bandits in the mountains, we can send Zhaojia after him. But he won't be so stupid; he'll probably run in the other direction. In that case, more intricate tactics will be required. It will be up to you to handle him."

"Excellent. We'll get much more that way."

"Good, then." Jianbo smiled. "Go back and resume your disguise. We'll arrive at dawn."

Zerong bid Jianbo goodbye and returned quickly to the nameless hamlet the same night.

At daybreak, leading Zhaojia's squad, Jianbo entered the little hamlet. The PLA men arrested the "trader", his "helper", and the self-styled Tinker, and detained them in a small house at the east end of the street.

Jianbo, his face stern, questioned the trader.

"Who are you?"

"I'm the outside man for the Decheng Trading Company in Peony River."

"Your name?"

"Yang Aiming."

"You don't look like a trader to me, with those long whiskers. The truth now — who are you?"

"Whiskers Yang. Everybody in Peony River knows me."

"Go back there then. We don't want any more of you crooked traders coming around to cheat these mountain folk. Our government will set up a market for them. Do I make myself clear?"

"Quite clear." The man who called himself Whiskers Yang bowed repeatedly. "Quite clear..."

Jianbo turned to the alleged Tinker.

"Who are you?"

"I'm a Tinker," the man replied, blinking his eyes.

"No one in this poor hamlet has any metal pots or pans. What could you mend around here? You must be a bandit."

"No, no, your excellency, I don't work in the mountains. I've only come to see my sister. All my life I've been a Tinker."

"Don't you know there are bandits around here? That you're risking your life to come?"

The Tinker twisted his mouth. "*Aiya*! I'll leave right away. I'll go tomorrow."

Just then an ailing man, and a woman holding a ten-year-old boy by the hand, entered the door. The man bowed repeatedly. "He's my wife's brother, captain. He's not a stranger. Our whole family vouches for him." As he said this, the man's face was tight with fear.

Jianbo rose. "Very well," he said to the Tinker and the two traders. "I'll give you till noon to clear out."

After the three men had departed, Jianbo led Zhaojia's squad due west in the direction of the steep mountain from which Zerong had first seen the hamlet.

The Tinker headed east. Zerong and Longlegs went along with him. They became quite friendly, and chatted about their respective trades. The Tinker spoke openly, without the least reservation.

Can he really be a Tinker? Zerong wondered. Why is he heading away from the mountains? If he's a contact man for the bandits, how can he talk so freely? Is he a good person — or a very clever bandit? If he's a good man, why is he taking such a sneaky route?...

Zerong was hesitant, doubtful, but his long experience as a scout taught him not to waver. He thought to himself: We mustn't underestimate the craftiness of these birds.

At dusk, the Tinker increased his pace, although he obviously was very tired. He limped a little too. But he gritted his teeth and pushed on as if racing to a destination. Several times Zerong and Longlegs urged him to stop and make camp, but each time he refused.

"This part of the forest is full of wild beasts," he said. "The nearer we get to the edge of it, the safer we'll be."

But even when they came to sparsely wooded clearings, the Tinker still insisted on going ahead. This aroused Zerong's suspicion. He gave Longlegs a slight nudge, indicating that he should keep on the alert.

It grew darker. In the southeastern sky the constellation Orion appeared. The men reached the foot of an ominous rocky peak. The Tinker proposed that they camp there.

Zerong and Longlegs looked up at the heavy pile of rock overhead and at the dark surrounding forest. Can there be bandits here? they thought in alarm. But feeling the hard pressure of the twenty-round automatics concealed in their waistbands, they grew calmer and settled down for the night.

Although it was very cold, the Tinker did not sleep together with them. He made himself a pallet of dry grass at the foot of a tall tree about ten paces away.

Zerong's heart beat fast. He was quite worn out, but he could not sleep. Before long, the Tinker began snoring loudly. Zerong's suspicions were slowly allayed by the rhythmic peaceful snores.

Icy night air seeped through Zerong's padded robe. Even a good sleeper like Longlegs was awakened by the cold. But the Tinker continued to snore. Zerong was both worried and delighted. Worried because he feared there might be bandits nearby — he and Longlegs were just two men with one pistol each. Delighted because the shrewd Tinker had made another slip. Although the frigid temperature forced him to turn frequently, he never stopped snoring, even when he rolled over on his side.

Zerong grinned. If that's what he wants, we'll play it that way too. Nudging Longlegs, he also started to snore, gradually increasing in volume. To make it look authentic, he lay motionless, letting the cold eat into his bones. You're pretty smart, he thought, but I'll be damned if I can't act this role better than you!

"Trader, trader," the Tinker whispered timidly. "Mr. Yang, Mr. Yang..."

Zerong squeezed the young scout's arm. With his other hand, he grasped the automatic in his waistband.

The Tinker stealthily rose from his pallet, stole past a few trees, and crept off in the direction of the rocky peak.

"You stay here," Zerong said to Longlegs. "Be ready for anything. I'm going to trail him." His voice was so low he could barely hear it himself.

Years of training had sharpened Zerong's vision. It was keen even in the night. Now, his eyes fixed on the white cloth band around the Tinker's waist, he followed softly, darting from tree to tree. Although the Tinker was jumpy as a gun-shy fox, he was unaware of the man stalking fifteen or sixteen paces behind.

After proceeding cautiously about two hundred metres, the Tinker seemed to gain confidence. He increased his stride and walked quickly to a few big trees at the foot of the rocky peak. There he bent and lifted a heavy stone from the mountainside. Zerong could hear him strain and grunt. The stone thudded to the ground, followed by a second and a third. The Tinker leaned panting against a tree and looked around.

Apparently satisfied, he again walked toward the rock mountainside. Something creaked, and the Tinker disappeared.

Like a cat chasing a mouse, Zerong crouched behind a big tree, his eyes piercing the darkness in the direction from which the sound had come. Suddenly a match flared, and then a lamp gleamed. Zerong's heart glowed like the flame. From inside his padded robe he brought out a small dagger that every man in the unit carried, and sliced a piece of bark from the large tree, revealing the white wood beneath. He took his directions from the North Star, then once more carefully examined the rocky peak. When he was sure he could find this place again, he walked softly toward the light. Hey! Before him was a little window one foot square.

Aided by the feeble glow of the lamp, he could see now that this was a small cave. The entrance was a little door woven of thin branches. The stones the Tinker had removed must have concealed the door and window. Inside, the only sound was the heavy breathing of the Tinker.

Zerong crept back to the concealment of the large tree. He kept his eyes on the secret cave.

About an hour later, the light in the cave went out, and the Tinker hurriedly emerged. Before Zerong could move, the Tinker walked quickly past him in the direction of their camp.

Damn, murmured Zerong. What will happen if he gets back first and finds I'm not there?

He thought fast, and swung off in a wide detour around the Tinker. But the man was travelling in a direct line, and Zerong was taking a circuitous route. The scout was unable to get ahead.

Reaching the camp site, the Tinker called in a low voice, "Trader, Mr. Yang..."

"What's the matter? Are you cold?" Zerong's friendly voice came from behind him.

"Oh!" the Tinker spun wildly around. "Mr. Yang, you ... you..."

"This blasted cold chilled my guts. I've been having the runs. I was just off in the bushes."

"Ah!" the Tinker feigned a sympathetic laugh. "That's too bad."

Bending over as if his stomach still pained him, Zerong walked back to his bedding. He adjusted the padded coat covering Longlegs, who was lying rigid and wide-awake, and crawled in beside him.

The next afternoon, the three men arrived in Pear Valley, a village of a hundred families at the edge of the forest. To lull the suspicions of the Tinker, the two scouts immediately bade him farewell and set out toward a hamlet to the west.

They returned at dusk, now dressed as PLA soldiers, and took posts in an old abandoned house on a hill at the east end of Pear Valley. From there they had a clear view of the street and all the courtyards.

The sun set.

At the east end of the village was a large prosperous-looking compound with whitewashed walls. With the accouterments of his trade hanging from a carrying pole on his shoulder, the Tinker slipped into this compound, furtive as a rat. Before long, a fat old man poked his head through the compound gateway, looked around, then slammed the gate and barred it.

Longlegs fretted impatiently.. "There's no doubt any more. That fat fellow's a big landlord. Let's nab them and be done with it."

Zerong smiled. "Be patent. The deeper the water, the more line we give. The more line we give, the bigger the fish we'll catch."

After dark, the mountain wind rose. It howled and moaned.

The two scouts came down from the hill and halted outside the large compound. They exchanged a few whispered words, scaled the wall, and stole into the rear courtyard. The loud wind muffled the sound of their footsteps. Outside the main building of the hollow square, the scouts stopped and listened beside a window. The place seemed empty. But a light was gleaming in a room in the eastern wing of the building. A pungent odor assailed the scouts' nostrils. Longlegs grasped the lapels of Zerong's coat.

"Opium," he whispered hoarsely.

The older scout made a gesture warning him to be silent. Zerong crept to the window, wet his finger, rubbed a hole in the paper pane and peered in.

Beside the window was a large *kang*. In the center of the *kang*, an opium lamp burned. The Tinker and the fat old man who had barred the gate lay like curled shrimps on either side of the lamp, sucking away for dear life on opium pipes.

The Tinker inhaled deeply, retaining the smoke for a long time before expelling it in a thick blue cloud.

When the two men had satisfied their craving they sat up.

His eyes bulging like a frog's, the Tinker said, "I've brought two hundred ounces today, Third Uncle." He walked over to his tinker's equipment and from a compartment took out two large black packages.

The fat old man also got down from the *kang*. He removed a pot-bellied idol from its niche in the wall and the Tinker put the packets into the hollow pedestal.

Pretty slick, bringing in all that opium without us seeing it, Zerong said to himself.

The two men returned to the *kang*.

"Why so little this time?" Fatty demanded, closing his eyes.

"You don't know the trouble I had, Third Uncle," the Tinker said in a low tone. "I couldn't make contact."

"What?" Fatty's eyes popped open.

"I was nearly held by the Reds." The Tinker drew closer. "Their army's gone into the mountains. They're at Nine Dragon Confluence, and that section behind. If this nephew of yours hadn't thought fast, they'd have seen through me. I just managed to talk them out of it. I didn't dare to make contact; I came right back. Two fellows who said they were traders from Peony City came down the mountain with me. Sons of bitches. Traders! Communist scouts, that's what they were! But they couldn't kid Luan Ping. I pretended not to know a thing. They were fooled and went away empty-handed." The Tinker laughed loudly. "Monkey Diao is probably cursing me. Waiting all day at Muffin Rock must have driven him crazy!"

Fatty gave a dry rasping laugh. "Nice work. You sure can wriggle out of a tight spot." He changed the subject. "The last couple of days they've started land reform at Monk Hamlet too. In places where they've finished they're going through it again to check against any slip-ups. Those dirty paupers are full of tricks." He coughed dejectly, like a man on the point of death.

The Tinker hung his head. "What about our family?" he asked dully.

"Everything's taken care of." Fatty's gloom did not vanish, but he appeared more confident. "Your aunt and my three daughters-in-law have moved in with your Third Sister's family in Peony River. Your oldest cousin faked his background and got a job in the Railway Administration. All our valuables and opium I've moved away. Let the dirty paupers come. They won't be able to get a thing out of me."

The two men laughed, but there was fear in their voices, and desolation.

"Third Uncle has vision," said the Tinker. "You're sharp and quick. But take my advice — if things look bad, head for the mountains. We've got plenty of grain and meat up there, and the old God of the Mountains protects us. But we're short of salt and medicine. Sell the black stuff, I say, and buy salt and medicine."

Fatty expelled a great breath. "We've got a lot of black stuff but very few customers. Old Jiang of Monk Hamlet — the paupers beat him to death. Feng the Third is in jail. Only Widow Liu is left, but she doesn't use much. I can only sell her a little."

For several minutes, the two sat in gloomy silence.

"You'll get rid of it gradually," the Tinker said without much conviction. "Things have been pretty tense lately. You'd better lie low. I'm going back to the mountains at dawn to hole up for a couple of days. I won't go near our other places for a while."

The lamp was extinguished. From within the room soon came the sound of snores.

Zerong and Longlegs climbed the wall and left the compound.

In a hushed excited voice Longlegs said, "Meat on the table! Let's take — the two together."

The older scout thought a moment. "Militarily, the old buzzard doesn't make any difference, and he may not know the location of the bandit lairs in the mountains. Leave him to the land reform team. If we arrest him now, the son who's wormed his way into the Railway Administration and the three daughters-in-law who are holding the family loot will all take off. This won't help our work, and the peasants will be losing property they ought to receive under the land reform."

Longlegs nodded. "Right. Leave him alone." He started to climb back over the wall. Zerong stopped him.

"If you beat the mule, you'll scare the horse. Didn't you hear him? Tomorrow, when he starts back for the mountains..." Zerong brought both hands together in a tight clutch.

"Good. We'll let him have his sleep first."

"Let's go. To catch a wolf, lay for him in his den."

When the Tinker returned to his secret cave, Zerong and Longlegs had already been waiting for a long time. They escorted him through the forest to Nine Dragon Confluence.

TRANSITION

To anger at the give-away of Chinese territory to foreign powers under the Versailles Treaty of 1919 was added nationwide fury at the collusion between the Peking warlord government and Japanese imperialism, at the exploitation of factory workers by Chinese and foreign bosses. There were big strikes and demonstrations.

New publications, periodicals and magazines proliferated. They called for "Science and Democracy", advocated everything from socialism, communism, anarchism, trade-union syndicalism, pragmatism and humanism to women's lib and birth control. Dissidents of every stripe were boldly rejecting the servile, backward, fusty old traditions fettering every aspect of Chinese life.

This broad, bold, unprecedent revolt became known in Chinese parlance as the May Fourth Movement. It brought danger to all who participated, for the ruling dictatorship — still essentially feudal despite its modern trappings — was strong and ruthless.

In this section, which we call Transition, we introduce literature reflecting not so much the shooting wars, but the mental and ethical conflicts which the radically changing Chinese scene engendered. We start with an extract from the novel *The Family*, written in the twenties by Ba Jin, describing the difficulties of breaking with the rigid patriarchal code within the home.

During the forties, Mao Zedong and other leaders were still directing the military and political activities of the revolution from the remote hills of Northwest China. Writers and artists, stifled by Chiang Kai-shek's Kuomintang regime and drawn by the new ideals, flocked to Yanan. Mao exhorted them to create for the "workers, peasants, and soldiers", who then constituted the bulk of the population.

While this was not easy for essentially city-bred intellectuals, they realized social revolutions could not be won with drawing-room comedies, and immersed themselves in the lives and minds of the rank and file. They produced little of note about the "workers", but particularly those who joined the Army or served as war correspondents did quite good novels about the "soldiers", as we have seen in our previous section on War and Revolution.

Their best works, however, during the Yanan days and thereafter, dealt with the "peasants". In a country where the vast majority till the soil, where the soldiers are "farm boys in uniform", where the factory machines are run by young people who left the fields only a few years before, there are few places in China, including government offices, which are not strongly influenced by traditional peasant concepts and practises. Every Chinese is steeped in them from birth. Intellectuals are no exception. They may strenuously oppose the effects of the hangover of feudal ideas, but they understand them thoroughly. No wonder they write about them so well.

One example is *The Marriage of Young Blacky*, an amusing, yet no-so-funny short story by peasant writer Zhao Shuli. He tells of a young couple's struggle to choose their own marriage partners in a village which had been "liberated" a few years earlier than the rest of the country.

Sun Li's *The Blacksmith and the Carpenter* is considered the best of his post-Liberation pieces. With deft, oblique touches, he probes into the minds and motivations of the main characters and the young people who surround them.

During the metamorphoses of the forties, fifties and sixties, the revolution led by Mao Zedong was revitalizing the "Sleeping Giant" of Asia. From *The Builders*, a novel by Liu Ching written in 1960, we offer extracts sketching a few typical rural personalities wondering whether to "build" their family fortunes, in the traditional feudal manner, or "build" for the good of all — and if so, how.

Ba Jin (1904-)

Ba Jin is the pen name of Li Feikan, born of a well-to-do family in Sichuan in 1904. As a child he studied with a private tutor. In 1920 he majored in English in the Sichuan Foreign Languages School, at the same time serving as editor on a number of magazines. He went to study in Shanghai in 1923, then to France in 1926. He was deeply influenced by the socialist concepts then spreading in China, especially those of the utopian socialists.

While in France and after his return to Shanghai in the late twenties he wrote a whole series of novels, including The Family, *his most famous. He intended it to be part of a trilogy entitled* Turbulent Currents.

Ba Jin continued writing novels and editing left-wing magazines, travelling all over China. He translated, from the French versions, Turgenev's Father and Son *and* Virgin Soil, *visited Japan in 1934, was a delegate to the Second World Peace Conference in 1950 in Warsaw, and went to Korea during the war in 1952 and again in 1953. Not surprisingly, his attitudes and literary style show marked foreign influences.*

Within the framework of describing a large disintegrating feudal household, The Family *bitterly attacks the stupid cruelties and hypocritical conventions of the day. Believed to be in part autobiographical, it seethes with the indignation of an educated youth exposed for the first time to progressive ideas from the outside world.*

Ba Jin writes poetically and with passion. The Family *made a strong impact on his contemporaries. It has been compared to Ibsen's famous drama The* Doll's House *because it inspired many young Chinese students to leave repressive home environments and strike out for themselves.*

Today, at 88, Ba Jin is still writing. His latest, Recollections, *contains much pungent comment on the "Cultural Revolution" and thereafter. It has been published in Hong Kong. His purpose, he says in his Epilogue, is to "tell the truth".*

THE FAMILY

The wind was blowing hard. Snowflakes, floating like cotton fluff from a ripped quilt, drifted down aimlessly. Layers of white were building up at the foot of the walls on both sides of the streets, providing broad borders for their dark muddy centers.

Pedestrians and sedan-chair porters struggled against the wind and snow, but to no avail. They looked weary, and the snowfall was becoming heavier. Snow filled the sky, falling everywhere — on umbrellas, on the sedan-chairs, on the reed capes of the chair-carriers, on the faces of the pedestrians.

The wind buffeted the umbrellas in all directions. It blew one or two out of their owners hands. Howling mournfully, the wind joined with the crunch of footsteps in the snow to create a strange, irritating music. The snowstorm will rule the world a long, long time, it seemed to warn the people on the streets, the bright warm sun of spring will never return...

It was nearly evening, but the street lamps had not yet been lit. Everything was gradually disappearing into a pall of grey. Water and mud filled the streets. The air was icy cold. Only one thought sustained the people struggling through these dismal surroundings — they would soon be back in the warmth and brightness of their homes.

"Walk faster, Juehui, or we'll be late for dinner," said a youth of eighteen. He carried an umbrella in one hand and held up the skirt of his cotton-padded gown with the other. His round face was red with cold as he turned around to speak to his brother. A pair of gold-rimmed spectacles rested on the bridge of his nose.

Juehui, the boy walking behind him, although the same size and wearing the same kind of clothes, was a bit younger. His face was thinner, his eyes were very bright.

"No we won't," Juehui replied. "We're almost there." But he quickened his pace, mud splashing the legs of his trousers.

The two brothers soon entered a quieter street. Here the oil lamps had been lit. Their dull gleam, casting pale shadows of the lamp posts on the snow, looked particularly lonely in the frigid windy atmosphere. Few persons were abroad, and these walked quickly, leaving their footprints in the snow and silently vanishing. The deep imprints rested exhausted, without even a thought of moving, until new feet pressed down upon them. Then they uttered low sighs and were transformed into queer shapes. On the interminably long, white-mantled street the regular patterns of footprints became only large and small dark shapeless holes.

A row of residential compounds, with large solid wooden gates painted black, stood motionless in the icy gale. Pairs of eternally mute stone lions crouched outside their entrances — one on each side. Opened gates gave the appearance of the mouths of fantastic beasts. Within were dark caverns; what was inside them, no one could see.

Each of the residences had a long history. Some had changed owners several times. Each had its secrets. When the black veneer peeled off the big gates they were painted again. But no matter what changes took place, the secrets were kept. No outsider was ever permitted to know them.

In the middle of this street, before the gates of an especially large compound, the two brothers halted. This was the mansion of the Gao family, of which they were members.

They scuffed their leather shoes on the flagstones, shook the snow from their clothing, and let their robes fall straight. Holding their umbrellas, they strode in, the sound of their footsteps quickly swallowed up in the dark cavern of the long entrance-way. Silence again descended on the street.

The outside of this compound resembled the others in that a pair of crouching stone lions flanked its entrance and two big red paper lanterns hung from the eaves of its gate. What made this place distinctive was the pair of large rectangular stone vats before the gate.

On the walls on either side of the entrance, hung vertically, were red veneered plaques inscribed with black ideographs. Reading from top to bottom, first the right board then the left, the wishful motto was set forth: Benevolent rulers, happy family, long life, good harvests.

Although the wind had died down completely, the air was still as cold as before. Night came, but did not bring darkness. The sky remained grey, the ground was paved with snow. In the large snow-covered courtyard, pots of golden plum blossoms were ranged on either side of a raised stone-flagged path. Coated with frosty white, the branches were like lovely jade.

(The traditional hollow-square Chinese courtyard contained the main building on the north side, facing south. In the center of this building was a large parlor, with one or two rooms adjacent on either side for bedrooms or studies. This main building was occupied by the master and mistress of the extended family.

On the east and west sides of the courtyard were smaller wings, each usually of three rooms, for the use of the eldest sons and their families, if they were married.

In wealthy households there might be additional courtyards extending outward and behind this one, each with gardens in the middle, some quite ornate, with servants' quarters on the perimeters, and the entire compound surrounded by a high wall. Generally, the buildings were one storey high, topped by tiled roofs.)

Advancing along a path through the garden, Juemin, the older of the two brothers, had just reached the steps of a one-storey wing on the left side of the courtyard, and was about to cross the threshold, when a girl's voice called:

"Second Young Master, Third Young Master, you've come back just in time. Dinner has just started. Hurry. We have guests."

The speaker was the bondmaid Mingfeng, a girl of sixteen. She wore her hair in a long single braid down her back. Her trim young figure was encased in a padded jacket of blue cloth. When she smiled, dimples appeared in the firm healthy flesh of her oval face. She regarded the brothers innocently with bright sparkling eyes, free of any timidity or shyness.

Standing behind Juemin, Juehui smiled at her.

"Right. We'll get rid of these umbrellas and be there directly," Juemin said. Without giving her another glance, he entered the door.

"Mingfeng, who are the guests?" Juehui called from the steps.

"Mrs. Zhang and Miss Jin. Hurry up." Mingfeng turned and went into the main building.

Juehui smiled after her retreating figure until the door closed behind her. Then he entered his own wing, bumping into his brother, who was coming out.

"What were you and Mingfeng talking about that kept you so long?" Juemin demanded. "Get a move on! The food will be all gone if you delay much longer."

"I'll go with you now. I don't have to change my clothes. They're not very wet." Juehui tossed his umbrella on the floor.

"Sloppy! Why can't you do things right? The old saying is certainly true — It's easier to move a mountain than change a man's character!" Though he spoke critically, Juemin still wore a pleasant expression. He picked up the dripping umbrella, opened it and carefully placed it on the floor.

"What can I do?" said Juehui watching with a grin. "That's the way I am. But I thought you were in a hurry. You're the one who's holding us up."

"You've got a sharp tongue. Nobody can out-talk you!" Juemin walked out as if in a great huff.

Juehui knew his brother as well as Juemin knew him, so he wasn't alarmed. Smiling, he followed behind Juemin, his mind filled with the pretty bondmaid. But his thoughts of her vanished at the scene which met his eye as he entered the main building.

Seated around a square table were six people. On the side farthest from the door — in the seats of honor, were his step-mother Madam Zhou and his aunt — his father's sister Mrs. Zhang. On the left side were his cousin Jin — Mrs. Zhang's daughter, and Ruijue — wife of his eldest brother Juexin. On the near side sat Juexin and their younger sister Shuhua. The two seats on the right side were vacant.

Juehui and his brother bowed to Mrs. Zhang and greeted Jin, then slipped into the two empty seats. A maid served them bowls of rice.

"Why are you two so late today?'" Madam Zhou, holding her rice bowl, asked kindly. "If your aunt hadn't come for a visit we would have finished eating long ago."

"We had no classes this afternoon, but Mr. Zhu wanted us to rehearse our play," Juemin replied.

"It must be cold outside after that heavy snowfall," said Mrs Zhang, half concerned, half for the sake of politeness. "Did you take sedan-chairs home?"

"No, we walked. We never take sedan-chairs!" said Juehui quickly.

"Juehui would never let it be said that he rode in a sedan-chair. He's a humanitarian," Juexin explained with a mocking grin.

Everyone laughed. Angry and embarrassed, Juehui kept his head down, concentrating on his food.

"It's not actually very cold outside, and the wind has stopped," Juemin replied courteously to his aunt. "We chatted as we walked, in fact we felt quite comfortable."

"When is your school going to put on that play you mentioned?" Jin asked him. She was a few months younger than Juemin. Jin was considered the most beautiful of all the girl relatives of the Gao Family, and the most vivacious. She had entered a girls' school at an early age, and was now a third-year student in the provincial Normal School for Girls.

"Probably when the next spring term begins. There's only a little more than a week of this term left. When does you winter vacation start?"

"We started last week. They say the school is short of money, that's why we were let off early this year." Jin had already finished eating and put down her bowl.

"All the provincial educational funds are being used for military purposes. Every school is in the same fix. The only difference with us is that our principal is bound by contracts with our foreign teachers. They get their salaries whether we hold classes or not. We cut our losses by holding class, so to speak...I hear our principal has some connection with the governor, so our money is not so tight." Juemin also put his bowl down. Mingfeng handed him a damp face-cloth.

"As long as you can go to school, what's the difference?" Juexin said.

"What's the name of their school?

I've forgotten," Mrs. Zhang asked Jin.

"Mama has a terrible memory," Jin said pleasantly. "They're in the Foreign Languages School. You've already asked several times."

"You're quite right, Jin. I'm getting old; my memory's failing me," Mrs. Zhang smiled. "I won a trick at mahjong today and forgot to take it."

By now everyone had finished eating and had wiped their faces with the damp cloths. "Let's go into the next room," Madam Zhou proposed, pushing back her chair and rising. The others also stood up, and all walked out together.

In the rear of the group, Juemin said to Jin in a low voice, "After next summer vacation our school is going to accept girl students."

Jin glowed with pleasure. She fixed her large limpid eyes on him as if he had given her the best possible news.

"Really?" she asked a trifle doubtfully. She was afraid Juemin might be teasing her.

"Really. Have I ever lied to you?" Juemin looked at his younger brother, standing beside him. "Ask Juehui if you don't believe me."

"It's not that I don't believe you, it's just that this good news came too suddenly," Jin replied with an excited laugh.

"It's true alright. But whether the plan can be put through or not is another question," said Juehui. "Sichuan has entirely too many feudal moralists, and their influence is very strong. They're sure to oppose this thing. Boys and girls in the same school? That's something they never thought of in their wildest dreams!" Juehui grew heated.

"It doesn't matter about them. As long as our principal sticks to his guns, we can do it," Juemin retorted, thinking to comfort Jin. "Our principal says if no girls have the courage to register, he'll get his wife to put her name down!"

"I'm going to be the first to apply" Jin said firmly.

"Jin, why don't you come in here?" Mrs. Zhang called from the next room. "Why are you still standing there by the door?"

"Ask your mother if you can come to our room," Juemin urged Jin quietly. "I'll tell you the whole story in detail."

Jin nodded. She walked over to her mother and said a few words in her ear. Mrs. Zhang laughed. "Very well, but don't be too long."

As the girl and the two brothers were leaving the main building, Jin could hear the clicking of the ivory pieces on the wooden table. She knew her mother was good for at least four games of mahjong.

"This term we finished reading *Treasure Island*. Next term we're going to do Tolstoi's *Resurrection*," Juemin said to Jin with a pleased smile as they walked down the steps. "Our Chinese literature teacher is the man who wrote that article 'Cannible Confucian Morality' in the *New Youth* magazine. Isn't that wonderful?"

"You're really lucky," cried Jin, her face flushing with admiration."We always get old-fashioned scholars for our 'lit teachers, the kind whose favorite texts are books like *Selected Ancient Essays*. As for English, we've been on Chambers' English Reader for the past few years, and now I hear we'll be switching to *Tales from Shakespeare* — always the same dull old antiques!... I'd give anything if your school would lift its ban on girl students right now and let me transfer."

"What's wrong with Chambers' English Reader?" Juehui queried sarcastically. "It's already been translated into Chinese under the title *Smiles from the Poets*!"

Jin gave him a severe glance. "You're always joking. We're talking seriously."

"Alright, I'll shut up," said Juehui with a grin. "You two go ahead and talk." He slowed down to let Juemin and Jin enter the wing first, while he paused in the doorway and gazed around the courtyard.

Lights were burning brightly in both the left and right sections of the main building as well as in the wing opposite the one in which the two brothers lived. Mahjong tiles clicked in the left section of the main building. All sides of the courtyard were alive with voices. How beautiful the snow-covered garden was, how pure! Juehui wanted to shout for joy, to laugh loud and clear. He flung his arms wide, greeting the broad vistas before him. He felt free, unrestrained.

He remembered how the Old Sea Dog in *Treasure Island* pounded the table at the inn and roared for rum. The gusto of it all surged up within him. Throwing back his head, he shouted:

"Mingfeng, bring three cups of tea!"

There was a call of acknowledgment, and a few minutes later

the girl emerged from the left section of the main building with the tea.

"Why only two cups? I distinctly asked for three!" Juehui was still shouting and Mingfeng, as she came up to him, was startled. Her hands trembled, spilling some of the tea.

"I've only got two hands," she said, smiling.

"Clever, aren't you? You could have brought a tray." Juehui laughed. "Alright, take these in to Miss Jin and Second Young Master." He pressed back against the side of the doorway to let her go by.

After a moment, hearing her returning footsteps, Juehui planted his legs wide in the doorway and stood facing the courtyard. She came up quietly behind him and, after a pause, said:

"Third Young Master, let me pass." Her voice was not very loud. Either Juehui didn't hear, or he pretended not to. In any event, he continued to stand where he was.

"Mingfeng...Mingfeng!" Madam Zhou, Juehui's stepmother, was calling from the main building.

"Let me go. Madam Zhou wants me," Mingfeng pleaded. "She'll scold me if I'm late."

"What if she does?" Juehui turned and smiled. "Just tell her I asked you to do something for me."

"She won't believe me. If I make her angry, she'll give me the devil after the guests leave." The girl's voice was low, audible only to Juehui.

The voice of another girl, Juehui's sister Shuhua, came ringing across the courtyard. "Mingfeng, Madam wants you to put tobacco in the water-pipes!"

Juehui stepped aside and Mingfeng hurried past. Shuhua came out of the main building. "Where have you been?" she demanded of Mingfeng. "Why don't you answer when you're called?"

"I brought some tea for Third Young Master," Mingfeng answered, hanging her head. Her voice was emotionless.

"Bringing tea shouldn't take all that time! You're not a mute. Why didn't you answer when I called you?" Shuhua was only fourteen, but she had already learned how to scold the bondmaids, just like her elders, and she did it very naturally. "Now get in there. If Madam Zhou knew you deliberately refused to answer, she'd tell you a thing or two!"

Shuhua turned and went back into the house. Mingfeng quietly followed her.

Juehui had heard every syllable of the exchange, and the words cut him like the blows of a whip. His face burned with shame. It was he who had brought this on Mingfeng. His sister's attitude sickened him. He had wanted to come forward and defend Mingfeng, but something had held him back. He had stood silently in the dark, watching, as though it had nothing to do with him.

Alone in the courtyard, he could still see Mingfeng's lovely face. It was subservient, uncomplaining. Like the sea, it accepted everything, swallowed everything, without a sound.

From his room, another feminine voice reached his ear, and he pictured another girl. Her face was also beautiful, but it reflected very different kinds of emotion. Resistance, ardor, determination, refusal to submit to the least injustice. The expressions on the two faces were manifestations of two different ways of life, two different fates. Somehow, even though the latter girl enjoyed a much greater abundance of happiness and gaiety, more of his sympathy and affection lay with the former.

The face of the first girl again loomed large in his mind, drawing him with its docile, beseeching expression. He wanted to comfort her, to offer her some kind of consolation. But what could he give her? Her fate was predetermined before she came into the world. Many other girls in her circumstances had suffered the same fate. Of course, she couldn't be any exception. Juehui wanted to cry out against the unfairness, to fight it, to change it. Suddenly, a strange thought came to him. After a moment, a faint laugh escaped him.

"It could never be. That sort of thing just can't be done," he said half-aloud.

Ah, if it only could, he mused. But when he thought of the consequences that might ensue, his courage left him. It's only a dream, he said to himself with a wry smile, only a dream.

Dream or no, the idea fascinated him and he was reluctant to abandon it. Suppose she had Jin's social status? he wondered.

There'd be no question about it! he told himself positively. For the moment it seemed to him that she really was a girl like Jin and that his relationship with her was quite ordinary.

Then he laughed, laughed at himself. Preposterous! Anyhow, who says that I love her? She's just fun to be with.

Gradually Mingfeng's submissive face was replaced in his mind by the stubborn, ardent visage of the other girl. But soon this too faded.

"'Can a man remain at home while the Huns are still undefeated?'" Although he didn't usually care for that hoary aphorism, it now seemed to contain a miraculous solution to all his problems. He boldly shouted it aloud. His "Huns" were not foreign invaders, nor was he intending to take up sword and spear to slay them on a battlefield. What the cry meant to him was that a real man ought to cast off family ties; he should go out into the world and perform great deeds. As to what kind of deeds these should be, he had only the vaguest notion.

Juehui strode into the room with the heroic quotation still on his lips.

"He's gone crazy again!" Juemin, standing beside his desk, looked around at the sound of Juehui's voice. He laughed as he addressed this remark to Jin, who was seated in a cane armchair. Jin glanced at Juehui. "Don't you know he's a great hero?" she asked with an amused smile.

"More likely than not, he's the Old Sea Dog. The Old Sea Dog was also a great hero!" Juemin said, laughing. Jin laughed too.

"Anyhow, the Old Sea Dog was a lot better than Dr. Liversey," Juehui retorted warmly, irked by their laughter. "Dr. Liversey was only one of the gentry."

"Now what in the world do you mean by that?" Juemin queried, half surprised, half in jest. "Aren't you also going to be one of the gentry?"

"No, I'm not!" Juehui cried. "Just because our grandfather and father are members of the gentry, does that mean we also have to become gentry?" He clamped his lips together and waited for his brother to reply.

Juemin had only been joking, but seeing that Juehui was really angry, he tried to find words to calm him. For the moment, however, he could think of nothing appropriate, and could only stare at Juehui in stupefaction. Jin, seated off to one side, was observing the two brothers, but she did not speak.

"I've had enough of this kind of life!" Juehui could contain himself no longer. "Why does Juexin sigh all day long? Isn't it because he can't stand being one of the gentry, because he can't stand the oppressive atmosphere of this gentry household? You know it is... We've got four generations under one roof — only one generation less that the ideal fam — but never a day goes by without open quarrels and secret wrangles. They're all trying to grab a bit more of the family property..."

Juehui was almost choking with rage. He had a lot more to say but he couldn't get the words out. What was infuriating him, in fact, was not his eldest brother's fate, but that of the girl whose expression was so docile. He felt he was being cut off from her by an invisible high wall, and this wall was his gentry family. It prevent him from attaining the object of his desire; therefore he hated it.

Juemin looked at his brother's red face and flashing eyes. He came up, grasped Juehui's hand, and patted him on the shoulder.

"I shouldn't have teased you," he said in an agitated voice. "You're right. Your unhappiness is my unhappiness. We two will always stand side by side." He still didn't know about the girl in Juehui's heart.

Juehui, quickly mollified, mutely nodded.

Jin rose and walked over. She addressed Juehui in a voice that trembled. "I shouldn't have laughed at you either. I want to stick together with both of you, always. I have to fight too. My situation is even worse than yours."

They looked at her. There was a melancholy light in her lovely eyes. Her usual vivaciousness was gone. A troubled expression bespoke her inner struggle. The boys had never seen her like this before. They knew what was disturbing her. She had spoken correctly — her situation was much worse than theirs. They were touched by her rare melancholy. They were ready to sacrifice themselves completely, if only it would bring this girl's wishes to an early fulfilment. It was just an idle hope, for there was nothing specific they could do, but they felt it was their duty to help. The boys forgot their own problems and concentrated on hers.

"Don't worry, we'll figure something out," Juemin assured her. "I'm a firm believer in 'Where there's will, there's a way.' Remember when we first wanted to go to a public school? *Ye-ye (pronounced "Yeah-yeah", meaning "Grandfather")* was dead set against it. But in the end we won out."

Jin steadied herself with one hand on the desk. She gazed at them as if in a dream.

"Juemin is right. Don't worry about a thing," Juehui entreated. "Just continue reviewing your lessons. Put in a lot of time on English. If you can pass the Foreign Languages School entrance exams, solving the other problems won't be so hard."

With deft fingers Jin adjusted her hair. She smiled, but there was a note of concern in her voice. "I hope so. There's no question about Mama; she's sure to let me transfer. But I'm afraid my grandmother won't agree, and there's bound to be a lot of talk among our relatives. Take your family — except for you two, everyone else will probably be opposed."

"What have they got to do with you? Going to school is your own affair. Besides, you're not a member of our family." Juehui was a little surprised that Jin should have mentioned the Gao family. Although Jin's mother was a daughter of Ye — the Venerable Master Gao, when she married she came under the jurisdiction of her husband's family, according to custom, and her original home no longer had any say in her affairs.

"You don't know what Mama had to put up with when I entered the provincial Normal School for Girls. Our relatives said, 'A big girl like her, out on the street every day; what will people think! What well-brought-up young lady would ever act like that!' Mama is very old-fashioned. She's more enlightened than most of them, but she has her limits. She's willing to take the brunt on her shoulders, no matter how our relatives sneer, because she loves me. Not that she thinks it right for me to go to school. It wasn't easy for her to let me do even that. Now I'm going to ask to enter a boys' school, to sit in the same classroom with male students! Can you think of one of our relatives who would dare approve of such a thing!"

The more she talked the more excited Jin became. She was standing very straight, her shining eyes fixed on Juemin's face, as if seeking the answer from him.

"Our Big Brother wouldn't oppose it," Juemin said.

"If Juexin were the only one, what use would that be?" Jin retorted. "Aunt Zhou will be against it, and it will only give Aunt Wang and Aunt Shen more to gossip about."

"Let them talk!" Juehui interjected. "They've nothing to do but stuff themselves all day. Naturally, they're full of gossip. Even if you never did anything wrong, they'd invent something to criticize. Since they're going to sneer anyhow, let them."

"Jin, there's something in what he says. Make up your mind," Juemin urged.

"I'm deciding right now." Jin's face suddenly grew radiant, and her usual vivacity and firmness flooded back. "I know that a high price must be paid for any reform to be put through, that many sacrifices must be made. I'm ready to be the victim."

"If you're determined as all that, you're sure to succeed," said Juemin soothingly.

Smiling, Jin said with her old stubbornness, "Whether I succeed or not doesn't matter very much. But I'm going to make the try." The brothers gazed at her admiringly.

In the next room the clock struck nine. They talked for almost another hour, until Jin rose and smoothed her hair.

"I must be going. Those four games of mahjong are probably over by now." She walked toward the door, then turned to say, "Come and see us when you have time. I'm home all day with nothing to do."

"We will," the brothers replied in unison. They accompanied her to the outside steps and watched until she disappeared into the main building. It was cold in the courtyard, but there was considerable warmth in the hearts of the two brothers as they returned to their room.

"Jin is certainly a brave girl," said Juemin. He lapsed into a reverie, but soon again burst out: "Even a vivacious girl like Jin has problems. That's something I would never have believed."

"Everyone has his troubles. I've got mine too," said Juehui. He abruptly broke off, as if he had revealed more than he had intended.

"You have troubles?" Juemin asked, surprised. "What's wrong?"

Juehui blushed. "Nothing. I was only kidding."

Juemin looked at him suspiciously.

"Mrs. Zhang's sedan-chair!" the clear crisp voice of Mingfeng was calling outside.

"Mrs. Zhang's sedan-chair!" echoed the hoarse tones of Yuan, a middle-aged male servant. A few minutes later the inner compound gates swung open and two men came into the courtyard carrying a sedan-chair. They set it down beside the steps of the main building.

On the street, the watchman's gong resounded deep and mournful — once, twice. It was ten o'clock.

The night died, and with it the glow of the electric lights died too. Darkness ruled the big compound. The dismal cry the electric lamps uttered as they expired still quivered in the air. Although the sound was low, it penetrated everywhere; even the corners of the room seemed to echo with soft weeping. The time for happiness had passed. Now was the hour of tragic tears.

Lying in their beds, stripped of the masks they had worn all day, people took stock of themselves. They opened their hearts and examined their innermost secrets, peering into the recesses of their souls. Stricken with remorse and anger, they wept over the waste, the losses, the bitterness of the day gone by. Of course there were a few pleased individuals among them, but these were already wrapped in satisfied slumber. The rest were disappointed, miserable creatures in unwarm beds, tearfully bemoaning their fate.

Whether in the brightness of the day or the darkness of the night the world has always had these two different aspects for these two different kinds of people.

In the female servants' room a wick floating in an earthen cup of oil sputtered feebly and grew dim, deepening the darkness of the humble quarters. Two women were snoring lustily on wooden beds on the right side of the room. On the left were two other beds, one occupied by Mama Huang, an elderly servant whose hair was streaked with grey, the other by the sixteen-year-old bondmaid, Mingfeng. The girl was sitting up, gazing dully at the lamp wick.

After working hard all day, now that the madams and misses of the household had retired and she had temporarily recovered her freedom, Mingfeng might quite reasonably have gone to sleep early. But lately, these hours of freedom had become especially dear to her; she treasured every moment of them. Thinking, remembering, she felt very much at peace. No one disturbed her. The noisy commands, the scoldings that were dinned in her ears from morning till night, were finally stilled.

During the day, wearing her mask like everyone else, she rushed around busily, a pleasant smile on her face. Now, in the precious hours of freedom, she could take the mask off; she could unlock her mind and spread out its secrets for her heart to see.

I've been here for seven years. That was the first thought. It had been constantly tormenting her of late. Seven years is a long time! She often marvelled that they should have gone by so uneventfully. She had wept many tears in that period, received many a curse and many a blow. But these had become commonplace, mere frills to her dull existence. Unavoidable things which, while she didn't relish them, had to be endured. All that happened in the world was decreed by an omnipotent being. It was her fate to be where she was and what she was. This was her simple belief, and it coincided with what others had told her.

But something else was now stirring in her heart. Though she was not yet aware of it, it was beginning to waken, bringing her hope.

More than seven years I've been here. It's soon going to be eight. She was swept with a wave of revulsion for the emptiness of life. Like other girls in her position, she began to bemoan her fate. When the Eldest Young Miss was still alive she had often talked to me about a home of my own. Who knows where my final home will be!

Ahead Mingfeng could see only a dreary wildnerness, without a trace of light anywhere. The familiar face of the Eldest Young Miss again floated before her... If only she were still alive, there would be someone who cared for me. She helped me understand many things, she taught me to read and write. Now she's dead. The good don't live very long!...Tears filled Mingfeng's eyes.

How much longer must I go on like this? she asked herself tragically. She remembered a snowy day seven years ago. A fierce-looking woman had led her from the side of her father, bereft over the loss of his wife, and brought her to this wealthy household. From then on orders, exhausting toil, tears, curses and blows became the principal elements of her existence. A life of dullness, of drab, unvarying monotony.

Like other girls her age, she had dreamed beautiful dreams, but they all passed quickly, blotted out by reality. She had dreamed of lovely baubles, of beautiful clothes, of delicious food, of warm bedding, of all the things the young ladies she waited on possessed. She even prayed that these wonderful objects might soon be hers. But the days continued to flit by, bearing her pain with them. Nothing new ever came her way, not even a new hope.

Fate, everything is decided by Fate. When she was beaten and cursed she used these words to console herself. Suppose I had been fated to be a young lady too? Mingfeng luxuriated in fanciful imaginings. She wore pretty clothes; she had parents who loved and cherished her; she was admired by young gentlemen. One of them came and took her away to his home, and there they lived together happily ever after.

How silly. Of course it could never happen! she scolded herself with a smile. I'll never have a home like that. Her smile faded and her face fell. She knew very well what would happen to her. When she reached the proper age, Madam would say to her, "You've worked here long enough." And she would be placed in a sedan-chair and carried to the home of a man Madam had chosen, a man Mingfeng had never seen. He might be thirty or forty years old. Thereafter she'd toil in his house, work for him, bear him children. Or perhaps after a few weeks she'd come back here to serve the same wealthy family, the only difference being that now she would not be scolded or beaten so frequently, and would receive a small wage which she would have to turn over to her husband. Isn't that what happened to Madam Shen's maid Xi Er?

How terrible! That kind of home is no home at all!... Mingfeng shivered. She remembered when Xi Er returned after her marriage, her long single braid now done up in a bun on the back of her head. Mingfeng often saw her alone in the garden, furtively weeping. Sometimes Xi Er told of the brutality of her husband. All this gave Mingfeng a frightening premonition of what her own destiny would be.

Darkness, only darkness! I'd be better off dead, like the Eldest Young Mistress! Mingfeng thought bitterly. The murkiness of the room closed in on her as the wick again dwindled. She could hear the snores of her companions. Listlessly she rose and adjusted the wick. The room brightened and her heart felt a bit lighter. She looked at the stout Sister Zhang, sleeping buried in bed clothes; only a tangled mop of hair and half a fat face were visible. The woman emitted queer regular little snores that sounded like yelps. Emerging half-muffled from beneath the thick comforters they were particularly frightening. Her massive body a great lump on the bed, the stout maid slept very deeply; she never stirred.

Like a pig, thought Mingfeng with a wry smile. But her heart was heavy. She was still surrounded by darkness, darkness filled with evil grinning faces. Some of them grew angry, opened their mouths, shouted at her. Frightened, she covered her eyes with her hands and sank down on the bed again in a sitting position.

Outside, the wind began to howl. It shook the window frames, causing the paper pasted over the wooden lattice-work to cry out dismally. Icy air seeped in through the paper and the room became cold. The lamp flame flickered. A chill crept up Mingfeng's sleeves to her body. With a shiver, she removed her hands from her eyes and gazed around.

I'd better go to sleep, she thought dully, opening the buttons of her padded jacket. She slipped it off. Two mounds of firm young flesh pressed against her undershirt.

I'm growing up, Mingfeng sighed. Who knows what kind of a home I'll have... The face of a smiling young man appeared before her. She recognized him and her heart burst into flower. Warmed by a thread of hope, she prayed that he would stretch forth his hand. Perhaps he could rescue her from her present life. The face gradually floated away into the sky, higher and higher until it vanished. And her dream-filled eyes found themselves looking only at the dirty ceiling.

A cold gust swept across her exposed breasts, wrenching her back to reality. She rubbed her eyes and sighed. Only a dream! After a final lingering glance around the room, she gathered her courage and removed her warm cotton-padded trousers. Piling them and the padded jacket on top of the bedding, with a quick motion she plunged beneath the covers.

She had nothing. The phrase the Eldest Young Miss had always used in talking of woman's lot revolved in her brain — "wretched fate".

It cut her heart like a whip, and she began to weep beneath the bedding softly, so as not to disturb the others. The lamp flame dimmed. Outside, the high wind howled mournfully.

On the snow-covered street, the clash of the watchman's gong sounded with deep solemnity through the quiet night. Reverberating in the icy air, it rolled past the sedan carriers' footfalls in the snow.

The men carrying the sedan-chairs walked very slowly, as if fearful that if they overtook the gong sound they would lose this solemn friend. But after travelling two more blocks, the gong turned off, leaving only its fading regretful sound to linger in the ears of the sedan porters and their passengers.

Middle-aged servant Sheng led the way with a lantern, his head hunched between his shoulders against the cold. From time to time his sharp cough broke the rather frightening stillness.

The chair porters shouldered their heavy loads silently, walking more freely now, with large strides. It was bitterly cold and the icy snow stung the bare flesh of their straw-sandaled feet. But they were accustomed to this and they knew the road ahead was not long. They would soon reach their destination. Then they could while away their time beside the opium lamp or at the card table. Walking quietly, with even footfalls, they occasionally shifted the carrying pole of the sedan-chair from one shoulder to the other, or blew hot breath on one of their hands. Exertion sent warm blood coursing through their bodies. They began to perspire, the sweat on their backs soaking their tattered old padded jackets.

Jin's mother, Mrs. Zhang, sat in the leading sedan-chair. Although she had only just turned forty, she already showed signs of age. A few games of mahjong had exhausted her. Her mind was numb. At times the wind swept open the curtain of her sedan-chair, but she was unaware of it.

Jin, on the other hand, was very alert and excited. She was thinking of what was soon to happen, the first important event of her life. She could almost see it before her, adorable, dazzling. She wanted to grasp it, but she knew the moment she stretched out her hand, people would hinder her. Although not sure she could succeed, she was determined to try. Yet, in spite of having made up her mind, she still was a little worried that she would fail, and she was rather afraid. The complicated thoughts made her alternately happy and gloomy. Wrapped in her problems, Jin was oblivious to her surroundings. She came back to herself only when the sedan-chairs passed through the gates of her family compound and were set down in front of the main hall.

As usual, Jin first accompanied Mrs. Zhang to her room and watched the maid change her mother's clothes. Jin hung them in the closet.

"I don't know why I'm so tired today," Mrs. Zhang sighed. She had put on a fur-lined silk jacket and sat wearily in a cane chair beside the bed.

"You played too long today, Ma," Jin said with a smile. She sat down on a chair diagonally opposite. "Mahjong takes to much out of people, and you played twelve games."

"You always scold me for playing mahjong, but what else is there for a woman of my age to do?" Mrs. Zhang laughed. "Sit around all day reciting Buddhist scriptures, like your grandmother? I just couldn't do it."

"I'm not saying you shouldn't play, I only mean you shouldn't play too long."

"I know," said Mrs. Zhang pleasantly. She observed the maid still standing half-asleep on her feet beside the clothes closet. "Go to bed, Sister Li. I don't need you any more," she instructed.

After the maid had gone, Mrs. Zhang turned again to her daughter. "What were you saying? Oh, yes, that I shouldn't play too much mahjong. I know that. But somehow I seem to get tired even when I don't do anything tiring. A life with nothing to do is boring if it lasts too long. People who live too long are a nuisance, anyhow." Mrs. Zhang closed her eyes and folded her arms across her chest. She seemed to doze.

Except for the ticking of the clock, the room was very still. Evidently Jin would have no opportunity to discuss that important matter with her mother tonight. She stood up, thinking she had better waken her mother and put her to bed so that she wouldn't catch a chill.

But as Jin rose her mother opened her eyes and said, "Jin dear give me some tea."

The girl took a teapot from a low-burning charcoal brazier, poured out a cup and placed it on a stool beside her mother.

"Here's your tea, Ma," she said. She stood awkwardly. She felt her chance to speak had come, but she couldn't get the words out.

"You're tired too, Jin. Go to bed."

Jin hesitated. Finally she screwed up her courage. "Ma," she began. Her voice trembled a bit with excitement.

"What is it?"

"Ma," Jin said again. Head down, she toyed with the edge of her jacket. She spoke slowly. "Juemin says next year their school will be accepting girl students. I'd like to take the entrance exam."

"What are you saying? Girl students in a boys' school? You want to go there?" Mrs. Zhang couldn't believe her ears.

"Yes," Jin replied timidly. She explained, "There's nothing wrong with it. Peking University already has three girl students. Co-ed schools have been started in Nanking and Shanghai."

"What is the world coming to? It isn't enough to have schools for girls, now they want to have co-ed schools too!" Mrs. Zhang sighed. "When I was a girl, I never dreamed there'd be such things!"

The words struck Jin like a gourdful of cold water. Chilled and dazed, she stood in silence. But she refused to give up hope. Slowly, her courage returned. She said:

"Ma, times have changed. After all, it's more than twenty years since you were my age; something new comes into the world every day. Girls are human beings the same as boys. Why shouldn't they study in the same classroom?"

Mrs. Zhang laughed. "I won't try to argue the merits of the case; I'd never be able to out-talk you. I'm sure you can find lots of reasons in those new books of yours to use against me. You probably think I'm a reactionary old mossback."

Jin laughed too, then she pleaded, "Let me go, Ma. You usually trust me. You've never refused me anything!"

Mrs. Zhang weakened a little. "And I've taken a good deal of abuse for the same reason," she sighed. "I'm not afraid of gossip, and I do trust you. No matter what it's been, I've always done what you wanted... But this thing is too special. Your grandmother will be the first to oppose. Surely you don't want me to fall out with her because of this? And of course all our relatives will be sure to talk."

"Didn't you just say you're not afraid of gossip?" Jin retorted. "Grandma is in a nunnery. At most she visits us once a month, and then only stays two or three days. The last few months she hasn't come home at all. Besides, who cares what she says? Since she usually doesn't concern herself with family affairs, you can decide — like the time you let me go to the girls' normal school. Our relatives won't have any reason to oppose. If they want to gossip, we'll just ignore them."

After a silence, Mrs. Zhang said in a deflated voice, "I used to be brave, but I'm old now. I don't want to be the butt of any more idle chatter by our relatives. I want to live in peace another few days, without any trouble. You know I've been a devoted mother to you. Your father died when you were very young, leaving me with the full burden of bringing you up. I never bound your feet like the other girls. I let you study with your cousins' private tutor at your grandfather Gao's house. Later, in spite of everything, I sent you to a girls' school. Your cousin Shuzhen has tiny bound feet, and she can barely read. Even your cousin Shuhua has had very little schooling. On the whole you must admit I've treated you pretty well."

Mrs. Zhang was too weary to go on. But when she saw that Jin was on the verge of tears, her heart went out to the girl and she said kindly:

"Go to bed Jin dear. It's late. We can talk again about what will happen next autumn some other time. I'll do my best for you."

With a murmur of assent, the disappointed Jin walked out, crossed the small hall and went to her own room. Although downcast, she did not blame her mother, in fact she was grateful for her affection.

Jin's room was dreary, as if devoid of all hope. Even her dead father's picture, hanging on the wall, seemed to be weeping. Jin felt her eyes grow damp. She took off her skirt and laid it on the bed, then walked over to the desk, turned up the wick of the pewter lamp and sat down. Picking up a *New Youth* magazine, she idly thumbed through a few pages. The following words caught her eye:

"...I believe that before all else I am a human being, just as much as you are — or at least that I should try to become one... I can't be satisfied with what most people say... I must think things out for myself, and try to get clear about them..."

Lines from Ibsen's play *A Doll's House...*

To her they were a revelation, and her eyes grew bright. She saw clearly that her desire was not hopeless, that it all depended on her own efforts. In other words, there was still hope, and the fulfilment of that hope rested with her, not with others.

With this realization, her despair melted away, and she cheerfully took her pen and wrote this letter to Jianju, one of the girls in her class:

> *Today, my cousins told me that the Foreign Languages School has decided to accept girl students, commencing next autumn. I am determined to take the entrance exam. What about you? Would you like to go with me? I hope you're willing to take the plunge. We have to fight, no matter what the cost, to open a road for sisters who come after us.*
>
> *Please come and see me if you have time. I have a lot to tell you. My mother will be glad to see you, too.*
>
> *Jin*

Jin read through the finished letter, wrote in the date, then painstakingly added puctuation marks, which had only recently come into vogue. Her mother despised letters written in colloquial. She said they were "...much longer than the classical style, and unbearably vulgar!" But Jin liked them, and she studied the colloquial letters in the "To The Editor" column of *New Youth* as a means of improving her own style.

To Juemin and Juehui, Juexin was "Big Brother". Though born of the same mother (*men in wealthy families often had more than one wife*) and living in the same house, his position was entirely different from theirs. In the large Gao family, he was the eldest son of an eldest son, and for that reason his destiny was fixed from the moment he came into the world.

Handsome and intelligent, he was his father's favorite. His private tutor also spoke highly of him. People predicted that he would do big things, and his parents considered themselves fortunate to be blessed with such a son.

Brought up with loving care, after studying with a private tutor for a number of years, Juexin entered middle school. One of the school's best students, he graduated four years later at the top of his class. He was very interested in physics and chemistry and hoped to go on to a university in Shanghai or Peking, or perhaps study abroad, in Germany. His mind was full of beautiful dreams. At that time he was the envy of his classmates.

In his fourth year at middle school, he lost his mother. His father later married again, this time to a younger woman who had been his mother's cousin. Juexin was aware of his loss, for he knew full well that nothing could replace the love of a mother. But her death left no irreparable wound in his heart; he was able to console himself with rosy dreams of his future. Moreover, he had someone who understood him and could comfort him — his pretty cousin Mei, "mei" for "plum blossom".

But then, one day, his dreams were shattered, cruelly and bitterly shattered. The evening he returned home carrying his diploma, the plaudits of his teachers and friends still ringing in his ears, his father called him into his room and said:

"Now that you've graduated, I want to arrange your marriage. Your grandfather is looking forward to having a great-grandson, and I, too, would like to hold a grandson in my arms. You're old enough to be married. I won't feel easy until I fulfil my obligation to find you a wife. Although I didn't accumulate much money in my years away from home as an official, I've put by enough for us to get along on. My health isn't what it used to be. I'm thinking of spending my time at home and having you help me run the household affairs. All the more reason you'll be needing a wife. I've already arranged a match with the Li family. The thirteenth of next month is an auspicious day. We'll announce the engagement then. You can be married within the year..."

The blow was too sudden. Although he understood everything his father said, somehow the meaning didn't fully register. He didn't dare look his father in the eye, although the older man was gazing at him kindly. Juexin didn't utter a word of protest, nor did such a thought ever occur to him. He merely nodded to indicate his compliance with his father's wishes.

But after he returned to his room and shut the door, he threw himself down on his bed, covered his head with the quilt and wept.

He wept for his broken dreams.

He had heard something about a match with a daughter of the Li family. But he had never been permitted to learn the whole story, and hadn't placed much credence in it. A number of gentlemen with unmarried daughters, impressed by his good looks and his success in his studies, had become interested in him. There had been a steady stream of matchmakers to his family's door.

His father weeded out the applicants until only two remained under consideration. It was difficult for Mr. Gao to make a choice; both of the persons serving as matchmakers were of equal prestige and importance. Finally, he decided to resort to divination. He wrote each of the girls' names on a slip of paper and rolled the slips up into balls. After praying for guidance before the family ancestral tablets, he picked one.

Thus the match with the Li family was decided. But it was only now that Juexin was informed of the result.

Yes, he had dreamed of romance. The one in his heart was the girl who understood him and who could comfort him — his cousin Mei. At one time he was sure she would be his future mate, and he had congratulated himself that this would be so, since in his family marriage between cousins was quite common.

He was deeply in love with Mei, but now his father had chosen another, a girl he had never seen, and said that he must marry within the year. What's more, his hopes of continuing his studies had burst like a bubble. It was a terrible shock to Juexin. His future was finished, his beautiful dreams vanished into thin air.

He cried his disappointment and bitterness. But the door was closed and Juexin's head was beneath the bedding. No one knew. He did not fight back, he never thought of resisting. He bemoaned his fate, but he accepted it. He complied with his father's will without a trace of resentment. But in his heart he wept for himself, wept for the girl he adored — Mei, his "plum blossom".

The day of his engagement he was teased and pulled about like a puppet, while at the same time being shown off as a treasure of rare worth. He was neither happy nor sad. Whatever people told him to do, he did, as if these acts were duties he was obliged to perform. In the evening, when the comedy had ended and the guests had departed, Juexin was exhausted. He went to bed and slept soundly.

After the engagement, he drifted aimlessly from day to day. He stacked his books neatly in the bookcase and didn't look at them again. He played mahjong, went to the opera, drank, and set about making the necessary preparations for his marriage, in accordance with his father's instructions. Juexin thought very little. He calmly await the advent of his bride.

In less than six months she arrived. To celebrate the marriage Juexin's father and grandfather had a stage specially built for the performance of theatricals in the garden.

The marriage ceremony turned out to be not as simple as Juexin had anticipated. He too, in effect, became an actor, and he had to perform for three days before he was able to obtain his bride. Again he was manipulated like a puppet, again he was displayed as a treasure of rare worth. He was neither happy nor sad — he was only tired, though roused a bit by the general excitement.

This time, however, after his performance was over and the guests departed, he was not able to forget everything and sleep. Because lying in bed beside him was a strange girl. He still had to continue playing a role.

Juexin was married. His grandfather had obtained a granddaughter-in-law, his father had obtained a daughter-in-law, and others had enjoyed a brief period of merry-making.

The marriage was by no means a total loss for Juexin. He had been joined in wedlock with a tender, sympathetic girl, just as pretty as the one he adored. He was satisfied. For a time he revelled in pleasures he had not believed possible, for a time he forgot his beautiful dreams, forgot the other girl, forgot his lost future. He was sated, he was intoxicated, intoxicated with the tenderness and love of the girl who was his bride. Constantly smiling, he hung about her room all day. People envied him his happiness, and he considered himself very lucky.

Thus one month passed.

One evening his father called him into his study and said:

"Now that you're married you should be earning your own living, or people will talk. I've raised you to manhood and found you a wife. I think we can say that I've fulfilled my duties as a father. From now on you must take care of yourself. We have enough money to send you to study in a university downriver. But in the first place you already have a wife; secondly the family property had not yet been shared out among me and my brothers, and I am in charge of the accounts. It would look like favoritism if I advanced money from the family funds for your university education. Besides, your grandfather might not agree.

"So I've found you a position in the West Sichuan Mercantile Corporation. The salary's not very large, but it will give you and your wife some spending money. Moreover, if you do your work diligently, you're sure to advance. You start tomorrow. I'll take you down myself. Our family owns some shares in the company and several of the directors are my friends. They'll look after you."

Juexin's father spoke in an even voice, as if discussing something quite commonplace. Juexin listened, and assented. He didn't say whether he was willing or unwilling. There was only one thought in his mind — "Everything is finished." Though he had many words in his heart, he spoke not a one.

The following day after the midday meal his father told him something of how a man going out in the world should behave, and Juexin made careful mental notes. Sedan-chairs brought him and his father to the door of the West Sichuan Mercantile Corporation.

Entering, he first met Manager Huang, a man of about forty with a mustache and a stooped back. Then Chen the accountant, who had a face like an old woman; Wang, the tall emaciated bill-collector; and two or three other ordinary-looking members of the office staff. The manager asked him a few questions. He answered simply, as if by rote. Although they all addressed him very politely, he could tell from their actions and the way they spoke that they were not the same as he. It occurred to him with some surprise that he had seldom met people of this sort before.

His father departed, leaving Juexin behind. He felt frightened and lonely, a castaway on a desert island. He was not given any work. He just sat in the manager's office and listened to the manager discuss things with various people. After two full hours of this, the manager suddenly noticed him again, and said courteously, "There's nothing for you to do today, Brother. Please come back tomorrow."

Like a pardoned prisoner, Juexin happily called a sedan-chair and gave his address. He kept urging the carriers to walk faster. It seemed to him that in all the world there was no place more wonderful than the Gao family compound.

On arriving home, he first reported to his grandfather, who gave him some instructions. Then he went to see his father, who gave him some more instructions. Finally, he returned to his own apartment. Only here, with his wife questioning him solicitously and at great length, did he find peace and relaxation.

The next day after breakfast he again went to the corporation and did not return home until five in the afternoon. That day he was given his own office. Under the guidance of the manager and his colleagues, he commenced to work.

Thus, this nineteen-year-old youth took his first big step into the world of business. Gradually, he grew accustomed to his environment and learned a new way of life. Gradually, he forgot all the knowledge he had acquired in his four years of middle school. He began to feel at home in his work. The first time he received his salary of thirty-two dollars, he was torn between joy and sorrow. It was the first time he had ever earned any money, yet the pay was also the first fruits of the sale of his career. But as the months went by, the regular installments of thirty-two dollars no longer aroused in him any special emotions.

Life was bearable, without happiness, without grief. Although he saw the same faces every day, heard the same uninteresting talk, did the same dull work, all was peaceful and secure. None of the family came to bother him at home. He and his wife were permitted to live quietly.

Less than six months later, another big change occurred in his life. An epidemic struck his father down. All the tears of Juexin and his brothers and sisters were unable to save him. After his father died, the family burdens were placed on Juexin's shoulders. In addition to looking after his step-mother, he also became responsible for his two younger sisters and his two young student brothers. Juexin was then only twenty years of age.

Sorrowfully, he wept for his departed father. He had not thought that fate could be so tragic. But gradually his grief dissipated. After his father was buried, Juexin virtually forgot him. Not only did he forget his father, he forgot everything that had passed, he forgot his own springtime. Calmly he placed the family burdens on his own young shoulders.

For the first few months they didn't seem very heavy; he was not conscious of any strain. But in a very short time many arrows, tangible and intangible, began flying in his direction. Some he was able to dodge, but several struck home. He discovered something new, he began to see another side of life in a gentry household. Beneath the surface of peace and affection lurked hatred and strife. He also had become a target of attack. Although his surroundings made him forget his springtime, the fires of youth still burned in his heart. He grew angry, he struggled, because he considered himself to be in the right. But his struggles only brought him more troubles and more enemies.

The Gao family was divided into four households. Originally, Juexin's grandfather had five sons, but the second son had died many years ago. Uncle Keming and his Third Household were on fairly good terms with the First Household, which Juexin now headed. But the Fourth and Fifth Households were very unfriendly to Juexin. The wives of both secretly waged a relentless battle against him and his First Household, and spread countless rumors about him.

Struggling didn't do the least bit of good. He was exhausted. What's the use of this endless strife? he wondered. Those women would never change, and he couldn't make them give in. Why waste energy looking for trouble? Juexin evolved a new way of managing affairs — or perhaps it would be better to say of managing the family. He ended his battle with the women. He pretended to go along with their wishes whenever he could. Treating them with deference, he joined them in mahjong, he helped them with their shopping... In brief, he sacrified a portion of his time to win his way into their good graces. All he wanted was peace and quiet.

Not long after, the older of his two young sisters died of tuberculosis. (*One of the most deadly and pervasive diseases ravaging old China, it was rampant among the impoverished millions. Frequently, even some of the rich were struck down.*) Although he mourned for her, his heart felt slightly eased, for her death lightened his burden somewhat.

Some time later, his first child was born — a boy. Juexin felt an immense gratitude to his wife. The coming of this son into the world brought him great happiness. He himself was a man without hope; he would never have the chance to fulfil his beautiful dreams. His only function in life was to bear a load on his shoulders, to maintain the family his father had left behind. But now he had a son, his own flesh and blood. He would raise the child lovingly, and see in him the realization of the career he had lost. The boy was part of him and the boy's happiness would be his own. Juexin found consolation in this thought. He felt that his sacrifices were not in vain.

Two years later, in 1919, the May Fourth Movement began. Fiery, bitter newspaper articles awakened in Juexin memories of his youth. Like his two younger brothers, he avidly read the Peking dispatches carried in the local press, and news of the big strike in Shanghai on June third which followed. When the local press reprinted articles from the *New Youth* and *Weekly Review* magazines, he hurried to the only bookstore in town that was selling these journals, and bought the latest issue of the first, and two or three issues of the second. Their words were like sparks, setting off a conflagration in the brothers' hearts. Aroused by the fresh approach and the ardent phrases, the young men found themselves in complete agreement with the writers' sentiments.

Thereafter, they bought up all the progressive magazines they could lay their hands on, including back numbers. Every night they took turns at reading aloud. Not even letters to the editor escaped their notice, and they had many lively discussions. The younger boys were more radical that Juexin in their approach. When they attacked the "compliant bow" philosophy of the conservative professor Liu Pannong, Juexin confessed he rather liked Tolstoy's "policy of non-resistance". Actually, he had read none of Tolstoy's writings on the subject, but had only seen it mentioned in *The Story of Ivan the Fool*.

Indeed, Juexin found the "compliant bow" philosophy and the "policy of non-resistance" most useful. It was thanks to them that he was able to reconcile, with no difficulty at all, the theories expressed in *New Youth* with the realities of his big family. They were a solace to him, permitting him to believe in the new theories while still conforming to the old feudal concepts. He saw no inconsistency.

Juexin became a man with a split personality. In the old society, in the midst of his old-fashioned family, he was a spineless, supine Young Master. In the company of his brothers, he was a youth of the new order.

Naturally, this way of life was something the younger boys could not understand. They berated Juexin for it frequently, and he placidly accepted their criticism. He continued to read new books and periodicals, and continued to live in the same old-fashioned manner.

He watched his first son learning to crawl, then to walk, then to speak a few simple words. The child was adorable, intelligent, and Juexin lavished nearly all his affection on him. "He's going to do all the things I couldn't," thought Juexin. He refused to hire a wet-nurse, insisting that his wife suckle the child herself. Fortunately, she had enough milk. Such goings-on were virtually unprecedented in a wealthy family, and they led to a great deal of gossip. But Juexin bore it all, convinced that he was acting in the child's best interests.

Every night, after his wife and child had retired, he would sit beside them, feasting his eyes on the baby sleeping in its mother's arms. Looking at the child's face, he was able to forget about himself completely. Juexin couldn't resist planting a kiss on the baby's satiny cheek. He softly breathed words of thanks and hope and love. Rather vague words, but they gushed naturally from his lips like water from a fountain.

Juexin didn't know that his parents had loved him with the same fervor when he was an infant. They too had breathed words of thanks and hope and love.

On Sunday, Juexin went as usual to the West Sichuan Mercantile Corporation. In that office there were no Sundays off.

He had no sooner sat down and taken a few sips of tea, than Juemin and Juehui arrived. They visited him at the office almost every Sunday. As had become their custom, they brought several new periodicals.

The company Juexin worked for, besides renting out shops in the arcade which it owned, ran a small power plant which supplied electricity — for a price — to its tenants and other neighboring shopkeepers. The arcade was very large, and housed all kinds of enterprises, including the manager's office of the West Sichuan Mercantile Corporation. Near the rear door of the arcade, in the left corner, was a bookstore specializing in new publications. Because of its proximity, the bookstore became very well known to the three brothers.

"Only a few issues of *New Tide* came this time. This was the only one left, and I grabbed it. A few minutes later and it would have been gone. We might have had to wait ages before getting to see a copy!" Juehui lay back in a reclining cane chair beside the window of Juexin's office, reverently holding a magazine with a white cover lettered in red. His face was wreathed in smiles.

"I left word with the bookseller — come what may, he must keep a copy for us of everything new that comes in," said Juexin, looking up from his account book.

"Leaving word isn't enough," Juehui explained excitedly. "There are too many people wanting them, mostly subscribers, too. The bookstore only gets three bundles at a time. In less than two days they're all gone." He turned to an editorial and began reading it with interest.

"More will be coming in. Didn't the bookseller say they're on the way? These three packages came special delivery." Juemin, who had just sat down, got up, walked over to the desk and picked up a copy of *Young China*. He seated himself beside the wall to the right.

None of the brothers spoke. Except for the sharp clicking of Juexin's abacus counters, all was still. The warm rays of the winter sun, filtered through the pale blue curtains, slanted into the room as only blurry shadows.

The door curtain was swept aside and Jin entered, followed by her mother and their male servant Sheng. Having seen them to their destination, Sheng left to wait outside.

Jin was dressed in a pale blue silk padded jacket and a dark blue skirt. There was a faint dusting of powder on her cheeks. A strand of hair curving down beside each ear flattered the oval configuration of her face. Beneath the neat bangs on her forehead long eyebrows arched over large eyes set on either side of a well-formed nose. Those eyes were exceptionally bright and penetrating. They shone with a warmth that not only added a glow to her enthusiastic vivacious face, but seemed to light up the room the moment she came in. She magnetized the attention of everyone in Juexin's office as she and her mother smilingly greeted them all.

"We hear that the department store has some new dress material.

I wonder whether they have anything nice we can buy," said Mrs. Zhang after a few minutes of general conversation.

"They have quite a variety now, mostly silks. I've seen them," Juexin replied promptly.

"Would you mind going with me some time?"

"Not at all. I'll be glad to. How about now?" asked Juexin cheerfully.

Mrs. Zhang was very pleased. "If you're not too busy, that would be fine." She rose and looked at Jin inquiringly.

"I'll wait for you here, Ma," Jin said with a smile. She also stood up and walked over to the desk. Juexin had already risen. He held aside the door curtain for Mrs. Zhang.

"I'll be back soon," Mrs. Zhang said as she crossed the threshold. Juexin followed her out.

"What are you reading?" Jin asked, noticing the magazine Juehui was holding.

Juehui looked at her. "*New Tide* — a new publication," he answered in a satisfied tone. He was clutching the magazine lovingly with both hands.

Jin laughed. "Don't hold it like that. I'm not going to take it from you."

Juehui hastily sat up and offered his magazine to the girl. "Take it, take it. I don't want you to say I hoard new magazines!"

Jin shook her head. "After you've all finished reading it, I'll take it home and go through it at my leisure."

Lying back in his reclining cane chair, Juehui resumed his reading. A moment later he asked, "Have you succeeded, Sister Jin? You're so happy today. Did your mother consent?"

"Not yet. I don't know what I'm so happy about. But it doesn't matter whether Ma agrees or not. I can make my own decisions. I'm a person, the same as the rest of you." She seated herself in Juexin's swivel chair and idly leafed through the account book on his desk.

"Well said. Bravo!" cried Juemin. "Spoken like a true New Woman!"

"Don't mock me," smiled Jin. Then her face fell and she said in a different tone of voice, "I have some special news for you. Your aunt Mrs. Jian has come back."

That was special news indeed. Everyone's mood changed instantly.

"What about Cousin Mei? Has she come back too?" Juehui sat up and asked anxiously.

"Yes. Mei's husband died a year after their marriage. She's a widow now. Her mother-in-law didn't treat her well, so she went back to her mother. They've come together to Chengdu."

"How do you know all this? asked Juemin, gazing round-eyed at Jin through his gold-rimmed spectacles.

"She came to the house to see me yesterday," replied Jin slowly.

"She came to your house? Is she still the same?" asked Juemin.

"She looks a little haggard, but not too thin. Maybe a little thinner than before. It's only in those limpid eyes of hers that you see she's been through a lot. But I didn't dare ask her too much, I was afraid to stir up old memories. The only things she talked about were the county town she had been living in — the people there, what it was like — and a little about herself. But she never mentioned Juexin or the Gao family."

Jin's voice had become very sad. Then in a different tone, she suddenly asked Juemin, "How does Big Brother feel about her?"

"He seems to have long since forgotten her. I've never heard him mention her name. He's very satisfied with Sister-in-law," Juemin retorted frankly.

Jin shook her head slightly. She said in a rather pained voice, "But Mei probably hasn't forgotten him so easily. I can tell from her eyes that she still thinks of him... Ma says I shouldn't tell Big Brother that Mei is here."

"It wouldn't matter. Anyhow Mei and her mother won't come to our house, so she and Juexin aren't likely to meet. Big Brother's forgotten the whole affair. Everything changes after a few years. What's there to worry about?" said Juehui.

"I agree it's better not to tell him," said Juemin. "If he's forgotten there's no sense in reminding him. And who can guarantee he's really forgotten her?"

"That's right," Jin nodded. "It's better not to say anything."

"I don't know who stirred up the trouble between our mother and Mrs. Jian, but they certainly ruined Mei's and Big Brother's happiness once and for all!" Juehui said angrily.

"You don't know? Well, I do. Ma told me the whole story. Even Big Brother himself doesn't know it," Jin said in a mournful voice. "Your father had already sent a matchmaker, and Mrs. Jian had consented. But then she took their horoscopes to a fortune-teller who said Juexin and Mei were ill-mated, and that if they married Mei would die young. So Mrs. Jian refused the match. But there was also another reason. She and your step-mother had a tiff over a mahjong game. Mrs. Jian felt very much aggrieved, and used breaking the match as a form of retaliation. Your step-mother had been quite fond of Mei — so was your whole family, for that matter — and she was put out when it was called off. Later, when Big Brother's engagement to a girl of the Li family was announced, Mrs. Jian was displeased with that too. The relations between the two mothers grew worse. Finally they stopped seeing each other altogether."

"So that's the way it was! We didn't know," said Juemin, surprised. "We didn't even know that their marriage had been proposed. In fact we blamed our father and step-mother for not knowing what Big Brother felt and not caring about his happiness. It wasn't their fault after all!"

"That's right. We all wanted Big Brother to marry Cousin Mei. When we heard of the engagement with the Li family, we felt a cruel wrong had been done to Mei. We thought Big Brother should have resisted. Instead, he gave in, like a fool," cried Juehui.

"Cousin Mei stopped coming to the house and, not long after, she left Chengdu," he continued. "When Big Brother married Sister-in-law, we were sorry for Cousin Mei and secretly blamed him. It's funny when you come to think of it. We were more upset about the thing than he was... We had believed he and Mei were fated for each other." Juehui smiled in spite of himself.

"I'm afraid we can't say they were really in love. It's just that they were about the same age and well-suited temperamentally," mused Juemin. "That's why Big Brother wasn't too hurt after they parted."

"You are the limit!" said Juehui. "'About the same age and well-suited temperamentally! What else do you want?"

The room was silent for a while. A face peered in through the door, looked around, then withdrew, muttering, "Oh, Young Master Gao has gone out."

"I've already decided to take the exam for your school," Jin suddenly announced to Juemin. "I'm working hard on my lessons now. Would you be willing to help me review my English?"

"Of course. What a question!" Juemin cried happily. "What about the time?"

"That's up to you. In the evening, naturally. We both have classes during the day.... I don't think we ought to wait till school starts next year. We can begin right now."

"Fine. I'll call at your house later and we can talk it over. — They've come back." Juemin had heard the voices of Juexin and Mrs. Zhang outside.

And indeed it was Juexin who held aside the door curtain to let Mrs. Zhang enter first. Then he came in, followed by Sheng, carrying the packages.

"Let's go, Jin. It's late," Mrs. Zhang had just sat down and taken a few sips of tea, when she addressed these words to her daughter. To winter vacations. Many less than the entire student body were present, and these were only from the more important schools. The turn-out was much smaller than for previous demonstrations. In all, there was a total of only about two hundred students.

Dusk had fallen. Lamps were being lit in the gathering gloom. The students began their march to the office of the governor.

Juehui looked around him tensely as he walked. Knots of people lined the streets, gazing at the students curiously. A few made guarded remarks. Some timidly hurried away.

"They must be out for another blasted check on enemy goods. Which store is going to catch it this time?" Juehui caught the sound of an out-of-town accent. He turned to look at the speaker and found himself confronted with a pair of small shifty eyes in a small pasty face. Scowling, Juehui bit his lips. He couldn't be sure he had heard correctly, so he continued to march.

It was night by the time they reached the governor's headquarters. The pressing darkness increased the tension in every student's heart, assailing them with a nameless fear. They had the peculiar feeling that this was not merely the darkness of night, but the darkness of society and the political situation. Against all these, alone among an indifferent populace, they pitted their youthful hearts.

On the field in front of the governor's compound a platoon of soldiers stood awaiting them with gleaming levelled bayonets, held chest high. The soldiers watched in grim silence as the students excitedly demanded to be let in. Neither side was willing to fall back. The students held a conference and decided to send a deputation of eight, but these too were stopped by the soldiers. Finally a junior officer emerged and addressed them curtly:

"Please leave, gentlemen. The governor has gone home."

The deputies replied courteously but firmly that if the governor was not in, his secretary would do just as well. But this was not of the slightest avail. The junior officer shook his head in a cold, pompous manner, as if to say — The power is in my hands now. I can handle you students myself!

When the deputies reported the results of this argument to their mates, the students were furious.

"Nothing doing!" they shouted. "The governor must come out!"

"We're going in! We're going in!"

"If the governor's not here, let his secretary come out!"

"Charge! Let's go in first and talk afterward!"

Heads were bobbing all over the field. A few students began to push forward but were held back by their mates.

"Quiet down, fellows. Order. We must keep order!" one of the deputies shouted.

"Order! Order!" Others took up the cry.

"Never mind about order," someone yelled. "The first thing is to get inside!"

"It can't be done. They've got guns!"

"Order! Order! Listen to our deputies!" was the cry of the majority.

Gradually the hubbub subsided. In the dark night a fine drizzle began to fall.

"Fellows, they won't let us in, and the governor refuses to send anyone out to see us. What shall we do? Shall we go back? Or shall we wait here?" So that everyone might hear him, a deputy shouted at the top of his lungs, his voice going hoarse with the effort.

"We won't go back!" roared the students.

"We insist on seeing someone in authority. Our demands must be met. We're not falling for any tricks!" several of the students cried.

The junior officer approached the deputies. "It's raining," he said in a more conciliatory tone. "I urge you to go home. I promise to deliver your request to the governor. There's no use your waiting out here all night." The deputies relayed his words to the students.

"No, we're not going!" was the noisy response. The whole field seethed with agitation. Finally, quiet was slowly restored.

"Alright, then. We're staying right here," a deputy shouted through cupped hands. "We deputies will make another try at reasoning with them. We're not leaving till they meet our demands!"

A few students clapped their hands, and in an instant the whole assembly burst into applause. The deputies set out. This time, eight of them were permitted to enter the governor's compound.

Juehui clapped with all his might as rain drenched his hatless head. Though at times he shaded his eyes with his hand or held his wrist over his forehead, his eyes continued to be blurred by the rain. He looked at the bayonets of the soldiers, at the two big lanterns hanging in the entrance-way, at the sea of heads all around him. Uncontrollable anger welled up within him. He wanted to shout, he was suffocating. The soldiers' attack in the theatre had been too sudden. Although there had been rumors that the authorities were planning some action against the students, no one had guessed it would take the form that it did.

"How despicable! Why are they treating us like this?" he asked himself. "Is love of country a crime? Are pure, sincere young people really harmful to the nation?" He didn't believe it.

A watchman's gong sounded twice in the distance. Nine p.m.!

Why haven't our deputies come back yet? Why is there still no news? the irritated students wondered. They began to stir uneasily. The rain was coming down hard now, soaking them from head to foot. Juehui could feel the cold seeping into his bones. He shivered. Then he thought: Is a little discomfort like this going to bother me?... Placing his hands in his sleeves, he raised his chest.

All around him students stood with hunched shoulders, their hair plastered on their foreheads by the rain. But they were not dismayed. One was saying to a classmate: "If we don't get any results, we won't go back. We can be just as brave as the Peking students. When they go out to make speeches, they bring packed suitcases with them — ready to go to jail. You mean to say we can't stand here one night to get our demands?"

Juehui heard these words clearly. He was moved almost to tears. He wanted to take a good look at the speaker, but the mist in his eyes prevented him from seeing clearly. Juehui felt a strong admiration for the boy, although he had said nothing out of the ordinary, nothing different from what Juehui himself might have said. Juehui forgot everything — his well-lit home, his warm bed. He would have been willing to do anything for the boy who had just spoken, even if it meant going though fire and water!

By the third watch — midnight — the deputies still had not returned, and there was no news. It was growing much colder. Cold and hungry and, most of all, weary of the indecision, boys were beginning to ask, "How much longer do we have to wait?"

The bayonets of the soldiers lined up before the entrance gleamed dully, as if in warning.

"Let's go back. We can decide our next step tomorrow. Hanging around here won't do any good," a few of the weaker boys suggested.

But none of the others responded. It looked as if the majority were willing to wait out the night.

After a long, uncomfortable period, someone said, "The deputies are coming out." A deep hush fell on the entire field.

"Fellows, the Department Chief is going to say a few words to us," announced one to the deputies.

"Gentlemen, the governor left for home hours ago. I'm sorry we had to keep you waiting all this time," said a crisp unfamiliar voice. "I have already conferred with your deputies on his behalf, and I have received your demands. Tomorrow, I shall present them to the governor. He, of course, will attend to them. You gentlemen may rest assured of that. He will also send a representative to call on the students who were hurt.

"And now it is getting late. Please go home. We don't want any of you catching cold. You know the governor has the greatest concern for all you gentlemen, so please go home. We wouldn't want anything unfortunate to happen to you."

The voice stopped and, at once, the students began talking among themselves.

"What is he saying? What does he mean by 'unfortunate'?" a classmate asked Juehui.

"He says the governor will attend to our demands, that we should go home. He doesn't take any responsibility himself. Pretty slick!" Juehui retorted indignantly.

"We might as well go home. Standing here won't get us anywhere... And that last thing he said — it's worth thinking over."

Another deputy came forward and addressed the students. "Did you hear what the Department Chief said, fellows? He has received our demands and the governor will attend to them. Why not wait and see? Now that we've got results, we can go home."

"Results? What results?" a number of students countered angrily. But most of the boys said, "Let's go home, then." It was not because they believed the words of the Department Chief, but rather because they realized that to stand all night in the open would be a useless sacrifice. The temperature was still falling and the rain was growing heavier. Everyone was cold and hungry. They had had enough.

"Alright, alright, we'll go home. We can talk some more about this tomorrow," was the feeling of most. Only a few wanted to stick it out, but there was not enough of them to make their view prevail.

The two hundred students began to leave the field.

Large raindrops pelted them without mercy, striking their heads and bodies fiercely, as if intent on leaving an indelible impression on their memories.

Because even the promise that a representative of the governor would call on the students who were hurt was not kept, two days later the students in all schools called off classes. Actually, this was only a gesture, since most of the schools were already closed for winter vacation.

The second day of the strike, on the insistence of the Foreign Languages School and the Higher Normal School, the Students Federation formally issued a strike proclamation. It contained a few disrespectful remarks about the governor. Several days of terror followed. There were frequent clashes between soldiers and students. The citizenry were apprehensive that the soldiers might once again turn into undisciplined mobs. Students did not dare appear on the streets alone, but walked only in organized groups of five or six. A student was badly beaten by three soldiers at dusk near the city's South Gate, while a policeman looked on from the sidelines, afraid to intervene.

Disorder reigned everywhere, but the authorities turned a blind eye. The governor seemed to have forgotten the students completely, perhaps because he was busy making preparations for his mother's birthday celebration. Soldiers grew increasingly arrogant, particularly demobilized wounded soldiers. Thrown out on their own, subject to no discipline whatsoever, the "wounded veterans" roved the streets at will (*demanding money and free merchandise*). No one dared to interfere.

But the students were not so easily bullied. They launched a "Self-Defence Drive to Preserve Respect for Students", they turned out leaflets, they made speeches. The Students Federation went into action with telegrams to leading social organizations all over the country requesting support. It sent representatives to other cities to explain the students' position. Most important of all, it enlisted the co-operation of other student federations. The drive grew to impressive proportions. But there was no sign of any action by the governor.

Juehui was much more active in all this than Juemin, who was occupied helping Jin review her English and was not very interested in anything else.

One afternoon, on returning home from a meeting of the Students Federation, Juehui was summoned to this grandfather's room.

Well over sixty, the old man lay in a reclining chair. His body looked very long to Juehui. Sparse white stubble sprouted on the jaws of his long, dark face, and there was a fringe of grey hair around his shiny bald head. Lying with eyes shut, the Venerable Master Gao dozed, snoring slightly.

Juehui stood timidly before his grandfather, afraid to call the old man, yet not daring to leave. At first, Juehui was very uneasy. The whole atmosphere of this room appraised him. He stood in silence, hoping that his grandfather would awaken soon so that he could quickly leave. But gradually his fear diminished, and he gazed with interest at the old man's dark face and bald head.

As long as Juehui could remember, there had always been a picture of a stern grandfather in his mind. A severe, forbidding man whom all feared and respected. Juehui had seldom exchanged more than a few words with his Ye-ye. Except for the two times during the day, once in the morning and once in the evening, when he formally called briefly to pay his respects, Juehui had little opportunity to come into contact with him. Juehui avoided him as much as possible, for he always felt awkward and over-awed in his presence. The old man seemed to him a person devoid of affection.

At the moment, his grandfather, lying weakly in the reclining chair, looked worn-out. Ye-ye probably wasn't always such an irritable old stick, thought Juehui. He recalled that many of his grandfather's poems had been dedicated to singsong girls, quite a few girls at that. Picturing how the old man probably looked in his youth, Juehui smiled. He must have been a dashing sort then. It was only later that he acquired his pious air... Of course that was thirty years ago. As he grew old, he turned into a crusty Confucian moralist.

Yet even now his grandfather still played around with the young female impersonators in the opera. The old man once invited one of them to the house and had his picture taken with him. The actor had worn his costume for the occasion. Juehui recalled seeing him putting on his powder and woman's wig in their guest room.

Of course nobody looked askance at that sort of thing in Chengdu. Not long ago, a few old-timers who had been officials under the deposed Qing dynasty — pillars of the Confucian Morals Society, no less — made a big splash in the local press, publishing a list they had compiled of the "best" female impersonators in the opera. Patronizing these actors was considered a sign of "refinement". Juehui's grandfather, as a well-known gentleman who had several collections of poems published, a connoisseur of ancient books and paintings, could not go against the fashion.

Yet how can you reconcile this "refinement" with the defence of "Confucian Morals"? Young Juehui couldn't figure it out.

His grandfather kept a concubine — Mistress Chen, a heavily made-up woman who reeked of perfume and simpered when she talked. She was not in the least attractive, but the old man, who bought her after his wife died, seemed to like her. They had been living together for nearly ten years. She had given birth to a son, but he fell ill and died at the age of five.

Mentally comparing his grandfather's elegant tastes in books and paintings with his fondness for this coarse woman, Juehui had to laugh.

People are certainly inconsistent, he mused. The more he puzzled over it, the less he understood the old man. His grandfather was an unfathomable mystery to him.

Suddenly the old man opened his eyes. He stared at Juehui in surprise, as if he didn't recognize him, and waved at him to leave the room. How strange! Had his grandfather summoned him and let him stand so long only to send him away without a word? About to ask, Juehui thought better of it when he saw his grandfather's irritated expression. But as he walked toward the door, his grandfather called

Juexin made respectful noises of assent, and shot a glance at Juehui indicating that he shouldn't try to argue. The younger boy's face was impassive.

"Alright, take him along. He's given me enough of a headache," the old man said listlessly, after a pause. He closed his eyes.

Juexin again murmured his compliance. At a signal to Juehui, the two brothers walked quietly out of the room.

After crossing the great hall, they entered the courtyard. Juehui drew a deep breath and said ironically, "My own master again, at last!" Juexin gave him a reproachful look, but he was unaware of it. Suddenly, Juehui asked seriously, "Well, Big Brother, what about it?"

"What else can we do? We'll have to carry out Ye-ye's orders. You just won't go out for a few days." Juexin helplessly spread his hands.

"But our students' drive is at its height. How can I stay home quietly at a time like this?" cried Juehui, aghast. He was beginning to realize that this thing was serious.

"That's what the old gentleman wants. What can we do?" said Juexin, unruffled. Lately he had been refusing to be upset by anything, big or small.

"There's your policy of non-resistance again! Why don't you become a nice docile Christian? When someone slaps your left cheek you can offer him your right," Juehui said hotly. He was letting out on Juexin all the emotion his grandfather's abuse had pent up in him.

"You are excitable," Juexin replied with a calm smile. "Why get angry with me? What's the good?"

"I insist on going out! I'm going to leave here right now! Let's see what he can do about it! Juehui stamped furiously.

"All that will happen is that I'll be scolded and lectured a few more times," said Juexin in a melancholy tone. Like his brother, he seemed more to be talking to himself than for others to hear.

Juehui gazed at him in silence.

"Let's speak frankly," urged Juexin, but his voice was even. "I hope you'll stay home a few days and not make Ye-ye angry. You're still young and impetuous. When Ye-ye talks to you, you ought to listen. Just let him talk. After he's finished and calmed down a little, say Yes a couple of times and walk out. Then you can forget the whole thing. It's much easier that way. Arguing with him will get you nowhere."

Juehui did not reply. He raised his head and looked at the blue sky. Though he didn't agree at all with his brother, he didn't want to argue. And there was something in what Juexin said. What was the point of wasting energy on something from which no good could come? But how could his young mind be forever weighing fine questions of possible personal profit and loss? Big Brother plainly didn't understand him.

It made Juehui's heart ache to see the clouds drift by. He was torn by conflicting desires. Finally he made up his mind.

"I won't go out for a few days," he said. "Not because I want to obey Ye-ye, but to save you trouble."

"Thanks very much," said Juexin with a smile of relief. "Of course, if you wanted to go out, I couldn't stop you. I'm at the office all day, usually. I just happened to have come home early today and ran into this business of yours. In all fairness to *Ye-ye*, he wants you to stay home for your own good."

"I know that," Juehui replied mechanically. He stood in the courtyard and watched Juexin walk away. He gazed idly at the potted flowers along the path. A few blossoms still remained on the plum trees. Their fragrance drifted to his nostrils. Breaking off a small branch, he snapped it into sections, plucked the blossoms and ground them into a soggy pulp between his palms. His hands, stained yellow with the juice, were steeped in perfume.

This act of vandalism somehow satisfied him. Some day, when his hands were bigger, if he could crush the old order between them in the same way, how wonderful that would be...

His mood changed, and he grew sad. He couldn't take part in the student movement.

"Contradictions, contradictions," he muttered. He knew contradictions existed not only between him and his grandfather, between him and his brother. There were also contradictions with himself.

You can lock up a person physically, but you cannot imprison his heart. Although Juehui did not leave home for the next few day, his thoughts were always with his schoolmates and their struggle. This was something his grandfather could not have foreseen.

Juehui tried to envisage what stage the student movement had reached. He avidly searched the local paper for news. Unfortunately, there was very little. He was able to get hold of a mimeographed weekly, put out by the Students Federation, which contained quite an amount of good news, and a number of stirring articles. Gradually the tension was subsiding, gradually the governor was relenting. Finally, he sent his Department Chief to call on the students who had been injured in the riots, and issued two conciliatory proclamations. Moreover he had his secretary write a letter in his name apologizing to the Students Federation and guaranteeing the safety of the students in the future.

Next, the local press carried an order by the city's garrison commander forbidding soldiers to strike students. It was said that two soldiers who confessed to having taken part in the theatre brawl were severely punished. Juexin saw the proclamation posted on the streets, and he told Juehui about it.

With the news improving from day to day, Juehui, a prisoner in his own home, grew increasingly restless. He paced alone in his room, too fretful at times even to read. Or he lay flat on his bed, staring up at the canopy above.

"'Home. Home, sweet home'!" he would fume. Hearing him, Juemin would smile and say nothing.

"What's so funny!" Juehui raged, on one of these occasions. "You go out every day, free as a bird. But watch out. Some fine day you're going to end up just like me!"

"My smiling has nothing to do with you. Can't I even smile?" retorted Juemin with a laugh.

"No, you can't. I won't let you smile. I won't let anyone smile!"

Juemin closed the book he had been reading and quietly left the room. He didn't want to argue.

"Home, a fine home! A narrow cage, that's what it is!" Juehui shouted, pacing the floor. "I'm going out. I must go out. Let's see what they're going to do about it!" And he rushed from the room.

Going down the steps into the courtyard, he spied Mistress Chen and Aunt Shen — the wife of his uncle Ke'an — sitting on the veranda outside his grandfather's room. Juehui hesitated. He made a detour around his brother Juexin's quarters and entered the large compound.

Passing through a moongate, he came to a man-made hill. The paved path he was following here forked into two branches. He chose the one to the left, which went up the slope. Narrow and twisting it led through a tunnel. When Juehui emerged again on the other side, the path started downward. A delicate fragrance assailed his nostrils, and he struck off in the direction from which it seemed to be coming. Moving down slowly through the bushes, he discovered another small path to the left. Just as he was turning to it, the view before him suddenly opened up, and he saw a great sea of pink blossoms. Below was a plum tree grove with branches in full flower. Entering a grove, he strolled along the petal-strewn ground, pushing aside the low-hanging boughs.

In the distance, he caught a glimpse of something blue shimmering through the haze of plum blossoms. As he drew nearer he saw it was a person dressed in blue coming in his direction over the zigzag stone bridge. A girl, wearing a long braid down her back. Juehui recognized the bondmaid Mingfeng.

Before he could call to her, she entered the pavillion on the isle in the middle of the lake. He waited for her to emerge on the near side. But after several minutes there was still no sign of her. Juehui was puzzled. Finally, she appeared, but she was not alone. With her was another girl, wearing a short purple jacket. The tall girl's back was toward him as she chatted with Mingfeng. He could see only her long plait, not her face. They came closer over the zigzag bridge leading from the near side of the isle, and he got a look at her. It was Jian'er, bondmaid in the household of his uncle Ke'an.

They soon neared the shore, and he hid among the plum trees.

"You go back first. Don't wait for me. I still have to gather some blossoms for Madam Zhou," said Mingfeng's clear voice.

"Alright. That Madam Wang of mine is a great talker. If I'm out too long she'll grumble at me for hours." Going through the grove of plums, Jian'er departed along the path by which Juehui had just come.

As soon as she disappeared around a bend, he stepped out and walked toward Mingfeng. She was breaking off a low-hanging branch.

"What are you doing, Mingfeng?" he called with a smile.

Concentrating on her task, Mingfeng hadn't seen him approach. She turned around, startled, on hearing his voice. She gave a relieved laugh when she recognized him.

"I couldn't imagine who it was! So it's you, Third Young Master!" She went on breaking the branch.

"Who told you to gather blossoms at this hour of the day? Don't you know that early morning is the best time?"

"Madam Zhou said Mrs. Zhang wants some. Second Young Master is going to take them over." Mingfeng stretched for a branch that was heavily laden with blossoms, but she couldn't reach it, even standing on tiptoe.

"I'll get it for you. You're still too short. In another year or so you might make it," said Juehui, grinning.

"Alright, you get it for me, please. But don't let Madam know." Mingfeng stepped aside to make room for Juehui.

"Why are you so afraid of Madam Zhou? She's not so bad. Has she scolded you again lately?" Juehui reached up and twisted the branch back and forth, twice. It snapped off. He handed it to Mingfeng.

"No, she doesn't scold me very often. But I'm always scared I'll do something wrong," she replied in a low voice, accepting the branch.

"That's called 'Once a slave, always a slave!'..." Juehui laughed, but he wasn't intending to deride Mingfeng.

The girl buried her face in the blossoms she was holding.

"Look, there's a good one," Juehui said cheerfully.

She raised her head and smiled. "Where?"

"Don't you see it? Over there." He pointed at a branch of a nearby tree, and her gaze followed his finger.

"Ah, yes. It has lovely blossoms. But it's too high."

"High? I can take care of that." Juehui measured the tree with his eye. "I'll climb up and break the branch off." He began unfastening his padded robe.

"No, don't," said Mingfeng. "If you fall you'll hurt yourself."

"It's alright." Juehui hung his robe over a branch of another tree. Underneath, he was wearing a close-fitting green padded jacket. As he started up the tree, he said to Mingfeng, "You stand here and hold the tree firm."

Setting his feet on two sturdy branches, he stretched his hand toward the blossom-laden bough he was after. It was out of reach, and his exertions shook the whole tree, bring down a shower of petals.

"Be careful, Third Young Master, be careful!" cried Mingfeng.

"Don't worry," he responded. Cautiously maneuvering himself into another position, he was able to grasp the elusive branch. With a few twists, he snapped it off. Looking down, he saw the girl's upturned face.

"Here, catch!" He tossed her the branch. When it was safely in Mingfeng's hand, he slowly climbed down.

"Enough," she said happily. "I've got three now. That's plenty."

"Right. Any more and Juemin won't be able to carry them all," laughed Juehui, taking up his robe. "Have you seen him around?"

"He's reciting by the fish pond. I heard his voice," Mingfeng replied, arranging the flowers in her hand. Observing that Juehui had only draped the robe over his shoulders, she urged, "Put it on. You'll catch cold that way."

He put his arms through the sleeves. The girl began walking off along the path. He called after her:

"Mingfeng..."

She stopped and turned around. "What is it?" she asked with a smile. He didn't answer but only stood smiling at her. She again turned and walked away.

Juehui hastily followed, calling her name. Again she halted and turned. "Yes?"

"Come over here," he pleaded.

She came toward him.

"You seem to be afraid of me lately. You don't even like to talk to me. What's wrong?" he asked, half in jest, toying with an overhanging branch.

"Who's afraid of you?" Mingfeng replied with a chortle of laughter. "I'm busy from morning till night. I just haven't the time for talk." She turned to go.

Juehui held out a restraining hand. "It's true. You are afraid of me! If you're so busy, how come you have time to play with Jian'er? I saw you two just now in the isle pavilion."

"What right have I to chat with you? You're a Young Master. I'm only a bondmaid," Mingfeng retorted distantly.

"But we used to play together all the time. Why should it be any different now?" was Juehui's warm rejoinder.

The girl's brilliant eyes swept his face. She dropped her head and replied in a low voice, "It's not the same now. We're both grown up."

"What difference does that make? Our hearts haven't become bad."

"People will talk if we're always together. There are plenty of gossipers around. It doesn't matter about me, but you should be careful. You have to uphold your dignity as one of the masters. It doesn't matter about me. I was fated to be just a cheap little bondmaid." Mingfeng spoke quietly, but there was a touch of bitterness in her voice.

"Don't leave. We'll find a place to sit down and have a long talk. I'll take the blossoms." Without waiting for an answer, he took the branches from her hands. Surveying them critically, he broke off two or three twigs and threw them away.

He set off along a small path between the plum grove and the edge of the lake, and she silently followed. From time to time he turned his head to ask her a question. She answered briefly, or responded with only a smile.

Leaving the grove, they crossed a rectangular flower terrace, then went through a small gate. About ten paces beyond was a tunnel. The tunnel was dark, but it was quite straight, and not very long. Inside, you could hear the gurgling of spring water. On the other side of the tunnel the path slanted upward. They mounted about two dozen steps, followed a few more twists and turns, and at last reached the top.

In the center of the small gravelled summit was a little stone table with a round stone stool on each of its four sides. A cypress, growing beside the flat face of a large boulder, spread its branches in a sheltering canopy.

All was still except for the chuckling of a hidden brook, flowing somewhere beneath the rocks.

"How peaceful," said Juehui. He placed the blossoms on the table. After wiping the dust off one of the stone stools, he sat down. Mingfeng seated herself opposite him. They couldn't see each other clearly because of the blossoms heaped between them on the little table.

With a laugh Juehui shifted the branches to the stool on his right. Pointing to the stool on his left, he said to Mingfeng, "Sit over here. Why are you afraid to be close to me?"

Silently, Mingfeng moved to the place he had indicated.

They faced each other, letting their eyes speak, letting their eyes say the many things words could not express.

"I must go. I can't stay too long in the garden. Madam will scold me if she finds out." Mingfeng stood up.

Taking her arm, Juehui pulled her down again to the seat. "It doesn't matter. She won't say anything. Don't go yet. We've just come. We haven't talked at all. I won't let you go!"

She shrank a bit from his touch, but made no further protest.

"Why don't you say anything? No one can hear us. Don't you like me any more?" Juehui teased. He pretended to be very downcast.

The girl remained silent. It was as if she hadn't heard him.

"You're probably tired of working for our family. I'll tell Madam that you're grown up now, to send you away," Juehui said idly, with affected unconcern. Actually he was watching her reaction closely.

Mingfeng turned pale, and the light went out of her eyes. But her trembling lips did not speak. Her eyes glistened like glass, and her lashes fluttered. "You mean it?" she asked. Tears rolled down her cheeks.

Juehui knew his teasing had gone too far. He hadn't meant to hurt her. He was only testing her. It had not occurred to him that his words could cause her so much pain. He was both satisfied and regretful over the results of his experiment.

"I'm only joking," he laughed. "You don't think I'd really send you away?" But his laughter was forced, for he had been very moved by her emotion.

"Who knows whether you would or not? You masters and mistresses are as changeable as the winds. When you're displeased there's no telling what you'll do," sobbed Mingfeng. "I've always known that sooner or later I'd go the road of Xi'er, but why must it be so soon?"

"What do you mean?" Juehui asked gently.

"What you said..." Mingfeng still wept.

"I was only teasing. I'll never let that happen to you," he said earnestly. Taking her hand and placing it on his knee, he caressed it soothingly.

"But suppose that's what Madam Zhou wants?" demanded Mingfeng, raising her tear-stained face.

He gazed into her eyes for a moment without replying. Then he said firmly, "I can take care of that, I can make her listen to me. I'll tell her I want to ma—" Mingfeng's hand over his mouth cut him short. He was quite sincere in what he was saying, although he hadn't really given the matter much thought.

"No, no, you mustn't do that!" the girl cried. "Madam would never agree. That would finish everything. You mustn't speak to her. I just wasn't fated..."

"Don't be so frightened." He removed her hand from his mouth. "Your face is all streaked with tears. Let me..." he carefully wiped her face with his handkerchief. This time she did not draw back. Wiping the tear stains, he said with a smile, "Women cry so easily." He laughed sadly.

Mingfeng smiled, but it was a melancholy smile, and she said slowly, "I won't cry any more after this. Working for your family I've shed too many tears already. Here together with you, I certainly shouldn't cry."

"Everything will be alright. We're both still young. When the time comes, I'll speak to Madam. I definitely will work something out, I mean it," he said comfortingly, still caressing her hand.

"I know your heart," she replied, touched. Somewhat reassured, she went on, half in reverie, "I've been dreaming about you a lot lately. Once I dreamed I was running through the mountains, chased by a pack of wild animals. Just as they almost caught me, someone rushed down the slope and drove them away. And who do you think it was? You! I've always thought of you as my savior."

"I didn't know. I didn't realize you had so much faith in me." Juehui's voice shook. He was deeply moved. "I haven't taken nearly good enough care of you. I don't know how to face you. Are you angry with me?"

"How could I be?" She shook her head and smiled. "All my life I've loved only three people. One was my mother. The second was the Elder Young Mistress. She taught me to read and to understand many things. She was always helping me. Now both of them are dead. Only one more remains..."

"Mingfeng, when I think of you I'm ashamed of myself. I live in comfort, while you have such a hard time. Even my little sister scolds you!"

"I'm used to it, after seven years. It's much better now, anyhow. I don't mind so much... I have only to see you, to think of you, and I can stand anything. I often speak your name to myself, though I'd never dare to say it aloud in anyone else's presence."

"You suffer too much, Mingfeng! At your age you ought to be in school. A bright girl like you. I bet you'd be even better than Jin... How wonderful it would be if you had been born in a rich family, or even in a family like Jin's," Juehui said regretfully.

"I never hoped to be a rich young miss. I'm not that lucky. All I want is that you don't send me away, that I stay here and be your bondmaid all my life... I'm so happy just being able to see you. As long as you're near me, my heart's at ease... You don't know how I respect you. But sometimes you're like the moon in the sky. I know I can't reach you."

"Don't talk like that. I'm just an ordinary person, the same as everyone else." His low voice trembled and tears rolled from his eyes.

"Be quiet," she warned suddenly, grasping his arm. "Listen. Someone's down there."

They both listened. The sound when it reached them was very faint. Mingled with the babble of the hidden spring, it was difficult to distinguish clearly. They finally recognized the voice of Juemin singing.

"Second Young Master is going back to the house." Juehui rose and walked to the edge of the hilltop. He could see a small figure in grey flitting through the pink haze of the plum blossoms. Turning to Mingfeng he said: "It's Juemin, alright."

Mingfeng hastily rose to her feet. "I must go back. I've been out here too long. It's probably nearly dinner time."

Juehui handed her the plum blossoms. "If Madam Zhou asks why you're so late, make up an excuse — anything will do. Say I asked you to do something for me."

"Alright. I'll go back first, so we won't be seen together." Mingfeng smiled at him, and started down the slope.

He walked with her a few steps, then stood and watched her slowly descend the stone stairway and disappear around the face of a bluff.

Alone, he paced the hilltop, all his thoughts devoted to Mingfeng. He walked over to the little table and sat down opposite the place she had just vacated. Resting his elbows on the stone surface and supporting his head in his hands, he gazed into the distance.

"You're so good, so truly pure..." he whispered.

After a while he rose abruptly, as if awakening from a dream. He looked all around him, then hurried down the path.

Zhao Shuli (1905-1970)

Zhao Shuli, born in Shanxi in 1905, was the peasant writer among peasants. He knew them better than anyone. Some say he wrote about them better than anyone. His first short story, The Marriage of Young Blacky *which we present here, was published in 1943. It was an immediate success — first and foremost among the peasants themselves. In the revolutionary base in the Taihang Mountains alone, where the author and the story were both located, it had a first edition sale of almost forty thousand copies. Local theatrical troupes immediately dramatized it and put it on the stage.*

He wrote other best sellers like the short story "Rhymes of Li Youcai" and the novel Changes in Li Village, *also dealing with the metamorphoses which have shaken the countryside.*

Zhao's style is warm and loving, with a deceptive simplicity, but he didn't hesitate to poke fun at backward rural types and stodgy officials. During the "Cultural Revolution" these humorous jibes were labelled smears against the "noble peasants" and the "leadership". Zhou Shuli was hounded to death in 1970.

The Marriage of Young Blacky *is one of his most popular stories. In his effortless almost casual style, Zhou Shuli shows how the battle to change backward ideas goes on long after the shooting stops.*

THE MARRIAGE OF YOUNG BLACKY

In the village of Liujia Valley were two oracles, a man and a woman. Everyone in the neighboring towns and hamlets knew about them. The man was called Liu the Sage. The woman was called Third Fairy.

Liu, who had been a small merchant, never made a move without first consulting the stars. Third Fairy was the wife of a fellow named Yu Fu. On the first and the fifteenth of each month she draped a red cloth over her head and strutted about, claiming to be a heavenly spirit.

Each of these oracles hated a particular phrase. Liu the Sage abhorred "Not right for sowing". Third Fairy abominated "The rice is overdone". Both had their reasons.

A number of years before, there had been a spring drought. Not until the third day of the fifth month did they finally get a little rain. The following morning everybody rushed out to sow millet. Liu the Sage checked the farmers' almanac and calculated on his fingers. Then he announced: "Today is not right for sowing." The fifth was Dragon-Boat Festival, and he had never worked on that day. The sixth according to his calculations was a lucky day, and he sowed his seed. But by then the soil had gone dry again. Less than half of his millet came up.

There was no more rain until the fifteenth. While others were out hoeing around their sprouts, Liu and his two sons had to re-sow their empty patches. A young neighbor, meeting him on the street that evening after supper, asked innocently: "Would you say today is right for sowing or not, uncle?" Liu the Sage glared at him and walked away. Everyone laughed, and the story spread rapidly.

One day a man came to ask Third Fairy's divine aid in curing an ailment. Seated behind an incense table, she pretended to go into a trance and sang incantations. The man knelt before her. Third Fairy's daughter Qin, who was then only nine, had put the rice on to boil for the noonday meal. Attracted by her mother's singing, she forgot about it, and slipped into the room to listen. When the man went out a moment to relieve himself, Third Fairy hissed at her daughter: "Take the pot off, quick. The rice is overdone." The man heard her. After he left he told everyone of these prosaic words he heard from a medium who was supposed to be communing with the gods. People who liked a joke often asked one another in her presence: "How's the rice? Is it overdone?"

Third Fairy had been "divinely gifted" for a full thirty years. It began when she was fifteen. The prettiest girl in the village, she had just married Yu Fu, a quiet, hard-working honest young man. Yu Fu's mother had died when he was a child, and when he and his father went out to work in the fields, the bride was left alone at home. Fearing she might be lonely, other young men of the village drifted in to keep her company. Soon there was a whole crowd of them, and the house rang with their laughter.

Yu Fu's father thought these goings-on disgraceful. He blew up and berated the young men so roundly they didn't dare show themselves again. The bride went into hysterics. She wept all day and the following night. In the morning she neither combed her hair nor washed her face. She wouldn't even eat. She just lay in bed and refused to leave it.

Father and son were helpless. An old woman neighbor invited a medium for them. The medium consulted the gods and said the bride had been possessed by a supernatural being called Third Fairy. The girl herself moaned and muttered a lot of mystic nonsense. Thereafter, on the first and fifteenth of each month a divine spirit was said to enter her body. People burned incense before her and begged for instructions on how to get rich or cure ailments. That was when her incense table was first set up.

Young men again started calling. Although they claimed they wanted to consult the heavenly oracle, what they really wanted was to view the heavenly image. Third Fairy guessed what was on their minds. She dressed in her best clothes and made herself up alluringly. It wasn't long before she had all the young men wrapped around her little finger.

That was thirty years before. Most of the young men of that day now wore beards, and the majority had grown children and daughters-in-law of their own. Except for one or two bachelors, few had time to idle with Third Fairy. But, although she was forty-five, Third Fairy still liked to play the coquette. She continued to wear embroidered shoes and trousers with fancy cuffs. The front of her head was bald, but she covered this with a black handkerchief. Unfortunately powder couldn't smooth over her wrinkled face. It only made it look like a frosted donkey turd.

Not satisfied with her few old bachelors, Third Fairy gathered round herself another troupe of youngsters, even more numerous and more mischievous than her admirers of former days.

What was it about Third Fairy that attracted so many young men? The answer lay in her daughter Qin.

Third Fairy gave birth to six children, but five of them died. Only Qin, a daughter, survived. At two or three, she was very cute. Third Fairy's admirers loved to hold the child in their arms. "She's mine," one would say, picking her up. "No, she's mine," another would insist, taking her over. By the time the girl was five or six, she realized there was something improper in these claims.

"If anyone says that again," her mother advised, "you just reply: 'I'm your aunt. Be more respectful to your elders'." Qin did so, and this put a stop to the insulting remarks.

Now she was eighteen. Idle gossips said she had it all over her mother at the same age. Young men sought every excuse to talk with her. When she went to wash clothes by the stream, the young men immediately found that their own clothes were dirty. When she gathered wild herbs, they discovered that wild herbs were exactly what they needed most.

At mealtime, neighbors like to bring their food over and chat with Third Fairy while they ate. Some lived at the other end of the village and the round trip was a full *li*, but they didn't mind. This had been going on for thirty years. But the present generation of young men began manifesting their enthusiasm only two or three years before. Third Fairy at first thought her own charms were the cause. But gradually she realized it was Qin the young men were interested in.

Qin was quite different from her mother. Although she too laughed and chatted, she was a prudent girl. The only boy with whom she was fairly friendly was Young Blacky, so called because of his darkly sunburned complexion. One day two summers before, she was home alone when Wang, another boy, dropped in.

"Here's my chance at last," he leered.

The girl's face stiffened. "You shouldn't talk like that. You're a big boy now."

"You don't have to put on an act with me," the boy sneered. "You'd soften up soon enough if I were Blacky. Why don't you give us a little taste? The pot has no right to call the kettle black." Seizing her arms, he whispered: "Come on. Quit pretending."

To his surprise she let out a scream: "Wang, what are you doing?"

Hastily he let go and slipped away. "Just wait," he muttered. "I'll get you yet."

Everyone in Liujia Valley hated Wang. Only his cousin Xing could get along with him. Wang's father had been a petty tyrant. For years his favorite sport had been to tie people up and beat them. By the time Wang was seventeen, he was his father's worthy assistant. Xing, too, learned to play jackal to the tiger. Any time the old man wanted a dirty job done, he had only to give the order to Wang and Xing.

In the early years of the War Against Japanese Aggression, the countryside was overrun with traitors, enemy spies, deserters and bandits. Wang's father was dead by then and the two cousins did the inside work for a gang of deserters. They told them whom to kidnap, then acted as intermediaries to arrange the ransom, giving each side the impression that they were their friends. Later, the Communist-led Eighth Route Army came and smashed the deserter and bandit gangs, and the two cousins returned to Liujia Valley.

The peasants living in this remote mountain region were then rather timid. After months of chaos during which many people were killed, the Liujia Valley residents were even less inclined to stick their necks out. Other villages formed new administrations and set up societies to help the war effort, but no one in Liujia was willing to hold any post. Even the mayor had to be appointed by the county government.

Not long after, the county authorities sent people to supervise elections of village officers. Wang and Xing thought this was their chance to seize power. The villagers were only too glad to get someone to serve. Xing was chosen chairman of the military committee. Wang was elected political committeeman. Wang's wife became head of the women's association. A few old men were pressured into accepting the remaining offices. But of course an old man couldn't be the leader of the Anti-Japanese Youth Vanguard. Xing nominated Young Blacky for no other reason except that he was a nice-looking boy. Although Blacky's father, Liu the Sage, didn't like the idea, he didn't dare oppose Xing, and the boy was elected.

The mayor was not a native, and knew little about village affairs. Wang and Xing were able to ride roughshod over everyone even more easily than before. They had only to deceive the mayor and no one could refuse to do their bidding.

Young Blacky was the second son of Liu the Sage. Once in a counter-assault he killed two of the enemy and was awarded the title of Sharpshooter. During Spring Festival he and a group of amateurs toured the local villages and staged theatricals. He was so handsome the women couldn't take their eyes off him.

He never went to school, but he learned to read and write a little from his father. Instead of the classics or the standard texts, they used the old man's prognostication books. Then only six, Young

"She has only a father, and he's a refugee who's gone heaven knows where. There's no place to send her back to. I know the law says she's too young to be engaged, but lots of girls in our village are, at her age. Be merciful and let this engagement take place."

"Any party to an illegal engagement who's not willing can break it."

"But both families agree."

The district chief asked Young Blacky: "Do you agree?"

"No, I don't," replied the boy.

Liu the Sage glared at him. "That's not for you to decide."

"You didn't ask his consent when you made the engagement," said the district chief. "He doesn't need yours to break it. Today people choose their own partners in marriage, old neighbor. You have no say in the matter. If that little girl you're raising has no other home, You can consider her your daughter."

"I can do that, alright. But I must beg you to be merciful and not let him become engaged to Qin."

"You can't interfere in that."

"Be merciful, I beg you. Their horoscopes don't match. They'd be miserable all their lives," cried Liu. He turned to Young Blacky. "Don't be such a muddle-head. This will affect your whole life."

"Old neighbor," said the district chief, "don't you be such a muddle-head. Your son would really be miserable all his life if you forced him to marry a twelve-year-old girl. I'm telling you this for your own good. If Young Blacky and Qin want to get married, they can whether you agree or not. You can go home now. The little girl can be your daughter if she has no place else to go."

Before Liu the Sage could renew his pleas for the district chief to "be merciful", a messenger escorted him out the door.

Third Fairy had gone to Liu the Sage's home that night for two reasons. First, she wanted to show what a rumpus she could raise if she really tried. Second, she wanted to provide a cover for her actual feelings. As a matter of fact, she was quite happy that Qin had got into trouble, and when she returned home that night she slept well.

The next morning she continued lolling comfortably in bed. Though her husband was very anxious over the arrest of their daughter, he had no idea what to do about it. Too timid to call Third Fairy, he cooked breakfast himself. When it was nearly ready, she leisurely rose and began combing her hair.

"Are you going to see about Qin?" he asked.

"What for?" retorted Third Fairy. "Let her get out of this scrape herself, if she's so smart."

Her husband dared say no more. He put the cooked food on the side of the stove to keep it warm until Third Fairy finished making up.

As they were starting their meal the messenger arrived from the district with a summons for Third Fairy. She seemed quite pleased.

"Our daughter is grown now and we can't handle her any more," she drawled. "We hope the district chief will punish her."

After breakfast she put on her best clothes — a new kerchief, embroidered shoes, fancy-hemmed trousers. She added another layer of powder and stuck several ornaments in her hair. Then she told her husband to saddle the donkey. She mounted and, with him driving the beast from behind, rode to the district government office.

The messenger led her to the chief's room. She dropped to her knees and kowtowed.

"Please give me justice, your honor," she intoned.

The chief, who had been writing at his desk, saw a woman kneeling before him with lowered head, her hair full of silver ornaments. He thought it was a young wife who had sought his help two days before, after quarrelling with her mother-in-law.

"Doesn't your mother-in-law have a guarantor?" he asked. "Why don't you go to him?"

Bewildered, Third Fairy raised her head. When the chief saw a middle-aged woman, her face caked with powder, he realized his mistake. The messenger quickly explained:

"This is Qin's mother."

The chief looked her over. "So you're Qin's mother. Get up. No need to put on an act. I know the whole story. Get up."

Third Fairy rose to her feet. The chief asked:

"How old are you?"

"Forty-five."

"Why do you deck yourself out like that? Don't you know what you look like?"

A girl of ten or so who had been standing at the door, watching, giggled. "Go outside and play," the messenger ordered. The girl fled.

"Can you invoke the spirits?" the chief demanded.

Third Fairy did not reply. The chief asked her:

"Did you find a suitor for your daughter?"

"Yes."

"How much did he give you?"

"Three thousand five hundred."

"What else?"

"Some silks and jewelry."

"Did you talk it over with your daughter first?"

"No."

"Does she agree to the match?"

"I don't know."

"I'll call her and you can ask," said the chief. He turned to the messenger. "Bring Qin here."

The little girl who had been chased away spread the story that the chief was questioning a forty-five-year-old woman who powdered her face and wore embroidered shoes. The neighborhood women came flocking to see, filling half the courtyard.

"Just look at that," they chattered. "Forty-five, if she's a day."

"How do you like those trousers?"

"And those shoes!"

Third Fairy, who hadn't blushed in years, felt herself reddening. Perspiration rolled down her cheeks. The messenger, escorting Qin, said to the women in a voice deliberately loud so that Third Fairy could hear:

"What are you gaping at? She's human, isn't she? Haven't you ever seen anyone like that before? Make way, make way."

The women burst into laughter.

When Qin arrived, the chief said to Third Fairy: "Ask your daughter whether she's willing."

But Third Fairy had ears only for the women in the courtyard. "Forty-five," they were saying, "and she wears embroidered shoes." Sweating with embarrassment, Third Fairy kept mopping her face. She couldn't utter a word.

The ladies outside changed the subject. "That's her daughter... Doesn't make up nearly so fancy as her mother... They say she can invoke the spirits..."

One of them who knew the story of "the rice is over-done" told it in full. By then Third Fairy was ready to die.

"If you won't ask your daughter I'll ask her for you," said the district chief. He addressed himself to Qin: "Are you willing to marry the man your mother has chosen?"

"No. I don't even know him."

"Did you hear that?" the chief asked Third Fairy. He explained about the freedom of choice provisions in the Marriage Law, and said that Qin's engagement to Young Blacky was entirely legal. He advised Third Fairy to return the money and gifts to Brigadier Wu and let Qin marry Young Blacky.

Very ashamed, Third Fairy agreed to everything.

When the three militiamen arrived in Liujia and said that the district had arrested Xing and Wang and were sending a clerk to investigate their crimes, the villagers were delighted. After the noon-day meal, a mass meeting was called in the temple yard. The mayor explained the purpose of the meeting and asked everyone to expose the evil Xing and Wang had done.

People were afraid of retaliation if the two rascals couldn't be overthrown, and at first no one spoke. A few of the more timid even whispered: "Enduring silence brings peace."

"That's what I once thought," said a young man who had been victimized by the two scoundrels. "But the more I endured, the less peace I had. If you fellows won't speak out, I will."

He told how Wang had brought bandits to his house to extort money from him, and related four or five other crimes that Wang committed. "That's all I'll say for now. Let some of the others speak," he said. "Then I'll go on."

That broke the ice. Peasants rose one after another to expose the wickedness of Xing and Wang — blackmail, driving people to suicide, robbery, rape. They sent militiamen out to cut their fire-wood, they ordered villagers to hoe their fields. They confiscated grain, imposed taxes, used the militia as their private police... By sunset, fifty or sixty illegal acts had been revealed.

On the basis of this evidence, the two were sent up to the county court for a formal trial. There, besides being ordered to pay compensation for all the damage they had caused, they were each sentenced to fifteen years in prison.

When the results of the mass meeting became known, the villagers took courage. New cadres were elected. No one dared to cast a vote for any rascal. Even Wang's wife, who was voted out of office, changed her tune. "I'll be progressive from now on," she avowed.

There was a metamorphosis in our two oracles as well.

Third Fairy had been mortified by the stares of the women that day in the district chief's office. When she returned home she took a long look at herself in the mirror. She really was ridiculously over-dressed. A woman with a daughter who'd soon be married — who was she trying to fool?

She made up her mind. From head to toe she converted her appearance to one more suitable to her age. The incense table with which she had been invoking the spirits for the past thirty years, she quietly dismantled.

When Liu the Sage got back from the district office that day, he again bemoaned to his wife the fact that Qin and Young Blacky's horoscopes didn't match.

"It's time you got rid of those astrology charts," his wife said. "All your life you've never even broken wind without first consulting them. You said Blacky was in terrible trouble, but nothing happened. It seems to me Qin is a nice girl. She'll be a good wife to our son. What is this nonsense 'their horoscopes don't match'? Have you forgotten 'not ripe right for sowing'?"

With his wife no longer believing in his occult powers, Liu the Sage lost courage. He never tried to demonstrate them again.

Qin and Young Blacky also came home. They observed that the mood of their parents had changed and asked neighbors to put in a word for them. The two oracles, deciding to sail with the wind, consented to their marriage.

Both families joined in the wedding preparations. After the ceremony, Qin moved in with Young Blacky. They were very happy. Neighbors said they were an ideal couple.

In the privacy of their room the newlyweds often joked. Young Blacky mimicked Third Fairy and chanted: "Marriages are ordained in heaven." Qin, imitating Liu the Sage, cried: "District chief, be merciful. Their horoscopes don't match!"

Once, naughty children, listening at their window, overheard them. The result was that our oracles were given new nicknames. Third Fairy was called "Heaven-Ordained Marriage", and Liu became known as "Unmatched Horoscope".

Sun Li (1913-   )

Sun Li was born in the countryside of Hebei province in 1913. During the war against Japan he worked in the mountain area as a newspaper correspondent, editor and teacher. He studied in the Literature and Art Academy in Yan'an in 1943. His well-known short story "Lotus Creek" was written at that time. After the Japanese surrendered in 1945, he returned to central Hebei to join in the Land Reform. He edited the literary column of the Tientsin Daily *after the liberation of that city in 1949.*

Most of his works concern the struggles prior to the establishment of the new government. They include a novel The Stormy Years, *and several shorter pieces. His stories are clean, well-constructed, and portray women sensitively and sympathetically.*

Published in 1962, The Blacksmith and the Carpenter, *a novelette, is considered the best of his post-Liberation pieces. It is set in a village in the early days of New China. On a small quiet canvass, Sun Li paints a tightly packed picture of rather astonishing characters, mixing and clashing as they seek, or refuse, to adjust and adapt.*

THE BLACKSMITH AND THE CARPENTER

What things in childhood leave the deepest impressions? If you grew up in a village in the old days, you know how impoverished material life was and how few cultural activities there were. You saw an opera only once every several years when some travelling company stopped by. Once a year you might hear the drums and cymbals of a touring variety troupe. Except for the fields and cemeteries and abandoned kilns and willow groves in the outskirts, there were few places that were any fun for the children.

And so, the ringing of a hammer in anyone's courtyard drew them immediately. They would flock in whenever a villager hired a carpenter to build a cart or put up a door. A long carpenter's bench with a wedge on one end would be placed in the courtyard. On this would be laid a board that was to be planed. Then the carpenter astride the bench would lean forward and push the plane and shavings like strips of satin would come curling out and fall to the ground. The children would rush forward but, just as they got their hands on them, the owner of the house, watching the work, would bark:

"Get out of here, you kids. Go outside and play."

Yet that slithering sound was so fascinating! And how charming the art of the carpenter was! And in the corner of the compound wall the crackling fire — for heating fish glue and straightening warped boards — that was too hard to leave. Particularly since most of the carpentry work was done in winter. A good fire was doubly appealing then.

Sooner or later, however, the children, reluctantly, would have to go. Let the lovely ring of hammers sound far beyond the compound walls. May those gleaming flames dance forever before their eyes.

The children often had a ridiculous thought: Why can't we invite a carpenter to work at our house? When they got home they would express this wish to their father during the evening meal. He would get angry and say:

"We hire a carpenter! We haven't been able to afford one for generations. Maybe we'll start with yours, little wretch, if you're fated to be rich! Or I could send you to Old Li to be his apprentice. You can fool all day with hammers and awls."

(*Men are usually hailed as "Old" so-and-so on reaching middle-age, long before they actually become old. The appelation may continue in their later years, as well. It is a sign of respectful familiarity.)*

Old Li was the village's only carpenter. Tall, he had a brown beard and a pock-marked face. There seemed little likelihood of anyone becoming Old Li's apprentice. The children knew he wasn't taking on any. He had six boys of his own, and not one of them was a carpenter. They spent all day with wicker baskets on their backs, picking dried bean stalks for fuel, just like the other kids.

But hope springs eternal, and there were always chances for enjoyment. If it were late spring or early summer, the village street would resound with clanging and the roar of a fiery furnace. The clanging seemed especially heroic, the flames especially fierce. You could hear and see them from ever so far! They meant that Old Fu's travelling blacksmith forge had come once more to the village.

He came every year, as punctually as the swallows returning to the eaves at nesting time. Just before the wheat harvest and the busy autumn season, sickles and hoes and all sorts of tools had to be mended and other implements forged. As soon as he appeared, people brought out their worn and broken farm tools, and the scrap metal they had been saving for the repairs.

In the course of fifty years, Old Fu's lean face had assumed the color of the pincers he held in his left hand and the hammer he wielded with his right and the anvil resting on the big wooden block. Even the short beard that fringed his face was rusty in hue. He worked stripped to the waist. The oilcloth apron covering his legs was so pitied with holes, large and small, burned through by flying sparks of many years, that it resembled a hornet's nest. On his feet Fu wore a pair of very tattered stockings, also intended as a protection against the sparks that flew each time his hammer struck the glowing metal.

He had two apprentices. The older one swung the sledge hammer and sharpened tools, the younger worked the bellows and cooked their food. His grimy face streaked with sweat, the younger boy would stand proudly, his head high, his feet planted firmly one before the other, pulling and pushing the piston of the big wheezing bellows, while the village children who had gathered round gazed at him with the utmost admiration. "Watch out!" he would cry softly as Old Fu drew a cherry-red piece of iron from the forge. The kids would hurriedly scatter, and the ringing big hammer would send sparks flying after them in all directions. If their mothers didn't call them home, the kids would remain indefinitely. They had no idea what was being made. Was it a ring for a door-knocker, or a chain of iron circles? Ah, children! While you silently watch, what is really going on in your minds?

The blacksmith's team spent over a month in this village every year, rising early and going to bed late. At daybreak, when everyone else was wrapped in his quilt, the sound of their hammers resounded down the village street; the fire in their forge still glowed long after dark. They slept beside the forge at night, in the open, for they had neither shed nor tent. Only in the rainy season did they dismantle their portable furnace and wheel it into a villager's home.

Usually they stayed with Old Li, the carpenter. Old Li was very poor. His wife had died, leaving him with six children. A few years before, steeling his heart, he had sent the oldest boy to Tianjin to learn commercial trading; the others he boarded among relatives and friends. Then, shouldering his carpenter's kit, he had set out for the northeast provinces. In those distant parts he endured many hardships and saw much that was new. But in the end he returned home empty-handed. He and a few of his kids set up house in an unused compound. He was having an increasingly difficult time making ends meet.

Old Li was a friendly fellow. He knew the hardships a man faced when working away from home. He and the blacksmith were good friends. He addressed Old Fu affectionately as "relative".

When the rains came the blacksmith's team set up shop in the carpenter's mill shed. As a token of thanks to his "relative", in his spare time Old Fu would repair and sharpen the carpenter's tools. And Old Li, when he wasn't busy, would replace the handles of the blacksmith's hammers and mend his bellows, without charge.

No one was sure what was behind this appellation "relative" which the two men used so freely. Did Old Li want one of his sons to accept Old Fu as his foster father? Or had they arranged a match with Old Fu's daughter?

"What sort of 'relatives' are you, anyhow?" people would ask inquisitively. "Foster relatives, or relatives by marriage?"

"Foster relatives?" Old Li was a talkative fellow who liked to laugh. "I have six boys. If you want a foster son, take your pick."

"Relatives by marriage? Why not?" Old Fu, who seldom joked, this time also laughed. "I've a growing daughter at home, you know."

But whenever Old Fu mentioned his daughter, his ruddy face grew somber, like a glowing red iron billet after being plunged into the water bucket. His wife had died, and Nine, their only child, was left at home alone.

"Bring the girl with you next year." The two old friends were seated opposite each other, smoking their pipes in the old mill shed one evening. Old Fu wasn't saying a word, and Li made this proposal because he knew it would open his friend's tightly locked mouth and release some of the bitterness pent up in his heart.

"That would mean another mouth to feed." Old Fu spoke with downcast eyes. "Girls are a nuisance to have around."

"Look at me," said Old Li, trying to hold back the tears in his eyes. "I've got six kids."

They were revealing their innermost thoughts, but it was difficult for them to go on. For although each longed to help the other, both knew they were powerless. Even words of comfort seemed to be in vain.

At that moment, Six, Li's youngest son, came in to tell his father it was time to go to bed. Fu raised his head and looked at the boy.

"It seems to me Six is the most intelligent, the most quick-witted, of your six children."

"I wish you'd take him on as your apprentice," said Li, hugging the boy to his chest. "Is Nine as old as he?"

"How old is Six?"

"Nine," the boy answered for himself.

"My girl is nine years old too. But she's a head shorter than you. She'll have to call you Big Brother."

The following year when the wheat was ripe, Fu did indeed bring his daughter from their old home. He fixed a small perch for her on one side of his wheelbarrow. She sat cross-legged on a bit of old padding, leaning inward and holding on with her right hand.. They travelled for five or six days, eating plenty of dust, and stopping at little inns. But the child was very gay. To be with her father, her only dear one, to be together for a long time — nothing could make her happier.

Arriving in the village, they went directly to Old Li's house. The carpenter was delighted. He summoned all the little girls in the neighborhood to play with the small guest.

"What's your name?" they asked her.

"I'm called Nine."

"You mean you're the ninth child?"

"No, I'm the only one."

"Then why are you called Nine?" The girls were puzzled. "Here you get your nickname according to the order you're born in. Like Six, for instance. He was the sixth child in the family."

"That was the name my ma gave me before she died," the little newcomer said sadly. "I was born on the ninth day of the ninth month."

"Oh." The girls understood. "And where you come from, they still wear braids?"

"Yes," the guest said shyly. The woollen thread binding the end of her single thick braid was a dazzling shade of red!

She got to know the local girls well after playing with them a few days, and Six too. She and Six formed a close affection, just like their fathers.

Old Fu was too busy working to look after his daughter. One night he made her and Six an axe head each. Old Li fitted the handles. During the day they sent the two children into the hills to cut brushwood. A big rattan basket on his back, axe in hand, Six proudly led the way. Nine followed, carrying a somewhat smaller basket. They went far into the hills.

Six didn't like to cut brushwood near the village. He preferred uninhabited places, new places which he could imagine he was discovering. But he didn't do much work, wasting most of his time along the road. He would suddenly flush a bird brooding eggs and chase it in its short bursts of flight. Brooders always fly close to the ground, and never very far. The bird seemed to be teasing him, taking off each time he nearly caught up.

Or he would pursue a half-grown rabbit. Sure he could nab it, he was always disappointed.

"Let's cut some brush," Nine would urge.

"What's the hurry?" Six would retort. "As long as we bring back a full basket each before dark it'll be alright."

"Is there any rule that says we can't gather two baskets apiece?"

"Even if we each collect three, we'll never get rich!" Six would rebuke her.

One day he was walking slowly through the grass, watching the ground. Marking a certain spot, he stopped and examined the surroundings. He threw his basket aside and called Nine.

"Stay here and guard this burrow entrance. Don't let him escape."

He returned to the marked place, leaned over and began to dig, his small axe flying.

That evening, the children returned home happily with a short-tailed little mole. They put it in a wooden box. Carpenters' homes are full of wooden boxes.

The next morning the wind was very strong, and the children remained at home. After his father left for work, Six brought out the mole.

"He's been in that box all night," he said to Nine. "He must be stifling. We ought to let him run around a bit."

"Suppose we can't catch him again?"

"Just guard that water drain and nothing will happen." Six put the mole down on the floor. At first it crouched motionless at the boy's feet. But then Six "whoosh"-ed at it, and stamped his feet. The little animal scampered along the base of the wall, and popped into a rat hole.

Six was frantic. "Is there any water in the vat?" he asked Nine.

The vat was empty. Six grabbed a ladle, scooped some brine juice from the pickling jug and poured it into the hole. But it did no good. He started for the pickling jug again.

"Your father will scold you," Nine warned. "Salt is expensive."

The boy angrily flung the ladle to the ground with such force that it split.

Playing together that day was a failure. Six was unhappy over the loss of his mole. Nine felt badly about the wasted brine juice. A poor family's child, she had learned to cherish very needle and thread.

The wind blew harder and the children took refuge in the old mill shed. A seldom-used stone mill stood in the middle. Nine sat on the dusty stone roller base. Six crawled into the big winnowing machine, curling up like a shrimp, nose toward the ceiling.

"Come on in," he said to Nine. "There's still room."

"I won't," said Nine.

She was thinking, facing reality. Outside, the wind was howling. Spider-webs danced wildly in the eaves. A big spider was blown down by a fierce gust of wind. It hastily scurried back up its thread. I've no mother, Nine said to herself. My father is out working in that gale and my new friend is lying asleep in the winnowing machine...

Childhood memories of every kind remain long in people's hearts. When you're living in a skyscraper, will the recollection of that afternoon in the low-roofed mill shed surface often among your deepest thoughts?

That was in 1937, the year the War of Resistance Against Japan began. It was the first of the great storms that swept across the plain and shook the foundations of the old way of life. From that year on, people were tested in battle. They learned the meaning of class struggle. The vast majority, who had known nothing but hardship all their lives, as well as the children they formerly considered burdens and could never afford to educate, started to break the traditional fetters, tangible and intangible, that had bound them for so long. Two of Old Li's oldest sons joined the army.

What with all the troop movements and general chaos, Old Fu was unable to return to his home village. His daughter was with him, and he didn't want to risk the dangers of the long journey. During those years, carpenters and blacksmiths not only helped the needs of agriculture, they also aided the war effort. Old Fu's two apprentices went to work in an arsenal belonging to the Communist-led Eighth Route Army, then in a united front with the Kuomintang against the Japanese invaders. All that winter, Old Fu and his daughter shod horses for the cavalry that came and went in increasing numbers. To Nine the work was very exciting.

Once, she grew careless and looked up to watch some passing troops. The jittery horse she was shoeing kicked her, leaving her with a small permanent scar on her temple. But when the army first-aid man was bandaging her head, Nine didn't shed a tear.

Amid wind and rain and the roar of guns, suffering through hunger and cold, rejoicing in victory, the youngsters finished their childhood, their precious years of childhood. Because he got along well with people, Old Fu was known and liked by everyone in the surrounding villages. When he and Nine were refugees away from home, local women always volunteered to look after the girl. As soon as they heard she was the blacksmith's daughter they would offer to feed her and give her a place to live.

In the last two years of the war (*1944-45*), because she was more grown up and had acquired some experience in guerrilla tactics, Nine usually travelled with Six. The boy was bold and clever, and he took very good care of her. She was just reaching the age of understanding, and when they were together she felt fortunate to have such a companion. But it was more than that; there seemed to be a mutual reliance between them. They never ran into danger when they were together. At times she really believed Six's boastful claims.

"Just stick with me," he would say. "The Japanese devils are scared to come near me."

"All you can do is brag," Nine, walking behind, would scold him.

"Stick with me, and you'll never starve or go thirsty," Six would state cockily. "I can find food for you anywhere, like an old mother bird."

In Nine's eyes, Six was quite efficient. When it rained, he would find shelter for her, even in the wilds. When she was hungry, he would go off on long treks, and come back with something to eat. Many people were taking refuge out in the open; they generally were willing to help children. But more important, when she was with Six, Nine felt a kind of gratitude and joy that could overcome both hunger and cold.

After the Japanese surrendered, Old Fu was eager to go back to his native village with his daughter. They hadn't been home in several years.

The evening before they departed, Old Li heated a pot of wine and gave Old Fu a farewell dinner. Ordinarily, the old blacksmith wasn't very talkative, even when he drank. On the other hand, words gushed from Old Li's mouth as soon as wine touched his lips, like water pouring through a break in a Yellow River dyke.

But this night the two old friends sat with a vegetable oil lamp and the pot of wine between them, drinking in silence. Not until it was nearly time to say goodbye did Old Li manage to force out a few commonplace phrases. Then he lapsed again into silence, his head down.

This was an usual state for the carpenter. Old Fu asked him: "Is something troubling you, relative?"

"Yes, there is." Old Li suddenly grew animated. He had just been waiting for his friend's question. "I want to request a favor of you, relative. You know I have six sons, We're so poor — there isn't anything I hope for myself. But my boy, Six, believe me, he may amount to something."

"You've spoiled him a bit, relative," Old Fu interjected. "You can't be too soft with boys."

"It's this —" The carpenter refused to be diverted. "Let's not beat about the bush. Without being prejudiced, it seems to me that Nine and Six like each other pretty well. Of course, a pauper like me has no right to have a daughter-in-law, but, well, I can't help dreaming..."

He gulped down the remaining wine and again dropped his head.

"I know what you mean," said Old Fu. "You're poor, but am I any richer?"

"A man with a daughter naturally wants to find her a husband who's well off," Old Li mumbled.

"The kids are still young. Why not wait until Nine and I come again before we decide. What do you say?" With these cool words Old Fu concluded a meeting that should have warmed both parties' hearts. Old Li's enthusiasm at once diminished by half.

That evening Nine went around saying goodbye to the local women and girls. All hated to see her go; they trooped along with her as she went from door to door. Six tailed her every step.

"What are you following her for, you silly boy?" the women demanded. "You're not hiding out in the hills any more!"

"He's also come to say goodbye to Nine," explained some of the girls.

"Hurry home, Six, and go to bed," one of the older women scolded.

"I won't go to bed! I will follow her! What are you going to do about it?" Six muttered to himself.

Nine continued to chat and laugh with the others.

Early the next morning, Six and his father helped Nine and the blacksmith load the wheelbarrow. In the shadows, Nine said to Six softly:

"We'll be coming back."

After Old Fu and Nine left, there was no news of them. It was said that the region where their village was situated was occupied by Kuomintang troops.

During the past two years, the War of Liberation had swept the plains. In its wake had come momentous changes. Old Li, as a poor peasant and the father of two boys in the people's army, received a good allotment of land in the land reform. Later, his second son was killed in battle, and the carpenter was given a death benefit. When Tianjin was liberated, his oldest son, who was in business there, sent home some of his earnings. The family's standard of living rose precipitously.

Li was miserable when he learned that his second son had been killed. The boy had endured nothing but hardships from the day he was born. He and his brother Four had begged on the streets for a time after their mother died.

The carpenter was nearing sixty. Only Six and Four were at his side. For some reason Li didn't like Four much, and lavished his affection on Six. Now that life was better, he wanted Six to have some of the pleasures he and his other sons had lacked.

Six grew increasingly spoiled. Although quite big already, he was unwilling to work in the fields like Four. And he wouldn't even consider carrying manure or cleaning the pig pens. Since he couldn't very well remain idle, he took up a small trade. After autumn, he roasted shelled peanuts and sold them. In the winter evenings, he hawked hot beancurd on the street corner, banging a bamboo segment to attract attention. What he couldn't sell he ate himself. Every night, when his father was already in bed, Six would come home with a large bowl of hot beancurd spiced profusely with garlic and ginger, and place it down beside the old man's head.

"Eat, pa, it's nice and hot."

Old Li would sit up and eat the beancurd. How understanding the boy is, he would think to himself. What a filial son!

Sometimes, Six would bring a bowl to his brother Four who was giving the animals their nightly feed. Four had learned frugality as a child. He never would accept.

"Sell it," he would say. "It will be that much more money

earned. I'm going to bed anyhow. What's the point of eating?"

And Six would think: This fellow doesn't appreciate good treatment.

But whether he peddled peanuts or beancurd, Six was never able to earn any money. He had many friends. This one would grab a handful, that one would help himself to a bowl. Even when he kept a record, Six couldn't make himself go around and demand payment. At the end of the year, Four had to collect the bills for him.

The girls were the worst. Whenever they saw Six on the street, they would gather round and ask: "Are your peanuts crisp? Are they tasty?"

"Just try them!" Six would say with a laugh, quickly opening his cloth bag.

There was no charge for "trying", and the girls were many. Not only did each take a handful; Six generously helped them stuff their pockets, which were deep although their openings were small.

Of medium build, with very fair skin and an affable disposition, Six was a great favorite among the girls. He was not unaware of this, and took pains to consolidate and strengthen the good impression he was making.

After the war, he was the first man in the village to comb his hair long, with a part. Scorning the regular itinerant head shaver, on county fair days he would hurry to the county seat and have his hair done in a "modern" barber shop. He was also the only one in the village to use a flashlight at night. He played its beam all over the street. Laughing, the girls would surround him and say:

"Six, are you trying to blind me!"

"Six, let me have it a while!"

For rainy weather, he had a pair of shiny rubber half-boots. He would put these on and go calling, being especially courteous to those families possessing pretty daughters and flooded courtyards. When, peering through the window, a fair maiden would see him entering the yard she would hurry to the door and greet him.

"Six, you've come exactly at the right time. Take them off and lend them to me. I have to go to the outhouse."

"They're just your size," Six would say, pulling off the boots and handing them to her. "You ought to buy a pair."

"Where would I get enough money?" the girl would laugh. "The next time you go into town, buy me a pair of stockings, will you?"

"What color?"

"You decide. You're always buying things. You've got good taste." Thus expressing her confidence in him, the girl would reach into her pocket. "Here's some money."

"Not now. Wait till I've bought them."

But when, a few days later, he appeared with the stockings, although the girl would praise the quality and approve the size, the subject of money somehow didn't come up again.

Old Li was too involved in his new business to be concerned about his son's shortcomings. He had recently traded his old grey donkey for a roan horse. Although the horse was also a bit on the elderly side, its legs and color were good. The animal was much too handsome, in fact, for the dilapidated cart which had been allotted to Li during the land reform. After shopping around, Li brought home some logs of elm and locust. He had decided to build himself a big new cart.

The carpenter's skill at cart-making was famed near and far. He had built innumerable carts for others in his time. Now he was old. He would build a fine one to leave to his sons. The idea made Old Li very happy. In his search for proper lumber, he had come across a sandal-wood sapling. Carpenters love this kind of tree best of all. He planted it outside his bedroom window and tended it carefully. It would be the symbol of the new life he was starting. He also raised a flock of chickens in the yard and bought two new piglets for the pig pen.

He told Four to help him saw the logs into boards. In the courtyard the first log was propped up at one end so that it pointed into the sky like an anti-aircraft gun. The old man stood on the raised end, while Four sat on the ground, and both worked a two-man saw back and forth along a black line. Old Li kept complaining that Four was "stupid". He wasn't holding the saw to the line, he wasn't pushing it correctly...

Four proposed that Six take his place. The old man wouldn't agree. Four said he was playing favorites. Father and son wrangled loudly. The carpenter picked up an axe and chased Four all around the yard.

What Four hated worst was for anyone to say he was stupid. Ever since the War of Resistance Against Japan he had been studying hard, reading books and newspapers every day, going to school every night, and taking an active part in village youth work. He felt that he was more progressive than his father or Six, that he understood things much better.

Feeling lonely in the silence that followed the quarrel, the old man began to reminisce.

"When I was your age," he said to Four, "I was already a full-fledged craftsman, and not only in our county. Even in the compound. The old widow lay wheezing on the brick bed all day, not bothering about a thing.

That winter the carpenter wanted to move Four into one of the empty rooms and keep the horse and trough in an outer shed. He asked the widow's permission, but she flatly refused. She said the horse would drop its manure into her rice pot. The widow and Li had a violent quarrel. In a fit of rage the widow packed her things, moved out and went to live with her daughter. Rumor had it that Li had forced her to go, and this made a nasty impression in the village. Somehow the son in the army got word of it. He wrote a letter criticizing the old man.

Old Li felt badly about the matter for several days. He thought he had bought himself a packet of trouble. But since the place was his, why not move in? He chose an auspicious day and, together with his two sons, took occupancy of their new home. Their neighbors insisted that he serve drinks by way of celebration. He had no choice but to comply.

That night, Six returned very late. The old man was still awake, waiting for him.

"Why did I buy this cursed place, if not for you?" Li grumbled.

"It's awfully cold here," Six said in a muffled voice, his head beneath the quilts.

"You ought to behave better," Li admonished him, "instead of running around all day."

But Six was already asleep. His gentle rhythmic snores warmed Li's heart. For what could make an old man happier than to have his young son sleeping sweetly at his side?

That winter Six and a family of ne'er-do-wells formed a partnership to sell beef dumplings. Every evening, carrying a small wooden container on his back, Six hawked dumplings on the main street.

"Beef dumplings! Hot beef dumplings!"

Until late at night.

The dumplings were made at the west end of the village in the home of Stupid Li. Stupid's wife came from a family whose house had always been a popular hang-out for fancy ladies and gamblers. Fat and ugly, with a right foot that twisted inward, she had a darkly spotted face. On the lid of her left eye, which had been blind since her childhood, a large wart sprouted. In spite of several years in the new society she still retained her spoiled self-indulgent habits. A greedy eater, she could think up the most amazing devices to satisfy her rapacious appetite.

Stupid always had to make sure she approved before he ventured

finished, she halted and swept the grain together, then picked up her winnowing basket.

"I'm afraid that's still too coarse," a young man standing in the front ranks said. His name was Big Fellow.

In spite of his size, Big Fellow was extremely timid. But he could bear the silence no longer. He felt so sorry for Man'er that he screwed up his courage and took over for her at the roller. This remarkable action so astonished his mates they even forgot to tease him, as was their custom.

Suddenly, from the end of the street came a cry, one of those terrifying screeches which women alone at home utter when they are awakened from their dreams in the middle of a winter's night by a weasel getting at their hens.

It was Big Fellow's wife. He had been only a child when they married. She was eight years older than he, and she had suffered through a long period. (*This was one form of purchase-marriage in the old days in rural China. If the husband died before he was old enough to consummate the marriage, by custom the "wife" was nevertheless required to remain a chaste widow to the end of her days... Another form was the child-bride marriage. The girl in such marriages acted mainly as a wageless servant until she was mature enough to be a wife.*)

From the time Big Fellow reached the age of understanding his wife had loved him, and the more she loved him the more strictly she treated him. Big Fellow was afraid of her, the way he feared his older sister, or his mother. For many years not only had she looked after his wants, she had even taught him how to speak and behave. He had never thought her finding him in a chance encounter with another woman would evoke such a storm of rage. He stood holding the handle of the roller, gazing at his wife in stupefaction.

She charged up to him. "You shameless creature! It's almost time for me to cook supper and you still haven't fetched me any water. What are you doing here?"

"What?" Confronted by his wife's full fury in the presence of so many onlookers he didn't know what to say.

"Are you dumb, or only deaf?" Her voice grew sharper. "I asked you what you're doing here. You're almost eighteen. It's time you learned how to behave!"

"Excuse him this time, he's still only a child!" the young men hooted.

"A child is he?" Big Fellow's wife hated nothing more than for people to refer to her husband's youth. "Then what do you call a man? Are you children too? No pants-wetting kid would ever act in

such a disgusting manner! You're a pack of dogs! A little bitch trots down the street with her tail between her legs and you all swarm after her! You've been staring at her till you're glassy-eyed and stiff in the neck. I've been watching you for a long time; I've seen your wanton airs! Do you know what you look like? Get a bucketful of water from the well and take a good look at your reflection!"

This indiscriminate attack aroused great dissatisfaction among the young men, but none of them want to clash with her. With their eyes, with coughs, they encouraged Big Fellow, hoping he would pull the large wooden handle out of the stone roller and threaten her with it. But Big Fellow showed not the faintest sign of resistance. He even retreated a few steps, and seemed about to go home.

The young men watched Man'er as she winnowed the rice, her face scarlet. She was known for not being easily put upon, even by men. But today, under these circumstances, she hung her head in silence.

Battles don't remain at a standstill for long. Man'er's sister had already appeared at the west end of the street. She tore forward as if rushing to put out a fire. Because she was fat and had a twisted leg, and particularly because her vision was faulty, she ran like a soccer player jockeying a ball down the field — now bending forward at the waist, now flapping arms akimbo, now right and left foot mincing one over the other, now tripping and staggering across the ground.

"Who are you calling a little bitch?" she bellowed challengingly at Big Fellow's wife, while still ten meters away.

"Whoever the shoe fits, let her wear it!" the other woman retorted, straightening up.

"My sister is pure," cried Stupid's wife. "Her backside is cleaner than your face! You just tend to your little husband. Nobody can insult my sister and get away with it!" She dashed over to the roller to pull out the wooden handle, but Man'er prevented her.

"When did you turn into such a softy?" she berated Man'er. "Do you want me to lose face completely?"

Dragging out the handle, she ran full tilt at Big Fellow's wife. The latter calmly grasped the end of the handle and jerked it sharply toward herself. Stupid's wife fell flat on her face.

It was at this moment that Old Fu and his daughter, who had been away so long, returned to village.

As usual Old Fu was pushing his barrow with its portable blacksmith's furnace. Up front, pulling, was his daughter, Nine.

The blacksmith looked older and thinner. The barrow was quite dilapidated now; its creaks had lost their previous smartens. Nine

was taller, but her clothes were very tattered. Her face was drawn, dust coated her hair, her shoes were open at the toe. Only the joy shining in her eyes revealed how happy she was to return.

On the street corner, Old Fu set the barrow down and greeted everyone. Nine pulled the towel from around her neck and mopped her perspiring face.

"We're back again," said the blacksmith. Pointing at Man'er and Stupid's wife, he asked: "Why are they quarrelling?"

"No particular reason," the young men replied sarcastically. "They've eaten their fill and have nothing better to do. They're practicing acrobatics!"

"They shouldn't do that,'" Old Fu said seriously. "This village has always been in a liberated area. You're living in paradise. You should have seen our place. Life was terrible under Kuomintang occupation. When Nine and I went back, we fell into the net. Luckily, we lived through it."

"How is production down there now?" the young men asked.

"Just getting back to normal. But we had drought again this year," said Old Fu. "Life is good here. If you don't get along with each other, you'll be letting the Communist Party and Chairman Mao down. These last few years I've thought of you folks all the time. I knew you must be making fast progress in this old liberated area. Where's Six? Why isn't he here?"

While looking among the crowd, the blacksmith glanced at his daughter. Evidently she had also looked in vain, and now she was gazing at the beautiful girl with the lively eyes who was standing by the grist mill. Nine didn't know her. She assumed she must be someone's new bride from another village.

"I saw Six in the northern outskirts a while ago, flying his pigeons. Maybe he's gone home by now," a young man said. "You ought to go and see your old relative. Old Li has come up in the world these past two years."

Old Fu said goodbye and lifted the handles of his barrow. Nine took her place up front. As they walked off, she kept turning her head to stare at Man'er.

Old Li was overjoyed to see his old friend again. He led him to the new compound and showed him the cart he was building.

"We've been waiting for you, relative," the carpenter said excitedly. "Tomorrow, we'll set your forge up in the courtyard. See how big and light it is. Won't it be a pleasure to work here?"

"It's really fine," said Old Fu. "You could even build a carpentry shop here. There's plenty of room."

"When I finish this cart, I'm going to retire," Old Li said with

satisfaction. "You know, there's a lot of money in transport these days. Every time the cart wheels turn, the cash comes rolling in. Tianjin has been liberated, and my oldest boy has been doing very well in business there. Winter's only just begun, and he's bought me this. But how can I do any work wearing the thing?"

Looking at the fine black cloth robe whose flaps the carpenter raised high to show the thick fleece lining, Old Fu suddenly felt cold. It never occurred to Old Li that his guest, who had come so far, might want to rest. He told in detail his plan for building more rooms in the compound, then brought his "relative" to see his pig pens. Only after he had exhibited his horse as well did he finally lead Old Fu into the house and invite him to be seated.

Nine was about to follow when she happened to look up and see Six on the roof. He was waving to her and indicating that she should mount the ladder. Nine lightly clambered up. Screened behind a row of dry branches, Six was playing with a flock of tame pigeons. When the birds saw a stranger approaching, they took flight. The sun was sinking in the west, and scarlet clouds reflected pinkly on the flat white-plastered roof. Red and white pigeons wheeled overhead, chasing, soaring.

"I saw you long ago," said Six. "But I didn't dare call you because my father was there."

"What are you raising these pigeons for?"

"They're fun. A couple of days ago, my friend Yang Mao brought back a pair of pure white ones from Beijing, a foreign breed. They're real beauties. I'd like to buy them, but he won't sell at any price."

"Didn't the Youth League criticize you?"

"I'm not a member." Six waved his arms at the pigeons to make them fly higher and then lower. "Are you?"

"I just joined," said Nine. She fell silent.

"When you learn how to play with these birds, they're great sport." Six stood up and shouted to the sky: "Here pigeon-pigeon!"

Obediently, one by one, the birds returned to the roof.

"Six, who's that girl?" Nine suddenly noticed on a roof several courtyards away the beauty she had seen at the grist mill. The girl was gazing in their direction, smiling challengingly, with an expression difficult to fathom.

"That's Stupid Li's young sister-in-law, Man'er. The dumplings must be ready. I've got to load my hamper. Let's go down."

At supper time, Six still hadn't come back. Four was delighted when he learned that Nine was also a Youth Leaguer.

"Did you bring your credentials?" he asked. "You can join our

study group tonight."

"I carry then wherever I go," Nine laughed. "I'd like very much to be in your study group. What's your job in the League branch, Brother Four?"

"I'm responsible for public education. There's a lot of sand in this region and the winds are strong. In spring, we never have enough rain. Our superiors are urging us to dig wells and plant trees, and bring irrigation to our parched fields so that we can grow rice. It's a fine plan, but many people in the village don't understand how important it is."

"But you do, of course," Old Li growled caustically. "You've got to stop being such a blasted busy-body. You're bringing down curses on my head."

"Why hasn't Six joined the League?" Nine asked.

"Who knows?" replied Four. "He says there's something wrong with his brain. The minute a meeting starts, his head aches. Does he look like a boy with a weak brain to you?"

"You ought to help him. His interest seems to be in other things."

"Maybe if you talk to him, it'll be better. He has no respect for me at all," Four sighed. "In our family my prestige is very low."

"Stuff and nonsense," snorted Old Li. "Outside, your prestige is high, and where does it get you?"

"It's good for young people to be progressive," Old Fu said soothingly. "If it weren't for this new society, relative, would you be getting along so well?"

"True," Old Li conceded. "The times keep improving. But in our private lives, the old ways are still the best."

Because Nine was very concerned, Four agreed that they should talk to Six together. After he had fed the stock, Four gathered his study material and took a small oil lamp. He left the house with Nine, asking the two old men to open the compound gate for them when they came back.

"Why are you taking that lamp?" asked Nine.

"It's our group's study lamp. I can't leave it in the classroom. People might waste the oil."

On hearing the word "oil", Old Li shouted after him: "Four! Are you using our oil again? The Youth League of yours is a league of paupers! You work for them and give them free oil, to boot! Son of a bitch! Your prestige is high because you swipe out damned lamp oil!"

The boy did not reply. When he and Nine reached the street, he halted and said: "Six sells meat dumplings at night. I don't know

whether he's started yet or not."

But that night Six was not hawking dumplings. In place of his clear young shout was the raucous bellow of Stupid Li:

"Beef dumplings! Steaming hot meat dumplings!"

Four asked him where Six was.

"How do I know?" Stupid retorted solely. "I'm not his boss."

As Four and Nine walked to the west end of the village, they heard Six's voice coming from a large courtyard. Through the partly open gate they could see several trees and some piles of brushwood. A tall poplar reared up beside the compound wall. Beneath this tree, Six and a girl were standing very close together.

Nine halted at the gate. Four impetuously pushed it open, entered and shouted: "Six!"

The girl leaped as if she had been shot.

"What are you yelling about?" Six demanded in a low angry voice.

"What?" Four hadn't moderated his voice. "What's the secret?"

"Quit that noise!" Six whispered frantically.

Four said no more, but he struck a match and lit the small lamp. Holding it high, he looked around.

"Old Lord of the Heavens!" Six dashed over to him and with one puff blew the lamp out. "Do you have to shine that wretched lamp all over the place!"

"Is some dirty business going on here that can't be exposed to the light?" said Four. With large strides he made a circuit of the poplar, unexpectedly bumping into Man'er who was hiding on the other side of the tree. The two began to wrangle loudly.

"Ruined!" Six stamped his foot. There was fluttering sound in the branches above. "The pigeons have flown!"

"Only one of them is gone." Man'er stopped shouting at Four to look up. "Everybody keep quiet!"

They didn't know what sex it was, but the bird that had flown off couldn't bear to leave its mate. It circled once in the dark sky, and returned to the branch. It was only then that Six told his brother softly that Yang Mao's foreign-breed pigeons had escaped; he was just in the process of catching them.

In the black night the tall poplar seemed to reach up to caress the stars, and its bark was a smooth and shiny as a girl's skin. Six had already removed his shoes and socks. Spitting on his hands, he started up the tree.

"Are you trying to kill yourself in this darkness?" said Four. "I'll go home and tell pa!"

"Stop playing the big brother," said Man'er. "Those birds cost

thirty yuan each. You're a good student. Figure out what two of them will bring."

Nine could restrain herself no longer. "Six," she called, "they're not worth risking your neck for!"

"Tsk-tsk," said Man'er mockingly. "Words from someone who really cares about you."

"Who are you?" Nine demanded. "We've never met; why should you want to pick a quarrel?"

"Who am I?" Man'er laughed coldly. "I'm exactly the same kind as you!"

"Don't fight," Six pleaded. "You'll scare the birds off again. Here pigeon-pigeon!"

He quickly scrambled up to the crotch of the big branch.

"Let's go," Four said to Nine. "There's nothing we can do. If he falls and kills himself, it'll be his own fault."

Extremely angry and uneasy, Nine left with Four.

"A fine pair," Man'er drawled.

"What?" cried Six, up in the tree.

"I'm talking about the pigeons. They're on that south branch."

Four and Nine could hear her keeping up a flow of derisive comment, while directing Six's dangerous operations.

In a compound that had been confiscated from a landlord during the land reform, Nine met the members of the village Youth League. Many were old friends, and they greeted her warmly. Four lit the lamp and led them to a large room in the west wing which was used in common by the Youth League and the local theatrical company.

The room was frigid, for all the windows were broken. Ripped and hanging in patches, the flowered paper ceiling was covered with dust and cobwebs. One of the double doors was missing. A small blackboard hung on one wall; before it stood an old oil-stained table for six. Low platforms of bricks laid with mud fillers could serve as either benches or desks. The girls, in their thin clothes, found the bricks icy cold, but they remained seated quietly.

Four and a young fellow called Kitchen Stove were the teachers. Crowding close to the little lamp, they told the Youth Leaguers how to explain to the peasants the advantages of digging well and planting trees. The Youth Leaguers talked it over.

As the night deepened, the room became colder than the air outside. But the young people went on talking earnestly.

"Comrades, we must change our village into a place of prosperity and plenty," said Four. "Then our Youth League won't have to meet in a cold room like this. We'll build ourselves a fine club house."

"You're getting too far off the subject," Kitchen Stove warned him. "The question at hand is how to overcome the obstacles in the way of our educating the public."

"It seems to me there are two," said Four. "The first is Li the Seventh's big rubber-tired cart. It's earning a lot of money on transport jobs and is making people see only what's right in front of their noses. It's encouraging selfish capitalist-type thinking. The second is Stupid Li's dumpling business. All the carrying-on there is enticing young people away from their proper work. If we want to succeed in our propaganda, we've got to limit Li the Seventh's transport hauls and put an end to Stupid Li's dumpling business. Otherwise we'll just be making a lot of empty talk. As long as they've got something concrete to offer, our efforts are in vain."

"I agree with you," said Kitchen Stove. "But in the first place Six is your brother. It's up to you to get him out of the bad environment. Second, your father is building a large cart too; he wants to take the road to private wealth. These two big obstacles are right in your own family. What are you going to do about them?"

"The problem is this," Four said frankly. "My father doesn't listen to me. I asked him: 'Are you against the call of the Party? He said: 'I support it one hundred percent.' I said: 'Then let's dig a well here this winter.' He said: 'There's no hurry about it. That's my difficulty. But I'm certainly not going to give up.'"

"I can help," said Nine. "I look at it differently than the rest of you. Old men can be won over. When we were living at home, my father liked to hear me talk about the new thinking. As to Six, we ought to help him progress too."

"Right!" cried the girls sitting behind her. None of them had spoken for some time, and now they all burst out in chorus.

Kitchen Stove laughed. "Helping Six progress isn't going to be easy. That Man'er has a much greater attraction for him than our Youth League."

The girls disagreed.

"If you don't believe me, just try and pull him away from her," Kitchen Stove said gloomily, coming down from the teacher's platform.

After the meeting ended, they returned, singing, to their homes. The girls insisted that Nine sleep with them. Kitchen Stove had a large family and little space; every winter, he lived with Four. It was more convenient that way for studying and arguing together.

Kitchen Stove went to Four's house. Four fed the stock, then shared with Kitchen Stove a couple of leftover sweet potatoes. As the boys got into bed, Kitchen Stove grinned.

"These quilts are cold. With neither wood to heat the platform bed nor wives to warm us, we're in a bad way."

"Don't surrender!" cried Four, taking a breath of icy air. "If you want to remain a bachelor, you must have the courage to persist!"

"Are you sure we have to remain bachelors? Better not jump to conclusions!"

In the next room, the roan horse was munching hay. Although his teeth were old, they made a noise like grating iron. But the boys soon fell asleep. Shimmering moon beams shone in through the window.

At this time Six and Man'er were still in the empty courtyard. Six had long since caught the pigeons. When he slid down from the tree, Ma'er pulled him to a large stack of wheat stalks, and the two buried themselves in the soft warm pile. Tying the pigeons' wings with a red woollen thread, Man'er played with the birds merrily, now making them kiss, now placing one on top of the other in a mating position.

"I'll sell them and buy you a padded tunic," Six said to her. "I'll gladly share everything with you. You've helped me a lot."

"Our friendship isn't based on material things," said Man'er seriously. "Give that robe to Nine. Buy her one."

"Why?"

"Because her face is black," said Man'er, repressing a giggle. "A true blacksmith's daughter!"

"She's a good worker. And she's in the Youth League."

"What if she is? At home I was in the Youth League too. They criticized me. I left them flat and came straight to my sister's. As for working in the fields, you call that a woman's special talent?"

"What is a woman's special talent, then?"

Man'er smilingly raised her head. Six stared at her lovely face, even more alluring in the moonlight. He soon learned the answer to his question...

As dawn approached, a heavy mist spread, and frost coated the branches and grass and the eaves of the houses. Only then did Six and Man'er rise and brush the wheat stalks from their hair and clothing. They discovered that one of the precious foreign-breed pigeons had been crushed to death under Man'er's body.

Six was very distraught. He would have given anything to bring it back to life. But its heart had ceased to beat; beneath its wings it was already cool.

At Stupid's house, they found the compound gate and house door closed but not locked. Their late return evoked no surprise from Man'er's sister. Stupid didn't even hear them come in. He continued snoring beneath his quilts.

Man'er told her sister how she had helped Six catch the pigeons, and how badly Six felt because one of the birds had been crushed.

"What difference does it make?" Stupid's wife laughed. "Scald it, pluck out its feathers, and we'll save four ounces of beef for our dumplings! A cold night like this, I thought you were out on regular business, not playing around chasing pigeons. Hah! Come up on the platform bed, quick. Get under my covers and warm up."

Opening her bedding, she crawled out naked, and crept into the quilts with Stupid.

Six left at daybreak. He met the pigeons' owner, Yang Mao, at the compound gate.

Not very tall, smartly dressed, Yang had a small pointed head topped by a little felt skull-cap. But even this looked too big. His head kept nodding erratically, and his tiny round eyes moved with startling rapidity.

"You're up early, brother," he hailed Six.

"You too," said Six dejectedly. "What's on your mind?"

"Been looking for you." Yang Mao shoved his hands into the pockets of his tunic. "We've always been good friends. Give me back my pigeons. The female will be laying eggs this year. I'll give the first brood to you. I'm a man of my word."

Six did not reply.

"Or else — " Yang Mao came a step nearer, " — I trained a good rabbit hawk not long ago. The hunting season's just starting. I can give him to you."

Six remained silent.

"If it's money you want — naturally that could never come between us..." Yang Mao's lips trembled. He cocked his head to one side. "You can have that too. First give me my pigeons. I'll gradually raise some money."

"Let's talk about it some other time." Six began to walk away. "I'm going home to eat."

"What!" Yang's eyes glittered with agitation. "You're usually good to your friends. How can you treat me so badly? Give those pigeons back! Otherwise, you're a usurper!"

Six halted and turned. "What do you mean — usurper?"

"You've usurped my birds, and you usurped a girl who's somebody else's wife!"

"Did you see me do it?"

"Others have — with their own eyes! If they won't speak up, I'll expose you!"

The gate of Stupid Li's compound creaked and Man'er appeared. "Go ahead and expose," she said coolly. She evidently had just combed her hair and made up her face; her rouge was spread somewhat unevenly. Hands behind her back, she leaned against the gate post and faced Yang Mao.

"I'd like to see what you can expose. What proof have you got? Have you caught the man, or the woman? Let's hear it! Who told you to come here so early in the morning and spit turds all over the place? Now get out of here before I slap your face!"

Yang Mao formerly was a needle and thread pedlar. Every winter, he used to go to Baoding, buy up various items that women needed in the home around New Year's time, and sell them in the mountain villages on the other side of the railway. There were some strange stories about his wanderings through the mountains, all of them of a romantic nature. Though he worked at the trade for many years, Yang Mao was never able to earn much money. Now, the only thing he had left of that period was a small earthenware teapot with a blue glaze.

A few days before, a man had arrived from the provincial government, from all appearances a high-ranking *ganbu*. (*Any person with some authority in a governmental, semi-governmental, or military organization, from a petty functionary to a high official. "Ganbu" is frequently mistranslated as "cadre" — meaning a group of instructors.*) According to custom, such a person usually would be put up in the home of a local *ganbu*, or with one of the village activists. But he asked to be quartered with an ordinary family, saying he would also like to meet some of their backward elements. The village *ganbu* wanted to give the matter more thought. Could he be on some sort of special mission? But the vice-chairman of the village, who was always getting queer ideas, simply breezed right along. He led the comrade to the house of Yang Mao.

Yang Mao was a bachelor. He welcomed the guest and gave him a place on the platform bed — although on the least warmly heated section. The visitor's health was poor, so the village authorities also set up a small coal stove for him.

"Comrade Yang," said the provincial official, "there's nothing on the fire. I wonder if I you could borrow an iron kettle for me to boil some water in?"

"No need to borrow. I've a kettle here." Yang reached down to a shelf under the table, brought out his blue teapot, filled it with water, and placed it on the stove.

"Can you boil water in that crockery pot?"

"That's the beauty of this pot. It has an earthenware base and a porcelain glaze. It comes to a boil quickly and never leaks."

But the stove lid immediately became moist and began to hiss. At first the comrade from the province thought the outside of the teapot had got wet when it was being filled. He raised the teapot and looked. The bottom had several cracks which had widened with the heat. Not only wouldn't he have any water to drink — there was a danger that the fire would be extinguished.

"That pot's no use, Comrade Yang," he said. "It leaks."

"It does not!" cried Yang, his little eyes glaring. "If I say it doesn't leak, it doesn't leak!"

"But it's obviously leaking."

"Living here with me isn't suitable. Move to some else's house," Yang Mao said brusquely.

His guest was bewildered. He showed Yang — the water was leaking from the cracked base. Big drops were going hiss, hiss, hiss as they hit the hot stove.

Yang Mao wouldn't even turn his head.

The *ganbu* had no choice but to roll up his bedding and seek the vice-chairman. He told him what had happened. The vice-chairman laughed.

"You wanted to see something of the backward side of this village, comrade. Perhaps we can consider Yang Mao a typical example. I can tell you quite a bit about his background, if you're interested. When I was young, he and I formed a small trading partnership. As you can imagine, it was very hard to get along with him. He was quarrelsome and stubborn. He'd never admit an error. The least little thing and he'd ignore you, as if you didn't exist. But he knew every path in the Western Hills. So I controlled my temper and played along with him.

"He'd stay up in the hills until he went broke. Then he'd come home. It happened every year. He'd go broke not because he was lazy, or dissolute. It was always due to his peculiar emotional make-up. As soon as he entered the hills, he'd immediately start hunting for a beautiful woman. As to who was beautiful and who was ugly — that was entirely a question of his personal taste. That fellow, anything that belonged to him was good, nobody could criticize it. If he liked it, even a scrawny chick was a gorgeous phoenix.

"Every year, he was sure to meet one beauty. As soon as he discovered her, he'd head straight for her village and hawk his wares outside her door, regardless of wind or rain, and never go any place else. But in one little hamlet, after all how much could you sell? You'd soon eat up your capital.

"One winter he found another beautiful woman. She lived way up in the hills. I got a look at her from behind once, and it's true she wasn't bad looking. Dressed in clean blue homespun, nicely combed glossy back hair with a bun in the back — Yang Mao was enchanted. By the end of the lunar year I was ready to head for home, but he kept going to her village and sitting outside her door all day. When he got hungry he'd eat dry rations and take a sip of cold water from his teapot. Though he twirled his little hawker's drum till the skin on both sides was broken, the woman wouldn't come out any more.

"He couldn't stand it. One day he walked into her courtyard — and ran into her husband, who had just come home from the mountains. The man chased him out with a carrying pole and kicked his merchandise box and teapot down the slope. Yang Mao came rolling down next, his head split and bleeding. He was so dizzy he passed out. I rushed over to him and brought him round and put his things in order. There wasn't much damage to the merchandise, but the small teapot was cracked. I said: 'Yang Mao, your teapot's broken.' He was very annoyed. 'It's not broken,' he said. 'At most, it's got a tiny crack in it.' I said: 'That's right, a tiny crack — like that gash you've got in your skull!'

"That's the sort of fellow Yang Mao is, comrade. He still thinks of that woman to this very day. He says she loves him; it's only her husband who's standing in the way!...Don't be offended. I'll find you a place to stay. We've got another backward family in this village..."

Never in his life had Yang Mao seen such a beautiful girl. He was simply overwhelmed by Man'er's pink and white splendor. He hopped forward like a sparrow in the winter snow, his trunk rigid, his small pointed cranium aimed straight ahead. His eyes devoured Man'er, every inch of her, and he docilely accepted her upbraiding like a repentant sinner accepting a reprimand from Heaven.

But then the sound that was like music to his ears suddenly terminated. Man'er had gone in and slammed the door.

The blacksmith's work on Old Li's cart formally commenced. The smith's forge was set up in the yard of the newly bought compound. Early in the morning, the sky cleared, and Six's pigeons took off in soaring flight.

Old Li put the finishing touches to his carpentry. He was waiting now only for the metal fittings to be made and put on, and he would paint the cart. Old Fu had just lit the forge. Thick smoke billowed upwards, broke, and spread over the compound. Nine operated the bellows piston. Fu was told to practice swinging the big hammer.

Old Li brought out all the pieces of scrap metal he had been accumulating over the past few years, plus some iron he had recently bought, and tossed them down beside the forge.

Nine was lightly clad today. Her tunic was of unpadded blue cotton cloth. She wore a towel on her head, knotted in front covering her hair. Her face shining with pleasant anticipation, she worked the bellows piston easily and steadily.

Old Fu forged the first billet. Grasping it with his pincers, he placed it on the anvil. Four hurried over with the big hammer. Old Fu tapped on the anvil with a small hammer beside the glowing metal to indicate where to strike. But Four's aim was not good. Sometimes he hit against the anvil; sometimes he struck the small hammer. Nine left the bellows to show him how. With her friendly help, Four improved rapidly.

Old Li was doing carpentry work on the side but his main attention was on the forge. He berated Four continuously, calling him stupid, saying he was useless. During a rest break, the blacksmith went up to Old Li.

"You've become bad-tempered, relative," he said. "You can't treat children like that. It doesn't help them work better; it only makes them worse. When you keep picking on him, he doesn't know what to do with his hands and feet."

"How can you talk that way? Didn't you say I'm not strict enough with my boys? My whole heart is in that cart. The sooner it's finished, the sooner it'll start earning money. Relative, let's use our very best skill on this job!"

Building a friendship is as hard as raising a flowering shrub. A careless slip can make a shrub wither. As the two old men worked together on the cart, they gradually realized that it wasn't the same as in the old days. In the past when they were working together on a job, there was a close brotherly tie between them. Now, Fu felt that Old Li wasn't co-operating — he was supervising. Li was driving him hard. The carpenter showed dissatisfaction even when Old Fu stopped for a smoke. What depressed Old Fu most was that although he had returned at last after a long journey, Old Li didn't once mention the matter of Nine and Six. It was as if the carpenter had never proposed the match.

During the final few days of the metal work on the cart, Old Li gave no help at all. He paraded around in his new fleece-lined robe, issuing orders. Six was also dressed up like a guest. Sometimes he came to the courtyard and looked around, then vanished.

Old Fu wasn't feeling too well. Although the weather was quite cold, he wore only a tattered shirt, and he was working very hard. Every day, people came to watch. They were all old friends and acquaintances of the blacksmith. They used to admire the combined skills of the two artisans. Now, they could see that there was a separation between Old Fu's art and Old Li's business. People no longer paid any attention to Old Li's carpentry. They were merely curious whether his new enterprise would prosper.

The two old friends plainly had developed two different standpoints. Old Li was entirely aware of this, and Old Fu quickly became aware of it too. That was the root of the tragedy. It seemed to Old Fu that Old Li had now openly adopted the "bossy" attitude they had both despised and ridiculed for so many years, and was directing it against him. Of course, this wasn't the fault of the new society, it was a hang-over from the old.

As the blacksmith's work was drawing to a close, one day when they were eating together, Old Li smiled and said: "I've been living more and more frugally, relative. You mustn't laugh at me. I'm saving to build some rooms for Six and his brothers. I'm sure you don't care about money."

Assuming he was going to talk about Nine and Six's marriage, Old Fu raised his head and listened. To his surprise, Li's next remark was: "Why not just treat these days as if you were earning your keep in a famine period in your own village?"

This last sentence angered the blacksmith. He furiously pushed his bowl away and stood up. "Relative," he said, "I didn't come to you as a famine refugee!"

Old Fu called his daughter to bring a bucket of water. He extinguished the fire, loaded his equipment on his barrow and pushed it to the street. Several people tried to pacify him, but the blacksmith flatly refused to go back.

None of the villagers knew the real reason for the split between the two old friends. Neither Four nor Nine, both young and inexperienced, had ever suffered so painful a blow. Old Fu was miserable. He took Four aside and asked:

"Tell me, child. Whose fault do you think it is?"

"It happened at just the right time. Now you can help us solve a problem."

"What problem? Are you laughing at us two old men, child?"

"We young people want to organize a well-drilling brigade. This winter we want to sink pipes into all the old wells. We've already borrowed a borer, and we've got a lot of tools that need repair. We've been wanting to ask you to help, but we were afraid my pa wouldn't agree. Now that you've quarrelled with him, you can work with us."

"Have you iron and steel?"

"We'll each contribute some. There'll be enough. We'll take your equipment to the Youth League compound."

When the blacksmith arrived, the youngsters welcomed him ecstatically.

"You don't know how we need you, uncle! You must never leave. We've got it all arranged with the village authorities. You can have the east wing. We'll repair it nicely and paper the windows for you. You can live here as long as you like. In the evenings we'll bring brushwood and heat your platform bed."

Alone in his courtyard, Old Li sat on a log thinking dully. When Old Fu had walked out on him, he had said to himself: "That kind of friendship is just as well ended. He can't hurt me. I can get someone else to finish his work. He's not the only blacksmith under the sun." Li had picked up his axe and, with the hammer end, had angrily driven big nails into the cart's rear boards.

But gradually the carpenter cooled down. The hammering of the nails rang hollowly in the empty courtyard. Without the friendly accompaniment of the blacksmith's clanging hammer, Li suddenly found himself unable to work. He flung his axe aside and sat down.

His friendship with Old Fu had been years in the building. It had stood the test of many an adversity. Old Li rubbed his left foot. Once, when he and Old Fu were working on a job in another village, Li was unhappy and his axe had slipped, putting a nasty gash in his foot. He was far from home, with no relatives to help him, and had little money. In the several months needed to recuperate, it was Old Fu who got the doctor, paid for the medicines, carried Li on his back to the latrine, fetched him water and brought him food. Of course, Old Li had reciprocated. The same summer, Old Fu was scalded by molten metal. Old Li had looked after him just as faithfully.

The carpenter felt quite badly. "Why, after all, should Old Fu break off our friendship so abruptly? Is he jealous because I'm doing so well?" But Old Li knew the blacksmith wasn't that sort of person. "Have I changed? Do I scorn the poor and love the rich? Have I treated my old friend shabbily?" The carpenter thought back on his words and behavior since Old Fu's return, and his misery grew weighted with shame.

As Old Li sat brooding, Six came in. The carpenter looked at his son, the boy's body, his face. He could see there was nothing but dissolute failure. "I've thought only of constructing a cart and building rooms these past two years, all for him," Li said to himself. "Offending my friend was because of him too. The boy lives for pleasure. He never gives a thought to his father's feelings!"

"Is the food ready yet, pa?" Six asked lazily, standing beside the window in the sunlight.

"Ready, Just waiting for you!" Old Li jumped up, grabbed his axe and charged.

Six had a quick eye. He turned and ran. Shortly before, he had quarrelled again with Yang Mao on the street. Yang had learned that the male pigeon was dead, and was determined to go to Old Li and protest. Now, Six bumped into him at the compound gate. Clasping hands together in a respectful greeting, Six pleaded:

"Let's not fight over that pigeon, Brother Mao. Go in and soothe my father, quick! He wants to kill me!"

Yang Mao could never resist soft words. He at once undertook the mission and hurried inside. Spreading his arms, he halted Old Li at the gate.

"For my sake, uncle, let's go back inside. We can talk this over calmly."

He shunted Old Li into the courtyard, brought him a stool, handed him a cigarette. Squatting down beside him, Yang Mao urged:

"Get the cart finished soon. Don't miss the winter season. That's when the money is made! Look at Wang the Seventh. One trip to Dingzhou earns him scores of yuan. In three trips, even after deducting the cost of his meals and the horse's feed, he took in enough to build a big brick house,. There's a house like that for sale in the western part of the village, Uncle Li. The price is reasonable. Are you interested?"

"No," said the carpenter. "My heart is cold."

"All elderly people are the same," said Yang. "They hate to see their youngsters going wrong. When my pa was alive, you two were good friends. You know how strict he was with me, how much trouble he took. Of course, I can't say I ever earned the old gentleman much glory. But, in all fairness, I never made him lose face. I'm an honest fellow who's been around a lot. I'm always fighting injustice, and I'll do anything for a friend. Money is no object. It's true I haven't got anywhere till now, but that's because I was fated to hardship, not that I'm incapable. Brother Six isn't a bad sort, it seems to me. He's intelligent and sensible. A bit wild, perhaps, but all young fellows go through that period. You get the cart finished and give it to him. Once he has a legitimate job to do, he'll settle down. Don't you agree?"

Old Li's anger gradually abated as Yang Mao led him back to his original line of thinking. About that time, Four returned. Without a word, he went to feed the horse. He had something in his hand, partly concealed by his padded robe. He did his best to keep it out of his father's sight as he neared the door.

"What have you got there?" Old Li demanded.

"An old spade head," Four halted and showed it to the carpenter.

"Where did you get it? I've been looking all over for scrap. Why didn't you tell me?" Old Li asked angrily.

"I picked it up that year we dismantled the Japanese gun tower. It wasn't any use then, so I put it aside. Now, our superiors are calling on us to dig wells, and I'm thinking of repairing it."

The old man swore. "The whole damned family is turning against me!" He stood up. "Put that back where you found it. Your superiors call on you to dig wells; I call on you to build that cart! No one's going to do it for me. You hurry and cook some food; after you're full, you're going to help me drive nails!"

Again, Yang Mao hastened to intervene. Four had no choice but to make the meal. Later, he would find some way to get that old spade head out of the house.

Drawing Six into study and work, as Nine had proposed, was proving extremely difficult. He rarely would join in meetings or other activities. When cadres tried to get him to take part, he would insist that at the moment production was of primary importance. Making a great show of diligence, he would take a basket and trot off into the hills on the pretext of gathering brushwood.

The village authorities discussed the matter. Some thought they ought to try and reform Man'er first. Approaching Man'er was easy enough. Although the young men wouldn't go near — either because they were timid, or afraid of becoming suspicious — the girls certainly would talk with her.

Man'er would warmly greet any young woman who called on her. If she brought a baby, Man'er would feed it goodies, hold it in her arms and smother it with kisses. Even the shiest child became happy, snuggled against Man'er's bosom. And Man'er's lovely young visage glowing with warmth would add color to the baby's face. Laughing, Man'er would talk vivaciously, as if her lips were oiled. Her caller would warm to her in spite of herself, and when she criticized Man'er, her tone would automatically soften.

"A clever girl like you ought to study, Man'er," the woman might urge. "I'll call for you tonight, and we'll attend class in the night school together."

"Fine," Man'er would retort smilingly. "I've always wanted a chance to study. But you needn't call for me, sister. The streets are dark and you're carrying a baby. What if you should fall? I'll go myself. I know my way around this village perfectly."

"You'll be sure to go, then?"

"Definitely." Man'er would see her guest to the door and smile and wave to the baby. But after her visitor had turned the corner, Man'er's face would darken and she would think a moment. Then she would enter the house, change her clothes and go to her mother in the county town.

If any political campaign was going on in the village and frequent meetings were being held, Man'er wouldn't show her face for days. Once in a while she would put in an appearance at the night school. She always sat far from the lamp, in a dark corner of the room. After the lesson started and everyone was settling down, she would pretend to listen. But when the others grew absorbed, she would quietly slip away.

Whether living with her mother or with her sister, Man'er loved to go walking outside the village, alone. She was a night bird, revelling in the darkness. On hot summer evenings she flitted about like a fire-fly, engaging in wild flights of fancy. Intoxicated with nature, she would wander over the brambly dunes far from the village walls. She was quite fearless at night. Marauding foxes would run past her, insects would knock against her face or crawl over her body, but she would sit happily on a dark sand dune, letting the cool breezes caress her while the sun-baked sand warmed her beneath. In winter, the savage winds excited her. Whirling snowflakes, landing on her face, melted as if they had fallen on a slab of molten metal.

Every night she came home very late, when all was still. With skilful familiarity, she would round the wall, climb over the fence, and slip into bed so softly that no one was aware of her return. She would rise early the next morning and light the stove and cook breakfast, full of energy. There seemed no limit to her young vigor. Wasting her precious youth, she teetered constantly on the edge of a precipice.

Man'er was a girl of many talents. Everyone knew that if planted in suitable soil, she would bear rich fruit. No matter how intricate the pattern of a length of material, or how new the fashion of a pair of cloth shoes, she needed only a glance to be able to duplicate them, quickly and well. She had a sharp intellect. It penetrated immediately anything pointed out to her, like a finger poking through thin spring ice or a flimsy paper window.

When the whim took her, she would carry buckets to the garden to water the vegetables. She was a match for the strongest young man. In one morning she could scoop a well dry. And it was nothing for her to walk a dozen or more *li* to market with eighty catties of beans in baskets suspended from the ends of her shoulder pole. At such times, even many of the old folks in the village praised her. They hoped that some force could be found to pull her back on the right track.

That year, the new Marriage Law was proclaimed, and Man'er suddenly began to take an active part in public affairs. She voluntarily attended meetings, asked people to read the newspaper to her, grew quiet and thoughtful. The articles said that women and men were equal, that the women had already done a great deal of work and that in the future they would make an even larger and more important contribution to the nation.

But then Man'er heard some people propose an investigation of illicit relations between men and women in the village, and she stopped going to meetings and returned to her free-and-easy way of life. That was why the vice-chairman brought the provincial *ganbu* to live in the home of Stupid Li.

The same day, Man'er's mother arrived. Though over fifty, she still dressed very flashily. It was obvious she had made herself up carefully in preparation for this exploratory call.

"Man'er," she said, "your husband will be home soon. Your mother-in-law came to see me. It's almost New Year's time. You ought to go back and live there a while."

"I won't," said Man'er. "You and sister picked him without consulting me. Since you've taken over my marriage, you're the ones who should receive him when he comes back!"

"How dare you speak to me like that, you little snip! There's a lot of idle talk about the way you're running around here!"

Man'er sat on the edge of the platform bed and toyed with her shoes and socks. "Why should I pay any attention to it if it's only idle talk? Some people have nothing better to do than gossip!"

"It's giving you a bad name, pet," the mother retorted, clapping her hands together fretfully.

Man'er walked over to the mirror and combed her hair. "If I'm getting a bad name it's only because I'm following the example you two have set!"

"Who set you any examples?" her sister demanded. Man'er's quarrelling with her mother irritated her. "You're not fit to be my pupil. Just look at you. You've been making love with Six all winter and he hasn't even given you a pair of new padded trousers. And you have the nerve to criticize!"

"You go earn a pair for me then!" Having finished making up, Man'er flipped aside the door curtain and walked out.

She wandered into her sister's vegetable garden. It was near the big sand dune west of the village. Because Stupid Li and his wife were lazy and did nothing to stop it, over the years the dune had encroached into half the garden. A young peach tree was bent almost to the ground by the weight of it. Man'er dug the sand away, straightened the tree, and wrapped the trunk with straw.

She sat down on the sheltered side of the dune, out of the wind. A large rooster atop the dune crowed shrilly. A dry poplar leaf fell on her breast. Suddenly Man'er felt miserable. She covered her face and wept. At that moment she understood herself, pitied herself, hated herself. She had always been unloved, she was always travelling alone. But had she chosen the right road? Man'er began thinking back on the criticism and advice people had given her.

When her sister left to escort her mother to the edge of the village, Man'er returned home by another route. She found Stupid Li helping a government officer put a room in order. Man'er was surprised. She knew that because her sister's family was backward, dirty, and had an unsavory reputation, no *ganbu* had ever lived there before. The place they were readying, a room in the east wing, was full of rubbish. In the room next door, a little donkey was quartered.

Man'er observed that her brother-in-law appeared both respectful and uneasy in the presence of his guest. Stupid couldn't understand why, of all the people in the village, the authorities should have come to him with such a high-ranking official. As he clumsily helped with the moving, Stupid kept asking the guest for his instructions.

Judging by his dress and manner, it seemed to Man'er that the *ganbu* was out of harmony with the room being given him. His clothing showed that he was of provincial government rank, at least. Insisting on absolute cleanliness, he wielded the broom and swept out places that hadn't been touched in ages. For some reason, Man'er suddenly wanted to help him. She filled her own pretty basin with water and sprinkled the room to settle the dust.

"Who are you?" the *ganbu* asked her.

"She's my sister-in-law," said Stupid with some pride, yet slightly fearful.

"Oh, you must be Comrade Man'er, then," said the newcomer, looking at her intently. "The village authorities just told me about you."

"What did they say?" asked the girl, her head bent as she swept the floor.

"A few words can't tell a person's whole story. Living here in the same house, we'll be like one family. We'll gradually get to understand each other."

The *ganbu* placed his luggage on the platform bed. Man'er brought some kindling, scraped the top of the stove, scrubbed the pot, and filled it with water.

"This room has been empty for a long time," she said. "It's cold. I'll heat the platform bed for you."

"I'll do it," said Stupid, who was standing beside her.

The girl ignored him. When the water was hot, she poured it into her basin, then went out and brought her own soap in a container. Handing it to the *ganbu*, she said:

"You can wash your face. Have you any towels?"

That evening, the *ganbu* went out to a meeting. It was quite late by the time he returned. On the platform bed now stood a short-legged table that had been rubbed very clean. There was a thermos flask filled with boiled water on the table, and a brightly polished kerosene lamp, its flame turned low. He touched the platform. It was warm, heated by flues underneath.

The door of the north wing squeaked. Soon Man'er, covering her bosom, entered.

"Comrade, pour me a drink of water."

"It's late. Why aren't you asleep?" The *ganbu* handed her a filled bowl.

Man'er smiled. "I wanted to ask you. What's your job? Do you look after production?"

"I've come to learn about the people here."

"That's rich," Man'er laughed. "Government production administrators come to our village all the time. They only examine our millet and wheat. What do you want to see?"

The *ganbu* smiled but didn't answer. He looked at the young woman. Although it was late and they were alone together under circumstances that might easily be misunderstood, her expression was quite innocent. There wasn't even a hint of anything improper in her manner.

It's not easy to know a person, the *ganbu* thought. I can't figure her out.

"Finish the water and go to bed," he said. "Your sister must be waiting for you."

"She blew out the lamp and went to sleep long ago," said Man'er. "I'm tired and your platform bed is warm. Let me sit a while."

The provincial officer picked up a newspaper and began to read.

Was the girl as loose and shameless as the villagers said? Was this a device to get on the good side of him so that he wouldn't criticize her? Or was she just a naive, curious girl trying to be helpful?

"If you want to learn about people here," said Man'er, bowl in hand, "why don't you go to some activist's or model worker's home instead of coming to a rowdy place like this?"

"Rowdy?"

"Living here, you're like a snare set beside a pile of grain. The birds all give us a wide berth. It's not usually so quiet here. Usually, my sister's room is jammed every night."

"In that case, I'm interfering with your social life. I'll move tomorrow."

"That's up to you. I'm not Yang Mao. I'm not driving you away. What I mean is learning about people isn't like looking at a picture. You can't do it just sitting here, or in a short time either. Some people know how to put on an act. To your face they'll say all sorts of things. Others won't say a word, they'll just wait and see what kind of subjective judgment you'll make."

At first though her voice trembled she restrained her tears. Finally, she broke into sobs. Tears ran down her face on to her tunic.

Startled, the provincial officer put his newspaper aside. But Man'er said no more. She removed her head kerchief and wiped her eyes with it. Gravely, she put down the bowl, turned and left.

Stupid didn't feed the little donkey all night. It brayed and kicked in the room next door and gnawed its trough. Rats, either because the room was warm or because it contained a newcomer, grew lively. They scampered squeaking over the table, the platform bed and the window sills.

For a long time the provincial official was unable to fall asleep. He awoke very early the next morning. Man'er came running in, dressed in a red woollen jersey. Her collar was open and her sleeves pushed up. Her face and neck were wet. Evidently, she had just been washing. Reaching for something on the end of the platform bed, she leaned over the provincial officer. Her breasts brushed against his face. He could smell her warm fragrance. She found the soap container which she had loaned him the night before and hurried with it from the room.

The blacksmith's forge was set up in a new location.

"This time, I'm going to take charge," Nine told the young people. "We're the Well Diggers Youth Brigade!"

"We're with you," the youngsters said. "We'll take turns swinging the big hammer and pulling the piston bellows. Old uncle won't have to do a thing except stand on the side and supervise."

The metal they contributed was broken old scraps buried over the years beneath the earth or lying in various corners. Now these pieces would be melted down and forged together. They would be made into a sharp steel bit that could bore into the ground and bring up the spring waters. To the youngsters it was as if the mounting enthusiasm of each of them was being forged into a single powerful force for building up the nation.

Nine's face reflected the red flames of the forge. The small hammer in her hand beat out a clanging tatoo on the anvil. The sound had a competent ring to it, for she was no longer a beginner at this heavy work. When still a child she had helped her father make horseshoes and bridle bits for the mounts of innumerable cavalrymen. Now the sharp raps of the hammer ringing in her ears recalled memories of her childhood. During those years of warfare, echoing in the hoofbeats of the battle chargers on the paths that criss-crossed the plain was the beat of a heart, pure as gold, of a little girl making her first contribution to her country!

She could remember an even earlier period. Today's work could serve as a memorial to her mother, who had been poor all her life and died middle-aged. When Nine was born, her mother had placed her on a small platform bed near the forge. Day and night, Nine had heard the sounds of the blacksmith shop. Her mother had plied the piston bellows while singing the lullabies that put her to sleep. Even when Nine was still in the womb, her mother had engaged in this heavy work.

Now, in the bitterly cold morning, warm perspiration soaked through Nine's thin clothing. It was the first time she had ever worked with her own companions according to a plan they had all discussed. The young people virtually fought for the jobs, snatched at them, yet were concerned about and assisted one another. This, to Nine, was particularly new and exciting. It seemed to her that her father was stimulated too. In his long years of hardship and wandering from place to place, he had never dreamed that a blacksmith shop could present such a scene!

The first snow of the year had already fallen upon the plain when the young people began laboring out in the open. At noon, the snow glittering on the nearby sand dunes gradually melted. Most of the fields had been given their autumn ploughing, and the soft turned earth was moist. But the weather was already quite cold. The soil would freeze again in the mornings and in the evenings.

They set up high treadle wheels. Rising one after another on the vast plain, the tall structures were a new element, arousing longings and stirring the imagination. They evoked images of fluttering banners, of windmills in foreign stories, of water towers at railway stations, of the towers above mine shafts, of the wooden scaffolding for the large buildings being erected in the cities. As the young people laborer diligently to tap water sources, their songs whirled through the air like the treadle wheels on high.

Four, Kitchen Stove and Nine were on the same team. They brought their own dry rations and millet, and cooked them together at noon beside the well shaft, burning for fuel the fallen branches and dry reeds they cut in the overgrown cemetery.

"We're on a plain here," Four said to Nine, "and the village has sand dunes on three sides. The ones to the west have come down from the mountains. Their flow does more damage than the river's floods. When the spring winds blow, the sky is covered all day with flying yellow sand. It leaps over walls and fences, it rolls into the fields and vegetable gardens. It smothers the young garlic and scallion sprouts, fills the furrows of the wheat fields and buries young trees.

"After the big spring winds we have to sweep the sand from the fields. We have to get down on the ground and blow it from the pale tender sprouts bent beneath its weight, and let them see the sun again. The big winds blow so much sand into the streets you feel like you're walking on the beach by the river, it's that deep. It gets under the doors and breaks the paper window-panes. The women sweep a couple of dustpans full from their houses every day. The only way to stop the sand is to do what the government is calling on us to do — dig wells and plant trees."

"My father and I lived in the mountains," said Nine, "but we also had drought year after year. As long as I can remember, hot sandy winds blew in from the northwest every spring and beat for all they were worth against our little house. There used to be a stream in front of our door. In winter we could hear the water gurgling under the ice. But when spring came, it was gone. We had to live on chaff and leaves."

They talked and dreamed about the future. If, starting with their generation, nature could be transformed, if they could change the harsh road people had been travelling for so long, if they could bring in bumper harvests, raise forests of trees, make the springs gush, criss-cross the land with irrigation canals, what a happy world it would be!

On the sand dune to the south a tableau formed that was very much out of keeping with what they were discussing. Six, a hunting falcon on his right arm, led the way up the dune. Behind came Stupid Li and his wife, like a pair of attendants, each carrying a dead rabbit.

They stood behind Six, one to his left,one to his right, and gazed and pointed at something in the distance. And behind the dune, like a faint sprig of peach blossom, appeared Man'er's lustrous head.

"Your kid brother gets more complicated by the day, Four," said Kitchen Stove. "He's playing with falcons now."

"I can't make head or tail of those people," said Four. "Six and Yang Mao had a big fight over pigeons. The hatred between them was something enormous. But then Wang the Seventh hauled the three of them into town for a meal. The two became good friends again, and Yang Mao loaned Six his falcon."

"What do you mean the three of them?" queried Kitchen Stove.

"Man'er went too," said Four. "She's their focal point, their organizational center, the guide of all their actions. They can't do a thing without her. I've also heard that Yang Mao has become the best customer of Stupid Li's dumpling shop. He goes there every night and fills up. Stupid Li's wife told him: You only eat well and dress well. Your new life still can't be considered complete. I'm going to introduce you to a nice girl, but you have to treat me to a meal first... So Yang Mao invited her to a restaurant in town."

"Why not call him over and ask him to help us bore this well?" Kitchen Stove urged

While Four hesitated, Six and his entire retinue left the sand dune and disappeared in the opposite direction.

People usually comment upon passing incidents only casually. They don't always notice what a depressing effect they may have on those concerned. Nine sat gazing abstracted at the bare sand dune. She still was thinking of her childhood at home. After her mother died, Nine had frequently sat alone by her small window. Outside was a date tree where little birds gathered to enjoy the sun and avoid the wind. There they played, obviously very affectionate. Several, perching on a branch together, chirruped with perhaps the greatest fondness of all. Soon, one of them flew to another branch. Then, a sudden gust of wind, and all flew their separate ways.

In front of Nine's door, there had also been a tiny cove of reeds. When the river was low, little fish used to gather there and frolic around the reeds. But in summer, when the river rose, each went off on his own, no one knew where.

Such memories are painful, enervating. Nine stood up and said: "We've had plenty to eat and enough to drink. Let's get to work. I'll do a spell on the treadle wheel."

"Be careful you don't fall into the well shaft," laughed Kitchen Stove. "Can you people guess what I'm thinking? I'm thinking it's better not to eat Six's dumplings. There's nothing but rabbit meat in them!"

Nine climbed into the treadle wheel. She paced energetically, and the wheel rotated. Four looked up at her from the bottom of the shaft. He felt she made a moving and remarkable picture, framed in the rim of the well.

Nine worked with increasing skill and ease. The sun before her moved slowly toward the west. She could see a long distance. She could see the two tall flagpoles before the temple by the south gate of the county town, peasants carrying fertilizer to the fields, gathering fuel, pasturing cattle and sheep, tending vegetable gardens. She could see Six and Man'er chasing something in the open. She could hear the shouts of Stupid Li and his wife.

Four and Kitchen Stove, working below Nine, were discussing this.

"You're a good theorist, Four," Kitchen Stove yelled down from the rim of the shaft. "Explain this to me: Why is it that while we're laboring here, getting tired and cold, your brother is out there playing around, with a girl to keep him company? Is our road correct, or is theirs?"

"That's a very important point you raise. It's a question of how to look at life," the voice of Four replied hollowly from the bottom of the well. "Do you envy the way they're living?"

"Sometimes they make me sick. But sometimes I'm a little envious too."

"The way they look at things, they're sure they're right. But I don't envy them in the least. Sometimes they must feel ashamed of the way they live. Otherwise, when they saw us why did they sneak away?"

"And there's another old question: Why hasn't Six ever been able to reform?"

"I've been thinking about that myself these past couple of days. If we rely only on the strength of us few, it isn't going to be easy to get results. How does a fellow become politically conscious? Study is important, a person's experience is important. But more important is the influence of society. I think we can compare Six's mind with this parched land we're in the process of changing. If we do our work well, we can tap water on it, make it able to bear crops, even bumper crops. But all around are dust-laden winds and shifting sands that can close it off, bury it, turn it into an eternal desert where not an inch of grass will grow. We've got to strengthen the positive influences in our society. That means increasing the number of irrigated fields, cutting down the dry patches, tapping more and more sources of water until we've wiped out the sand storms."

It can be done, Nine said to herself on the treadle wheel. As she continued pacing, the scoops brought up earth and sand from the shaft bottom. She looked down. Fresh clean water had begun to seep through.

But what about love? It was not the same as the companionship of childhood, she thought gravely. Only a love that had a common revolutionary goal, a love formed in the course of long hard work together, could endure the many trials of life, could be truly firm and everlasting. Of course love could also be born in the midst of childish laughter, like a flower blooming on the unruffled surface of a placid lake. But it never could be compared with the flower growing high atop a mountain cliff — digging deep tenacious roots into the soil, able to withstand drought and wind and rain.

The provincial *ganbu* naturally hadn't come to the village for the sole purpose of learning about the local residents. But he had developed a warmth during his years of work that made him want to help people. He hoped that with his aid Man'er would change. He knew that it was only through study and effort on her part that she could change. And it would be very difficult, for he realized that he didn't really understand her yet.

That evening when Man'er returned victorious from her hunt, the *ganbu* was standing in the courtyard. Stupid Li's family lived in a broken-down compound. In the northwest corner of the crumpling compound wall, beside an old storage cellar for cabbages, was a half-dead elm tree. Extremely ugly, it was withered on top, and its trunk was split and warped. A big branch which should have been chopped up for firewood long ago hung over into a neighbor's courtyard, where it served as a roost for the neighbor's hens. Several of the birds had already flown up on it preparing to retire for the night.

When Man'er came home, she bore no traces of her wild running, her exultation, her weariness, in the fields. She returned after her sister and brother-in-law. Each bearing a dead rabbit, they had been covered with dust, and bone tired. But Man'er seemed to have made some preparations before entering the gate. Neat and clean, her hair smoothly combed, she strolled past the provincial *ganbu* with her usual easy step.

"Doing anything after dinner?" he asked.

"Not a thing," Man'er replied with a smile. "What's up?"

"The Youth Leaguers are having a study class tonight. Why don't you go and listen?"

"Will they let me?" Man'er asked with a sly laugh. "A backward character like me!"

"Of course. First cook dinner. Afterwards, we'll go together."

Man'er nodded. She made no reply, but the *ganbu* could see from her face as she turned away how displeased she was. She carried in an armful of brushwood and sat down before the stove. As she lit the fire, she kept shooting glances at him out of the corner of her eye. The *ganbu* remained standing by the door.

"Aren't you going to eat, comrade?" Man'er asked.

"Put some more rice in the pot," the *ganbu* smiled. "I'll have a meal with your family."

"Our food's no good," said Man'er. "You won't be able to eat it."

"Good or bad, I'll pay for my share," the *ganbu* laughed. He stood in the courtyard until Man'er finished cooking.

Man'er dawdled. she spent long enough to have cooked two meals. Several times she thought of running away from the house. But her intelligence told her the provincial *ganbu* intended to prevent her from doing that very thing — that was why he was watching her. And she knew his intentions were good. Assuming a tranquil air, she sat down and had dinner with him.

Her brother-in-law ate his meal in the next room. Her sister, sensing that something had come up between Man'er and the *ganbu*, stayed out of the way and didn't speak.

It was already dark by the time dinner was over. Man'er switched from the defensive to the offensive. Putting down her bowl, she said: "Let's go, comrade."

When they left the compound gate, Man'er ran on ahead, a small flashlight in her hand.

"You've got one of those gadgets," said the *ganbu*. "That's fine."

"I'll show you the path," she said. "We'll go round the outside of the village. It's shorter that way."

From the small lane she turned north and proceeded to the outskirts. Since she walked quickly and kept darting the flashlight, which wasn't very bright, in every direction, the *ganbu*, who was following behind, couldn't see a thing. He was only conscious that the path was extremely bumpy.

Man'er flew down from a small sand dune, then turned east, hugging the old village wall. This stretch was all soft sand, and was pitted with holes from uprooted trees. Stumbling and staggering on the uneven ground, the *ganbu* had to go slowly, depriving himself of her leadership and wildly darting flashlight.

"Where are you taking me?" the *ganbu* asked, half in jest. "This isn't the right path."

"What is the right path?" Man'er countered. "As long as it gets you there a little faster, it's good. Be careful. There's a well here. Don't fall in whatever you do."

Cautiously feeling the windlass, he skirted around the well. Beyond was a sharp incline, which Man'er leaped down. The provincial *ganbu* nearly skidded to the bottom.

"Watch out. Fence." Man'er edged between some clumps of brambles. The brambles caught on the *ganbu*'s clothing.

"Take this." Man'er turned and handed him the flashlight. She continued to walk ahead. Along a rubble-strewn path, she led him to the rear gate of a large temple compound. The *ganbu* had visited here before. As they walked through the main temple building, he played his flashlight on the idols lining the aisle. Grotesquely askew, they were missing arms or legs. Some had lost their eyes. Man'er nonchalantly slowed her pace.

"Ever go to any of our spring temple fairs, comrade?" she asked. "They were very exciting. When the wheat was half as high as a man, old ladies used to come from all over to pray, bringing their daughters with them. The village boys would lure the girls to the wheat fields outside the village. If you took a walk through there at night, you'd flush them like birds. They rose up out of the wheat, pair after pair, and flew away. It was very funny."

"What was so funny about it?" the *ganbu* demanded.

"I've only heard people talk," said Man'er. "I was never there when all the fun was on. During the War of Resistance against the Japanese, the guerillas in this village were very brave. They held out in the third temple building. Some of them sat on the idols' heads to keep watch for the enemy sweeping in this direction and fight them off. The temple nuns carried ammunition for the guerillas. Now all the nuns have gone back to ordinary life. The youngest and most beautiful married the son of the village vice-chairman.

"Those war stories are fine," said the *ganbu*.

Man'er halted. "Let's not go to the meeting, then. Let's go home, and I'll tell you stories all night".

The provincial *ganbu* shook his head.

"They won't attack me at the meeting?" she asked in a small voice as they emerged from the main building.

"Certainly not," the *ganbu* said. "Whatever are you thinking?"

"A nun hung herself here." Man'er pointed to a large tree in front of the temple. "Because they wouldn't let her marry the one she loved. I saw her when she was alive. She knew how to play the *sheng* pipes. She was very good-looking."

The *ganbu* didn't say anything. A wind scraped the tree-tops and the roofs.

"I'm afraid." Man'er whirled and virtually threw herself on his chest. Her voice trembled. He could hear her teeth chattering. Supporting her, he switched on the flashlight. Her face was deathly pale, her eyeballs turned up. She was muttering something he couldn't understand, and tears rolled from her eyes.

"What's the matter?" he exclaimed in agitation.

"I saw her! I saw her!" Man'er shouted.

Hysteria, the *ganbu* said to himself. I'd never have thought she was the type.

The first one Man'er's cries brought running in from the street was Six. He had just sent Yang Mao a rabbit and was on his way home. Only when Six entered did it occur to the *ganbu* that he was in quite a compromising situation. A dark night, a deserted spot, and alone with a girl having hysterics. He explained to Six how he and Man'er had happened to come here.

"Save me! Carry me home on your back!" Man'er groaned when she heard Six's voice.

"A good idea," said the *ganbu*. "Lend a hand and carry her. Do you know where she lives?"

"Yes," said Six. He squatted down and pulled Man'er's arms over his shoulders. Man'er was still crying, her tears falling on his neck. When he reached the street, she grew quiet. Pursing her lips, she blew a silent puff on the back of his neck. At first, Six had been rather worried. But when Man'er stealthily placed her mouth against his cheek and kissed him ardently, he knew there was nothing really wrong with her.

To Old Li the carpenter, Six's first day out with the new cart was a matter of the utmost importance. When the cart was finished, he used his years of knowledge to see to it that the paint dried quickly in spite of the winter cold. That evening, he prepared some wine and tidbits and invited Wang the Seventh to his home.

"Brother Seventh," he said, "I entrust my boy Six and my new cart to you. Teach him well, give him the benefit of your half a lifetime's experience as a carter. Teach him to follow the right road, and not tumble and turn over."

Wang the Seventh readily agreed. "Don't worry, brother," he said, "I won't let him lose out. We're planning to go to Stonegate on this trip. What sort of merchandise do you want us to bring back?"

"Whatever earns the biggest profit, naturally. You decide. But since it's a new cart, don't carry coal the first trip."

Wang the Seventh laughed. "It's coal that earns the biggest profit in winter. Well, I'll see when we get there. Maybe I'll load you with an assortment of mixed goods."

When they were both half drunk the carpenter said to Wang the Seventh: "I know there were some differences between us, brother, during the land reform days. But I never really considered you a rich peasant. I always thought of you as an upper-middle peasant. (*The category to which, by popular local vote, a peasant was relegated determined what share of the landlord's land and equipment he was entitled. Rich peasants had to contribute part of their own property to the general division.*)

"Of course your grandfather and your father were rich peasants, both generations. But even after you and your brothers divided up the family property, you were mainly a carter, and you didn't hire much help. To classify you as a rich peasant I thought was going a bit too far. Yet I didn't think you should be called an ordinary middle peasant — it seemed to me you were a little over that line. That was what the argument was about, at the time."

"That's all past now. What hurt me most was losing that mule of mine," said Wang the Seventh. "Later on, I sold a few things and bought him back. I've got a bad status here, I don't like meeting people from my own village. Now that I'm a carter I'm getting along alright, as you can see.

"To tell you the truth, as long as a man's got ability and ideas he can eat and drink well even if he doesn't farm. I neither save nor stint. When I'm home, I eat whatever Stupid Li's dumpling shop has to sell. When I'm on the road and stop at an inn, my food is nothing but the best. And when I set out again, I've a bottle of good grog in my tunic. Whenever I feel thirsty I've only to bend my head to take a swig."

"I admire you," said the carpenter. "Those other families all remained collapsed. You were the only one to recover fast."

The carpenter got up several times in the night to feed his horse. At the first cock's crow, he awakened Six and loaded the fodder. When the beast was being hitched, he helped with the harnessing, tightened the belly band and greased the axles. They finished breakfast before daylight, and Six drove the cart into the street. People who were up early praised the new vehicle. The carpenter walked backwards before it, smoothing out ruts with his feet and giving Six continual instructions.

Outside the village, Wang the Seventh's big cart, pulled by a smart pair, joined them and took the lead. Yang Mao, who was going to Stonegate to buy some things for the New Year holiday, rode with Wang. As they rolled out of the old stockade gate, Wang flourished his whip to rouse his pair, ran a few steps beside them, then jumped up and sat sideways on one of the shafts.

He looked back. Six, imitating him, leaped up and sat on a shaft of his own cart. The old carpenter, at the edge of the village, gazed after them. Only when Six's cart rounded a big sand dune and vanished did he return to the village.

The village mayor stopped Old Li at the crossroad and said he wished the carpenter would join the agricultural co-op. To ease his doubts, the mayor told him enthusiastically how other villages were also forming co-ops, and what they were paying to people who rented their animals and carts to the co-ops. (*These "elementary" co-ops had evolved from "mutual-aid teams" which were composed usually of neighbors who helped one another at planting and at harvest time. In the "advanced" co-ops, and subsequently the communes which followed, peasants sold their animals and farm equipment to the collectives outright. They also received a share of the harvest proceeds in accordance with the amount of labor they put in. The changes varied greatly in different parts of the countryside. It was not uncommon to have all three forms of organization existing simultaneously within the same area.*)

Old Li seemed not to hear anything the village chairman said. As he headed home, people got the impression that his manner, ordinarily so self-satisfied and full of verve, had suddenly become anxious and uneasy.

After rounding the sand dune, the carts halted abruptly. Man'er, hugging a small package, sat waiting beneath an old poplar tree. She stood up and climbed on to Six's cart.

Talking and laughing boisterously, Wang the Seventh swung his whip. Behind the two carts rose swirling columns of dust.

Every day when Nine returned home, Old Fu had dinner ready for her. He knew his daughter was doing heavy work. Just as when they were blacksmithing, he cooked up millet and served it thick. Every day, father and daughter sat on the platform bed a beside a small kerosene lamp and ate their evening meal.

He noticed that she spoke little the past couple of days. He assumed she was over-tired.

"Some mutual-aid teams gave me money today," he said. "I helped them recently on a few odd jobs. I didn't want it, but they said that since we were away from home and couldn't earn an income from our land, our living depended on my blacksmithing. They insisted that I take it. I thought: New Year is coming, you ought to have some new clothes."

"I can get along without them." The girl lowered her head. "I can mend and wash my old clothes for the New Year. But your padded robe is too ragged, pa, you need a new one."

"I'm an old man. There's no reason for me to dress up," said the father. "The mayor told me that some of the mutual-aid teams here are going to combine into a co-op next year. He hopes we'll join. I said I'd talk it over with you when you got home. Help me decide. Is it better to join, or not?"

"I'm for joining," the daughter smiled. "There's nothing I'd like better."

"That's how I feel too," the father said excitedly. "Of course we could go home and join there. But they're a step farther advanced here, and we have a lot of feeling for this village. It's just as well to join here. Then, the co-op will have both a blacksmith and a carpenter. That will be much more convenient for the work. But Old Li is so enchanted with carting, he doesn't want to join. And I haven't seen Six around these last few days, either. Have you?"

The girl didn't answer.

"Aren't you feeling well?" Old Fu looked at her attentively. "You don't seem to have any appetite."

"I'm alright," Nine said. "Just a little tired."

She went into the next room and began to clean the pot and bowls.

"My quarrel with Old Li," her father called through the door, "is just between him and me, just a tiff between two old men. It doesn't amount to anything. You shouldn't take it to heart.

"I haven't taken it to heart," said Nine. "Your health hasn't been so good this winter, pa. I wish you'd get more rest."

"Don't worry about me," Old Fu laughed. "I'll be alright when spring comes. There are no meetings tonight. After you've straightened things up, go to bed a bit earlier."

Nine spread her father's quilts on the platform bed. Closing the door of the room, she left for the home of the girls she was staying with.

The sky was very beautiful that night, and the moon was very round, very bright. Nine paused in the courtyard and listened. After her father blew out the lamp and lay down, he didn't cough nearly so much as he used to. Her heart eased and lightened. She felt that her emotions now were worthy of this clear winter's night, worthy of the bright moon overhead. Fixing her eyes on the round moon, it seemed to her that for the first time she could see clearly the adorable lively little rabbit which, according to myth, was outlined there.

Liu Qing (1916-1978)

Liu Qing was born in Shaanxi province in 1916. He started writing and translating at an early age, worked as an editor on student publications, joined the Communist Party in 1936, went to Yanan in 1938, and took part in the civil war against Chiang Kai-shek's Kuomintang dictatorship, known as the War of Liberation. His novel, Wall of Bronze, *about peasant participation in the battles in Northern Shaanxi province, was written after the People's Republic was established in 1949, and was published in 1951.*

He was one of the first to heed Mao Zedong's urging of city-bred authors to immerse themselves in the lives of the ordinary people. In 1952 he settled down in a small village not far from Xian, and was appointed secretary of the local county Communist Party committee. Living and working among the villagers, he became involved in their affairs and problems. As a result, The Builders, *published in 1962, rings with an intimate authenticity. The style is colorful and wryly humorous.*

Liu Qing was too popular to have suffered more than a relatively mild persecution during the "Cultural Revolution", which ended in 1976. He died two years later, in 1978.

The Builders *is set in a village in the early fifties. Peasants who had been going it alone for centuries, and had been constantly in poverty and debt, are suddenly confronted with a new alternative. They can group together temporarily at busy times in "mutual aid teams". Or, if they are more venturesome, they can form permanent "agricultural producers cooperatives". But this is not simply a change in economic forms. It calls for entirely new concepts. It affects private lives and personal relations. Many peasants are stimulated, some are hesitant, some are opposed.*

In this sample Liu Qing shows what this dilemma meant to several people in one corner of rural China.

THE BUILDERS

The roan mare tethered outside the high wall that enclosed Yao's handsome compound had started to shed her long winter hair, and the rich peasant was working her over with a curry-comb. Squatting, he cocked his head, covered by a felt skullcap, and watched from underneath the movement in the mare's distended belly. It wasn't a little mule that was twitching in there, but three hundred yuan. Maybe more, certainly not less.

Soon, Yao said happily to himself. In half a month at the most, she'll foal.

His wife was expecting a baby, his mare was going to produce a mule colt — an increase in his family and an increase in his property. The rich peasant's heart felt warm, joyful, comfortable beyond words.

"Dirty bastard. A fine people's deputy. What a son of a bitch." Who was that, cursing as he came up the lane? Yao turned his head and looked. Oho! Ex-corporal Bai.

Who's been stirring you up? Yao wondered contemptuously. He ignored Bai and went on examining the belly of his mare.

During Land Reform, and the subsequent re-check on the way it had been carried out, Bai's insane zealousness had made Yao quake with terror. He was afraid at the time that if the Communist Party believed the madman and classified him, Yao, as a landlord, his land and surplus property would be distributed. What's more, he would have to allow several poor peasants to use some of the rooms in his big compound.

Yao had been so distracted he couldn't eat or sleep. He wished he could take his pigsticker and kill Bai. Of course whenever Yao met him on the street, he forced himself to hail the rascal as if he were a village *ganbu*. "Had your meal yet?" Yao would ask courteously.

Now, humphf, now even Chenshan didn't scare him. Why should he worry about a piss-pot like Bai?

Yao stood up. With one hand he patted the mare's full round flank while with the other he squeezed the animal's teats. He wanted to make an exact estimate of when she would foal. Staring haughtily at the sky — Yao's right eye had a scarred lid — he assumed a chilly reserve, as if Bai were a complete stranger.

"Who says you can't push people around in the new society? Son of a bitch. He never lets me breathe."

After nearing Cengfu's thatched cottage Bai turned and started walking back. On the dirt path along the wall opposite Yao's compound he halted, hitched up his trousers and angrily squatted on his heels.

"Does that stinking bird think he can build a nest in my hair? I'll show him that Bai's a dangerous man to rile."

Yao thought it peculiar. Why should Bai curse a village *ganbu* in his presence? Was it being done deliberately for his benefit? If on the road to the Huangpao market he heard someone damn any of the supporters of the new society, Yao was always interested. He would automatically move closer and listen. It did his heart good.

But why should the fanatic of the Land Reform period come before him and revile a people's deputy? What for? In spite of himself, Yao left off examining the mare and turned around, rubbing his hands together to remove the dirt transferred to them from the mare's teats.

"What makes you so upset, this early hour of the morning?" he asked with a smile of curiosity.

"What? I'll tell you what. Last night at the school, Cengfu pointed his finger at my nose and lectured me. I don't have to take that from him. I've never done anything against him, but he wants to pin a counter-revolutionary label on me."

Oho! So the ex-corporal in the Kuomintang army had come to pick a quarrel with Cengfu. But Cengfu had gone off somewhere with his little boy. When Bai saw the lock on his door, he had raved even more wildly, and squatted down in front of the rich peasant.

Yao laughed.

"What are you talking about? How could he call one of the activists of the Land Reform a counter-revolutionary?

"Easy there. Who says I was an activist?"

"Didn't you run around like crazy? The only thing was, they didn't make you a village *ganbu*."

"Good brother Yao, don't spit in my face." Bai had the air of a man seeking forgiveness.

Yao ridiculed him with increasing boldness.

"I don't know why they didn't — the way you sucked up to them. You yelled 'Long live the Communist Party' so loud the whole world could hear you. But you got nothing for your pains."

Bai tilted his shaven pate, which was covered by a cloth turban. He heaved a long sigh. "Don't talk about the past," he begged. "Let's say that I was blind. Yao old man, I can't get along on these Tang Stream Flats."

"Why not? Isn't this a good place? 'The whole Lu River valley can't compare with a bend in the Tang,' as the saying goes."

Yao gazed at him mockingly. Bai drooped like a blade of grass stricken at the root. The rich peasant couldn't resist the temptation to get back at him. He lectured the soundrel in a loud voice:

"You needn't think we can have a Land Reform every year. The Land Reform team can't come each winter and clean people out, like harvesting a crop. You got a few *mu* (*one* mu *is about one sixth of an acre*), didn't you? You ought to buckle down and learn how to farm."

"Ai," Bai sighed again. "How can I farm? I've got no ox, I've got no donkey. I don't even have any food."

Yao immediately knew that something was amiss. He regretted having paid any attention to this shifty idler. He coughed once and, without a word, picked up his curry-comb from the hitching post and walked quickly toward his compound gate.

Bai hurriedly followed and caught up with him in the entrance way. Grasping the sleeve of Yao's clean black padded jacket, Bai looked at him with a rascally gaze.

"Lend me two measures of white rice."

"What? Where would I get — "

"I'll give you wheat in return as soon as the summer harvest is in."

"Huh. Listen to you. Let go of me. I haven't even got black rice."

"Good brother Yao. Don't hold a grudge against me. That great tide of two years ago hurt many good neighbors. It made us all enemies."

A moment before, Yao had been considering pushing Bai out into the lane and bolting the gate. But after hearing Bai's frank pleas, Yao had another idea.

The fellow's a dog, he said to himself. Throw him a scrap to eat, and he'll wag his tail. Stir him up and he'll attack you. I'll get him to turn his teeth on the village *ganbus*.

As Yao stood thinking, Bai could see that there was hope for him, and he laughed ingratiatingly.

"It was Blue Moth's idea. She told me to ask you for the rice."

Blue Moth was Bai's wife. Recalling his affair with her before Liberation, Yao smiled. The memory of Blue Moth's tender backside moved him more readily than Bai's fawning expression.

"Alright. Now let go of my sleeve."

Releasing the rich peasant, Bai revealed his discolored teeth in a broad grin.

"I have troubles, too," said Yao. "That's why I didn't dare go to the grain loan meeting last night."

"I know. Of course I know."

"We've got to do this quietly. You're not to breathe a word. I don't want people saying I've got a river of grain."

"Don't worry. I'm not a child. Those two measures of rice will take care of Blue Moth while I'm in Xian. When I come back at barley cutting time — "

"Well then, bring a sack after dark," Yao said generously.

That night Bai, a sack of grain on his back, bent far forward with his rump up, trotted like a dog out of the gate of the handsome compound. At that moment the harmony — born of mutual understanding and concern — which had prevailed in the rich peasant household during the dangerous years of struggle, ended abruptly.

Yao's mother, a fat old woman in her sixties, simply could not understand her son's foolish conduct. Famed throughout Guan Creek Hamlet for her "piety", she worshipped idols in her central apartment in the main wing, kowtowing three times a day and burning incense once in the morning and once at night. Her response to any evil word or deed was always one simple all-embracing phrase — "Buddha preserve us!" She had uttered it innumerable time in recent years during the class struggle that were part of the village mass campaigns. Ex-corporal Bai who, shouting and ranting, had demanded that her family be classified as landlords, had inspired her to tireless entreaties to the gods that they crush the wicked creature like a bug. Yet today her own son had given him a loan of grain. Buddha preserve us!

She followed Yao to the east wing and then to the west wing. When he went to the stable by the gate house to give his roan some hay, she followed him there too. She stood before him nagging, her loose lips never resting, demanding to know why he had loaned grain to Bai. It seemed to her that it would have been better to dump it in the trough and feed it to the horse, or scatter it in the courtyard for the chickens rather than lend it to that man whom the gods were surely going to punish.

A ladle in one hand, a stick in the other, Yaop was mixing a mash of bran and hay. His did his utmost to remain patient and not lose his temper with his religious mother.

"Ma," he said, "it has to do with the new society. You wouldn't understand."

"Yes I would. You tell me. I'll understand."

"What do you understand? Eh? What? When I bought a picture of Chairman Mao during the Land Reform, you wouldn't let me hang it. The true hero doesn't reveal his courage on his face; it's in his heart."

The old woman's flabby countenance registered a recognition of her error.

"If you had told me it was just to fool the village *ganbus*," she said, "would I have stopped you?"

"And then when the relative came visiting at New Year's time, you spilled everything. Luckily he was a rich relative. If he had been a poor one — "

When he thought of what an awful impression the exposure of his hypocrisy would have made upon his neighbors, Yao glared at his mother and banged the stick against the wooden trough.

"Buddha preserve us! Buddha preserve us!" The old woman piously lowered her head at the sight of her son's worldly display of temper. Supporting herself with her hands on the frame as she stepped backwards through the doorway, she hastily fled.

She continued to intone "Buddha preserve us!" as she walked across the flagstone-paved courtyard in the darkness and returned to her apartment in the east end of the main wing.

Yao went to his own apartment, which was in the west end of the main wing. His wife, over thirty but still girlishly petulant, sat pouting on the kang. With a twist of the hips, she turned her back on him when he came in. He could see her glossy black hair but not her rosy well-nourished face.

Yao took a paper spill from the drawer of the cupboard to light his water-pipe. He smiled, pleased at the woman's jealousy. Even after two or three years, it took only the shadow of a suspicion to kindle it again.

Wrapping himself in manly dignity, he lit the paper spill in the flame of the oil lamp, and started puffing his gurgling pipe. He was careful not to look in his wife's direction. Although he felt full of vigor after sending Bai off with the two measures of rice, he had no intention of reviving his affair with Blue Moth. Yao knew how careful a rich peasant had to be under the new government.

What made him so energetic was the fact that the scabby dog who had been attacking him for two or three years had come now to lick his hand. When the government gave Yao a new land deed and announced that his class status had been finally determined, he had sensed that he was safe. Bai's subservience today was a concrete proof, you might say, that Yao's instinct was correct. Of course, to have a fellow like Bai on your side didn't mean you were travelling in luck. But it was better than having him against you. Bai could make a lot of trouble.

Her pregnant abdomen protruding, Yao's wife began spreading the quilts for the night, flouncing and sulking to demonstrate her indignation. She waited for her husband to say something, but all she heard from him was the sound of his water-pipe. Unable to bear it, in the end she was the first to speak.

"You've only been behaving yourself a couple of years. Are you going to start running wild again?"

"What have I done now?

"You'd better be careful. That militia captain Yuwan is a tough young fellow. He's liable to tie you and Blue Moth together and haul you both down to the township government in Xiabao."

"Aiya! What do you take me for? In this society do you think I'd dare go to Blue Moth's hut even in my dreams?"

"Then what are you giving grain to Bai for?"

"Don't worry. He won't be eating it for nothing."

"Give him a *dan* of white rice, why don't you, and see whether he'll eat it for nothing." (*A* dan *is roughly equivalent to a bushel.*)

"I'll give him two *dan*," Yao snarled with a savage conspiratorial grimace. "I know what I'm doing. Two years ago when you heard him yelling 'long live the Communist Party,' didn't you tremble? If he'd got his teeth into me then, you'd have had to go down to the county jail if you wanted to see me."

The woman understood. Lowering her head, she glanced up at him and burst into giggles.

Yao's grandfather had died toward the end of the Qing dynasty at the turn of the century. In the paddy area today there were only a few old men over sixty who had ever seen him. It was said that he had expired from a peculiar slow disease sarcastically called "greed consumption."

Nearly everyone in Frog Flat had known Yao's father, whose nickname had been "Iron Claw" because he was so cruel and grasping. Most of the stories concerned his winnower. If a poor tenant farmer wanted to borrow it the answer was — "Nothing doing!" Iron Claw had written on it: "For rent, not for loan." The charge was a peck of grain per day. If you worked far into the night and couldn't return the winnower until the following morning, Iron Claw insisted on two day's rent. His face hardened if you mentioned your difficulties, and he said: "It's a rule. I can't make any exceptions."

That was the kind of blood circulating in Yao's robust body. His lifelong ambition had been to be able to sit down at the table as equals with the big landlords Tenant-Skinner Yang and Miser Lu. Being "King of Frog Flat" didn't satisfy him.

But the nationwide Liberation in 1949 shattered his dream. In the Land Reform which followed in 1950, the fields which he had been letting to tenant-peasants at exorbitant rents were confiscated. Another stroke of the pen wiped out his practice of usury. As to debts still owed him, a stroke of the pen wiped these out also — when the interest already paid equalled the amount of the original loan. At mass meetings, members of the Land Reform team (*Specialists sent by the county government.*) repeatedly stressed the need to isolate the rich peasants. They urged his neighbors to make a clear class distinction between themselves and him, to guard against the rich peasants' sabotage.

Ai! Before Liberation all matters of importance in Frog Flat had been decided by him. When he walked down the road between the paddy fields, the peasants working on both sides had always paused to greet him. Then the Land Reform threw him down to the lowest level in the village. All of Frog Flat was one family, but Yao was an outcast. This treatment infuriated him. Not only did he hate the Communist Party, he hated every peasant who supported it.

Dark red circles marked his broad lined forehead where the cautery cups had been, breaths hot as flame came from his big hairy nostrils. His lips were dry and cracked, there were blisters in corners of his bristly mouth. His large flashing eyes had lost their brilliance, his thunderous voice had been reduced to a hoarse whisper. For the past two days Guo Chenshan, chairman of the village deputies to the township government, had been lying on the small kang in his thatched cottage. (*The township government chooses deputies to the county government, which in turn elects deputies to the district, and so right up the line to each higher level of administration.*)

An ordinary cold or flu never could have felled this brawny peasant. A powerful fellow, in the past whenever he ran a fever, instead of taking medicine or lying down, he went out and worked like blazes. Invariably, the next day he was cured. But this time his illness was serious. He neither ate nor drank. He only covered his head with the quilt and slept heavily.

His mother tiptoed up to his bed and asked: "Chenshan, how about some fine noodles?"

"Don't want any," the chairman muttered nasally from beneath the bedding.

"How about a couple of eggs?"

"Can't eat a thing."

"Ai! Chenshan," the old woman cried with a worried frown. "You're the one who's always teaching others. You ought to know — man is iron, food is steel. When a person is ill even if he doesn't feel like eating, he ought to force himself to take a little. You're the one who's always teaching others."

"Go away, go away." The voice in the bedding was impatient.

But no mother in the world can be angry with her son for long. After a little while, the old woman again tiptoed to the bed.

"Chenshan, how do you feel now?"

"Mm." He didn't want to talk.

"Chenshan," his mother said anxiously, "this illness of yours doesn't look so good. Hadn't I better send Chenhai into Huangpao to get a doctor at the health center?"

"Don't need any."

"Then how about Dr. Gao in Xiabao?

"Please, ma."

"What is it?"

"Just let me sleep here quietly." The nasal voice inside the quilt trailed away.

Ancient superstition convinced the old woman that her son's ailment was not merely due to the chill he had caught while talking too long with Secretary Lu on the bank of the stream, the night of the low-interest grain loan meeting. She suspected that during the course of their conversation some demon had taken possession of Chenshan's body. After privately consulting with his wife and the wife of his younger brother Chenhai, she and the two wives, unknown to Chenshan, went to the path along the stream bank to "send off" the demon. The old woman knelt on the path, heaped together a pile of earth, inserted a couple of incense sticks and burned simulated paper money. Kowtowing, she pleaded with the demon to wait at the crossroads for a different victim.

But the next day the chairman of the village deputies was still unable to raise himself from his bed, although his forehead felt cooler to his mother's touch.

Wrapped in his quilt, Chenshan was miserable. When a man is down on his luck, he thought, he'll tumble even on a perfectly level road. Last winter, just as he was about to buy two *mu* of paddy, Shengbao had found out and told the Communist Party village branch. Chenshan had to criticize himself three times at Party rectification meetings. Recently, he took the grain he had originally set aside for the purchase of the land and invested it in the private brick and tile kiln outside Huangbao's north gate — to "aid national construction." (*In those times private enterprise was considered "bourgeois" and backward. For members of the Communist Party, who were supposed to be models of righteousness and morality, to engage in such activities was particularly reprehensible.*)

Who would have thought the township Party Secretary Lu would hear about it so quickly? That night he had followed the secretary to the stream and jawed with him for a long time, but Lu had refused to drop even a hint of who had informed him. Chenshan had staunchly denied that he had done any such thing.

"If it's not true," Lu had retorted, "what do you care who told me?"

Chenshan had repeated that he hadn't invested in the kiln. He suggested tentatively that even if he had, you couldn't compare it with buying land or with shameful acts of exploitation like practicing usury. It would merely be a form of supporting national construction.

"Hah, comrade," Secretary Lu had said, "you're a smart talker. If you're so eager to support national construction, why don't you do the same as Comrade Shengbao and organize a mutual-aid team to help the poor peasants increase output? You call investing your grain in a private kiln 'supporting national construction'? Comrade, you're in business. You needn't think you're so clever and everyone else is stupid. You've got seventy-two holes in your heart; others can see right through you, even though they may not say so."

Chenshan had flushed. What could he say? The secretary hadn't left him a leg to stand on.

Muffled in his bedding, he thought hard. How did Secretary Lu know? When and where had the news leaked out? Chenshan had kept it a secret even from his mother, his wife, his brother and his sister-in-law. When they had asked him why he was giving grain to the kiln owner, he had cautioned them: "Not a word. It's the food grain we've saved. I'm giving it as payment for bricks and tiles I'm asking him to make for us. If you want a tile-roofed house, keep your mouths shut."

The whole family was very thankful to the head of the house for his long-range planning, and they knew he had been "rectified" during the Party rectification meetings the previous winter. They would never betray him.

As to the kiln owner, he had needed the grain badly to pay his workmen. He had nearly prostrated himself when he pleaded with Chenshan to invest.

"Don't worry about a thing, chairman," he had assured Chenshan. "I know you Communists aren't allow to buy land, or lend money, or hire farm hands, or do business. This is a secret between you and me and the earth and the sky. If I leak a single word you can spit in my face. You can call me a baby and make me wear split pants!"

Of the few sharpers in the Huangbao market, the kiln owner was one of the sharpest. Would he do anything to hurt his own interests?

Ah! Chenshan finally dug it out of his memory. He recalled that on two of the occasions when he and the kiln owner had met and talked in the Huangbao market, Shengbao had seen them.

Him again, Chenshan fretted beneath his quilt. Him again. He's got a keen eye and a sensitive nose for this kind of business.

Unhappily he remembered that time in the first lunar month when district Party Secretary Wang came to Frog Flat to help strengthen the mutual aid teams. He, Chenshan, had felt pretty uncomfortable then. Knowing that he was in the wrong, he had kept his voice low. Even his body had seemed too large — a big target attracts attention. What's more, Secretary Wang and Shengbao had been so friendly. At night, they had shared the same kang. It had made Chenshan feel even worse. His heart had warned him: Be careful. He's liable to whisper a lot of nasty things about you in Secretary Wang's ear. You'd better be careful.

Now, in his sweat-smelly bedding, Chenshan angrily muttered: "Use your own ability to climb, Comrade Shengbao. Don't raise yourself by dirtying my name before a leader."

He wouldn't give Shengbao any credit. How much ability did that young fellow have after all?

If I were the same as you — no wife, no kids — my mutual aid team would be ten times better than yours. And I'm not bragging, Chenshan thought truculently inside his quilt.

Now that his imagination was heated, he wondered why he shouldn't work to build up the country's enterprises instead of his own family fortunes. He'd show Shengbao how a mutual-aid team could flourish. But as he rolled over in his bedding, Chenshan again changed his mind.

You shouldn't toss away your personal livelihood just to let off steam, he thought. Socialism was something people were only now beginning to talk about. Everywhere peasants were concernedly asking: When will we have socialism in our China? But no one could say exactly. Obviously the road ahead was a long one, and vague. Maybe this generation wouldn't reach socialism, maybe the journey would have to be finished by the next.

Thanks to Land Reform, Chenshan was lucky enough to get a solid basis for building up his family fortunes. He and his brother Chenhai had strength that would make an ox die of envy. The way they worked, there was no doubt they'd overtake the well-to-do middle peasant Shifu. This wasn't even counting the income they'd get from their youngest brother Chenchiang. Chenshan had sent him to Xian the first time the city put out a call to the countryside for workers. He started as an apprentice in a power plant. When he became a regular worker, he'd be able to send money home.

Nineteen Fifty-three, the first year of the country's First Five Year Plan, was the third year of Chenshan's own first five-year plan to build up his family fortunes. He had started in 1951. The goal was to catch up with Shifu on average land ownership per family member. That was as far as he wanted to go, not a step further. He absolutely wouldn't permit his family holdings to approach the size of those of his enemy, rich peasant Yao. That would be as incompatible with his "political nature" as fire is to water.

Rafter by rafter and beam by beam he stealthily prepared the materials for his tile-roofed house, to be built during his second five-year plan, beginning in 1956. First, he would erect the main building. Then, in the third year of his plan, in 1958, he would build the east and west wings. In the fifth year, 1960, he would put up the front building. He wouldn't move too fast. It wouldn't look right for a Communist.

Even so, the Party time and again prevented him from carrying out his plans. His first five-year plan had already been ruined. During the Party rectification campaign, it was denounced as a breach of Party discipline for a Communist to buy land. Chenshan had no choice but to advance the date of his second five-year plan. But who would have thought that the minute he poked his head out he'd be spotted by the secretary of the township Party branch.

At a Party rectification meeting the previous winter, Chenshan had made a fervid speech:

"A truer word was never spoken. When the men of the Red Army were crossing the snowy mountains and slogging over the swampy grasslands, they didn't know how long it would be before the whole country was liberated. But though their feet were torn and bleeding they marched on, and in a little over a decade they smashed old Chiang Kai-shek. Who can say? We may even reach socialism in another ten or twenty years."

As Chenshan, together with the other Communists, came out of the large gateway of the Xiabao township government, his mind was filled with lofty socialist ideals. Walking along a path through the paddy fields, after crossing a single plank footbridge over the Tang Stream, he had an intimate chat with Shengbao. They discussed how to strengthen the mutual-aid teams of Frog Flat, how to help the needy members who were having difficulty in their work and in their daily life, so that they wouldn't fall back in the old mire.

But as he lay on his kang that night, amid his wife and children, and listened to the mighty snores of his brother Chenhai in the west wing, and heard the ox crunching chopped corn stalks in the shed adjoining the east wing, and the cat which guarded their grain growling as it pounced on a rat on the shed's roof, Chenshan at once came back to reality.

His public duties were occupying too much of his time. Chenhai was always threatening to take his share of the farm and pull out. If Chenshan wanted to go at mutual-aid in earnest, Chenhai would never agree. Chenhai had only two kids, but Chenshan had a large brood and he wasn't as powerful a worker as his brother. Chenshan couldn't allow a break. It was out of the question. As the old saying goes: "The only thing a good property fears is to be split up." Separated from Chenhai, Chenshan and his family would be hard pressed. Together, the brothers had a substantial bit of land and their labor power was strong.

I'll be a plain ordinary Communist. I'll do a good job of my village administrative work and that's all, Chenshan thought. Glory — I haven't the conditions to win glory.

And so, the man who had made such a name for himself in Xiabao Township during the Land Reform came to a final decision. He would look after his own household, he wouldn't bother with the poor peasants and hired hands. But he never dreamed Secretary Lu would keep such a close check on him. Nor had he ever expected that the village administrative work would become so difficult that he couldn't get by with only going through the motions.

His mother brought in a bowl of hot noodles. Very colorful, it had red peppers, green garlic sprouts and golden drops of bean oil floating on the surface. It made your mouth water just to look at it. Carrying it over to her son, the old woman stirred the noodles a bit with a pair of chopsticks.

"See, Chenshan, your wife cooked this for you," she said. "You must try to eat a bowl or two."

Chenshan pushed aside the quilt, struggled to a sitting position and accepted the bowl. As he gazed at it, his brows knit in worried frown. What shall I do? he thought. The village administrative work is so hard, being a Communist is so hard. What shall I do?

This extremely grave question was giving him a splitting headache.

"You're the one who's always teaching others," his mother grumbled. "Show a little sense."

"Outside the house he's so clever, but at home he's all muddled," Chenshan's wife said irritably. She was suckling a baby. "Ma, leave him alone. Whether he eats or not is up to him."

With an effort, Chenshan raised some noodles with the chopsticks and put them in his mouth. He didn't even have a desire to chew. A Communist, he fretted inwardly, a Communist. Why is it so hard to be a Communist?

The question was tormenting him. And Secretary Lu had looked at him with such displeasure in his eyes. Suppose he left the Party? He'd get along.

He forced down the first mouthful of noodles, and picked up a second. Again he was unable to chew. Suddenly all the blood in his body seemed to rush to his brain. He could neither move nor think.

It seemed to Chenshan that he wasn't on the small kang inside his thatched cottage but on a boat on the Wei River. He was dizzy, he couldn't sit firm. His head heavy, his throat choked, there was a bitter taste in his mouth, he wanted to vomit. Horrible. The entire cottage was moving. The bamboo basket hanging from a rafter swung to and fro. The cupboard against the wall swayed visibly.

Somewhere outside the compound there seemed to be a huge explosion. Chenshan's ears rang, his bowl fell on the quilt, and he lost consciousness.

When he awakened, he was lying in bed with tears running down his bristly cheeks. Ashamed and unhappy, he assured the rest of the family that he was alright. He ordered them to leave and go about their business.

Chenshan. Chenshan. The failing that was a peasant characteristic for thousands of years has been welded so firmly into your big powerful frame that it's difficult to pry it loose. You're crammed with ideas from the old society. Secretary Lu has already criticized you. Have you the strength to rip out your deficiencies? Who is going to win the battle for your intellect — Chenshan the Communist, or Chenshan the peasant?

After the others had left, he lay alone beneath the quilt, his body drenched in cold sweat. What a pity. Instead of examining himself ideologically, Chenshan the Communist merely upbraided Chenshan the peasant-cum-earthenware pedlar:

What crazy idea has possessed you? he scolded. Do you really want to take the road to the edge of the cliff? Wake up. Open your eyes. How can you think of leaving the Party? You must stay in the Party, you must. If you leave the Party the peasants of Frog Flat will stab you to death with their eyes. Your enemy Yao will spit in your face...

In that instant Chenshan, the peasant who was working so hard to build up his family fortunes, could see it fairly clearly: The Party had great and limitless strength. It was effectively guiding the development of China's history. Its policies were influencing the life of every Chinese. The Party enabled those who had been starving to eat their fill. It made the extravagant frugal, brought honor to the laboring people, made the lazy diligent, forced tyrants to bend the knee, gave courage to the weak, brought stability to society and prosperity to the Huangbao market fairs.

And what about Chenshan himself? He had been an ordinary peasant. It was only after he began carrying out Party policies that people attached any importance to him. If he quit the Party, all he'd have left would be a big body capable of toting a two hundred catty load and the petty shrewdness of a peasant living from day to day.

He had always considered being "in the Party" more vital than anything. He never missed a Party meeting. If the Tang Stream rose the day a meeting was called in Huangbao, he walked far along the bank to a small bridge. If it had been washed away by the mountain torrent, he went all the way to the big Huangbao Bridge to get across. Was he going to let his desire to build up his family fortunes make him leave the Party? Nonsense.

Blabbermouth Sun called on the chairman of the village deputies and brought him some news from the hamlet: Blue Moth, wife of ex-corporal Bai, had revealed that rich peasant Yao had loaned them two pecks of white rice. After depositing the rice at home, Bai had gone off to Xian to buy old junk. In fact two needy peasants in Guan Creek Hamlet had secretly borrowed grain from Yao. Cengfu's brother Cengrong had also gone to the rich peasant's handsome tile-roofed compound. Cengfu was so furious he had stamped with rage. Many peasants upstream were going into the mountains with Shengbao's mutual-aid team to cut bamboo. Shengbao and Yuwan had talked middle peasant Iron Man into lending grain to the families of the needy peasants from his ward who were joining the expedition. Cengfu was organizing porters in Guan Creek Hamlet to carry out the bamboo brooms.

Chenshan listened, depressed. The chairman of the village deputies had lost his power to control the affairs of Frog Flat. Matters in the hamlet were developing quite independently of his influence. The rich peasants obviously no longer feared him, the poor peasants weren't looking to him for guidance any more. Shengbao and Yuwan had not asked him what they should beware of when they were up in the hills.

Blabbermouth's account ran on and on. As Chenshan listened, one thing became clear: by his go-it-alone approach to farming, he had removed himself from the ranks of the militants in Frog Flat. He had placed himself outside the ranks of the revolution. No wonder Secretary Lu had looked at him with displeasure.

"Enough, enough," Chenshan pleaded softly. "Don't say any more. I've got a headache. If you've something else to do, just run along. We can talk again some other time." Chenshan once more covered his head with the quilt.

Blinking, Blabbermouth gazed at him in surprise. He left the cottage disappointed. He had been intending to try and enlist the chairman's help in his quest for Kaixia after reporting the news. He hadn't realized that Chenshan was so ill. Ai!

As for Kaixia herself, her thoughts were as healthy as her rosy cheeks, her heart was as spotless as her sky-blue tunic. Like a bee seeking nectar, she diligently sought knowledge. She strove for progress and longed to win honor by contributing greater spiritual strength to society. To the twenty-one-year-old member of the Youth League branch committee, honor was everything. She simply could not understand how a person could live other than honorably in this great new society.

At twenty-one, Kaixia was in third year primary school. In the early fifties, only after the proclamation of the Marriage Law was formal attention paid to women's rights. Some country girls in the more enlightened families were able to start school. By then, most of them were in their teens.

An important reason for Kaixia's disdain of Blabbermouth, aside from the fact that he gazed at her lustfully, was his failure to be accepted into the Communist Party after the chairman had recommended him.

Humph! What kind of a youth is he? she thought. Can't even get into the Party!

Land, houses, carts, draught animals, clothing, farm implements, and other such items of private property in Kaixia's eyes had no more significance than the stones and gravel and grass on the banks of the Tang Stream. If, when the time came, she applied to join the Party and was refused, she wouldn't know how to face people. To be a Communist, to add one's own strength to the great collective strength of the Party — this, it seemed to Kaixia, was the very minimum requirement of an honorable existence.

But, lacking sufficient knowledge and experience, she saw only the glory of being a Communist. She did not realize that the inner thoughts and secret conduct of certain individuals bearing this honorable name made them unworthy of it. Pure and honorable herself, with no selfish desires, she was accustomed to viewing people she respected in the best possible light, and assuming the worst about people she disliked. When she heard that rich peasant Yao and well-to-do middle peasant Shifu had the temerity to openly oppose the low-interest grain loans to needy peasants, she was so enraged she wanted to pinch them, to spit in their faces.

At the same time she sympathized deeply with Chairman Chenshan, who was responsible for this work. Her relations with him ever since Liberation gave her no reason to doubt his good intentions. She forgave his lack of enthusiasm for his mutual-aid team because he had a large family. "Of course," honest Kaixia said to herself, "Shengbao's situation is much simpler."

And so the day when she returned home from the Xiabao primary school and heard from her mother that the chairman of the village deputies was ill, she threw down her school bag and hurried over to the cottage across the lane.

Chenshan acted quite differently from the way he behaved when Blabbermouth had visited him. Pushing aside the quilt, he squatted on the sleeping mat, his feet bare, and chatted with the girl standing at the foot of the *kang*.

When she saw how ill he looked — this man who had always been so concerned about her progress and future — Kaixia was shocked. It was only a few days since she had last seen him on the village streets, but he had changed enormously. Because Chenshan had been sleeping too long with his head under the covers, his broad face had become pasty and swollen. Its lines had deepened into wrinkles. His bristly cheeks were even more unkempt looking. Squatting on the kang in a shadowy corner, Chenshan had the appearance of a doddering old failure.

After asking a few questions about his illness, Kaixia inquired with concern why he hadn't called the doctor from the health center in Xiabao.

"Ah, forget it." Chenshan's voice was still hoarse. "Forget it. I'm much better today."

Indeed, as his mother and wife could testify, this important member of their family obviously was gradually recovering. He had regained a bit of spirit. Chenshan now wore a smile when he talked with Kaixia. They were sure that a smile and anxiety couldn't exist at the same time, nor could a forced smile mask any worry in his heart.

Chenshan had fought his way out of a dangerous state of mind. He was struggling to take a broader view, to look towards the light. As long as he and Yao were living in the same village, he warned himself, he could never leave the Party. The hatred between them could never be dispelled as long as they both were on this earth. Land Reform had given Chenshan a bit of solace, but it made Yao hate him all the more. The sole reason why Yao hadn't dared to bare his fangs was because Chenshan's position had been just. For Chenshan to quit the Party now would simply be looking for trouble. How could he stand up against Yao man to man?

Chenshan came to a decision. He would accept Secretary Lu's criticism. The rice which he had invested in the private kiln would become the purchase price of bricks and tiles. Then no one could say he was "in business". As to his mutual-aid team, he would simply bear up under Secretary Lu's reprimand and Secretary Wang's coldness. He'd wait and see how Shengbao made out with his team cutting bamboo in the hills, then he'd act. He couldn't risk the livelihood of the dozen or more people in the other mutual-aid teams on a gamble. And since he was unwilling to respond positively to the Party's call, of course he couldn't expect to be commended as he had been during the Land Reform. Well, Chenshan thought, he'd just plug along at earning a living.

Now that he had convinced himself, Chenshan's health improved considerably. He didn't have to wrap himself in the quilt any longer. His wife and mother saw only that he was feeling better. How could they know what a severe struggle he had been through? And innocent Kaixia. Never in her dreams could she imagine such complicated ideas. She could only see him squatting barefoot on the bed. How could she tell what he was thinking? In fact she even said to herself: Aiya, look what worrying over our village's needy peasants had done to our chairman. He must be very angry with Yao and Shifu... And for this, she respected Chenshan even more.

In her plaid cloth shoes, the member of the Youth League branch committee stood on the earthen floor of Chenshan's thatched cottage. To manifest her sympathy for the chairman, she angrily attacked Yao and Shifu for their opposition to the low-interest grain loans.

After his internal struggle, Chenshan now appeared calm and reasonable, and full of self-critical spirit.

"I have shortcomings," he admitted. "I have shortcomings. If in the first lunar month my family hadn't insisted that I take our small store of surplus grain and order bricks and tiles with it, would Yao and Shifu dare to act so bold today? (*After general discussions with their inhabitants villages set a different minimum quota of grain for each family, according to its size and labor skill, to sell to the government at fixed prices. Any grain gathered over and above that quota the family was free to consume or sell on the open market.*) If I had used that grain to help the needy peasants, I'd be in a position to talk firmly to those two. As it is — ai! I was as wrong. Wrong. I shouldn't have listened to my family. 'A family has many tongues but only one master.' We've been living in thatched cottages for generations. Why should we be in such a hurry to build a tile-roofed house?"

His pained and self-critical manner touched Kaixia's simple heart. Self-criticism to any degree is always welcomed. It is in no way demeaning. On the contrary, it arouses people's respect.

"Ai, good Kaixia," Chenshan continued dejectedly, "my family complained we have to repair the thatch every year. On this wild flat if the wind blows the roof away some dark night, we can't even get up in time to catch it... I thought to myself: It's true. Rather than no one being able to sleep whenever there's a wind...But who knew —" The chairman was simply too miserable for words.

Kaixia believed he was sorry. She knew that selfish family demands could be a pit for any Communist or Youth Leaguer. If you were the least bit careless, you could fall right in. As she stood rolling the edge of her blue cloth tunic, she wondered whether there was anything intelligent she could say to comfort the chairman.

"You've come just at the right time," Chenshan went on. "I've been meaning to tell you. I want you to ask your ma whether she's willing to join my mutual-aid team."

Kaixia was very surprised. "Haven't you already teamed up with Old Chin and his brother?"

"That's right. Old Chin and his brother both have draught animals. The team isn't carrying along a family which has none. That's my fault too."

"I'm afraid Old Chin wouldn't agree," Kaixia said doubtfully. "We've got no men in our family, and no ox. We're a burden. No mutual-aid team wants us."

"Don't worry. If he isn't willing, I'll talk to him."

Kaixia was delighted. You don't have to ask my ma," she said excitedly. "I guarantee she'll agree. You live right across the lane from us. You know how we manage. Every year we have to borrow a draught animal from our relatives to till our field."

Kaixia felt closer to Chenshan than ever. Here was a man who recognized his mistakes and corrected them. Kaixia had lost her father and had no brothers. She considered herself very fortunate to have this older man, this Communist, looking after her.

Chenshan gazed at the girl's happy face, lovely as a newly opened flower. "What about going to a factory? Have you made up your mind yet?"

"Not yet," Kaixia laughingly replied.

"What's taking you so long?"

Kaixia only smiled. She wanted to talk with Shengbao, but she still hadn't been able to find the chance. Of course that wasn't entirely true. It would be more accurate to say she was waiting for

full-grown bride. Such girls — "child-brides" — were virtually slaveys in the groom's family until they were old enough to bear children. Shengbao's "bride" had died the year before.)

He was her ideal. She couldn't say what it was about Shengbao's face, eyes, eyebrows, nose or mouth that attracted her. As a matter of fact, he was quite ordinary looking. His goodness, decency and courage, blending into an entity with his voice, face and body — these are what won our Kaixia.

What did she care whose son he was, how much land and how many houses he had, or whether his parents were amiable or crotchety. "No matter if he owns valley land. What matters is whether he'll make a good husband," as the local saying put it. Two years before, if both of them had been unattached as they were today, even the Old Lord of the Sky couldn't have stopped Kaixia from going to Shengbao's thatched cottage as his bride. Neither her mother, nor public opinion, nor the disapproving stares of Shengbao's father Liang the Third, would have outweighed her love. They didn't bother her a bit. Although she wasn't able to express her feelings very well in words, compared with those middle-school and university students who could define their love with such precision, she was infinitely more ardent, considerate and true.

But today, now that Shengbao was single again and she had ended her engagement, society had changed more than she had dreamed possible. The drums and gongs, the shouted slogans that had resounded in Frog Flat during Land Reform could no longer be heard. No more did you see people marching with red flags down the streets. Except for the occasional lowing of an ox, the bark of a dog, the clucking of a hen, the villages were deathly still. It was dull enough to drive you to distraction. At the same time, the factories springing up in the cities like mushrooms after rain were beckoning to her. Kaixia was really troubled. She wasn't one of those frivolous girls. How could she toss aside her love, abandon Shengbao, and fly off, with no regard for anyone but herself?

"You've had three years of school. The men who've proposed are all educated, while that Shengbao of yours has only learned a couple of words in the literacy class." That was how Kaixia's mother looked at it. The widow didn't say so aloud, but her daughter could see it in her face. Ha, poor old backward feudal brain, thought Kaixai. Is your daughter going to school just to raise her status so as to find a better husband? She's not that kind of a cheap baggage.

The girl knew what little difference the three years of schooling had actually made in her. Whereas Shengbao, even when he was still the captain of the militia, even before he had joined the Communist

Party, was plainly a man who was going to do big things. She could tell it from the way he talked and handled his affairs. Kaixia remembered many times like this: Shenbao would be standing in a public meeting, his manner neither forward nor apologetic. He would listen quietly while someone else was speaking, seldom interrupting. But when he finally spoke, he would express himself much better than the others. His words would be well balanced and would attract everyone's attention. On each such occasion, Kaixia would feel herself irresistibly drawn to him. Shengbao — a poor village boy without a selfish thought in his head. This too tugged Kaixia's heart strings.

But Kaixia also had this sort of feeling: Shengbao is a fine boy, it's true, but who knows how many years it will be until the countryside gets to socialism? A few dozen, at least. And the selfish forces trying to build up their private property are so fierce. No matter how good he is, how much of a wave can he stir up with his one little mutual-aid team? I'd better just attend to my own future and not be ruled by emotion.

Kaixia wanted to get married not because she was looking for someone to provide her with food and clothing, and even less to satisfy a physical craving, but because she had an honest desire to help build a new society, husband and wife together. It was for this reason she thought that leaving Shengbao to work in a factory was right. The decision, she felt, was patriotic, forward-going and positive. For several days her mind was at ease.

But when she heard that Shengbao had organized a large group of men and they were getting ready to go to Mount Chongnan and strike back at the boycott of the low-interest grain loans by the forces of private expansion, Kaixia again was moved. Dear Shengbao. To take such a step in the spring of 1953 was not easy. Many residents of Frog Flat were looking forward to a long era free of harsh taxes, marauding soldiers and bandits, tyrannical landlords, robbers and thieves — a period in which only they, ordinary peasants, and no others would be allowed to compete for property and profit!

Shengbao was starting a new battle at the head of a group of poor peasants, the most reliable of the masses. His brave action made Kaixia waver about entering a factory. Several times she had thought of confiding in his sister Xiulan. But she realized that no intermediary can ever convey the full import of the original words. Kaixia would have to talk with Shengbao directly. She definitely would find a chance before he went off to the mountains. They'd have a good long chat, in detail, unhurried.

The chance Kaixia was waiting for came at last. Sunday also

happened to be market day in Huangbao Town. She had learned from Xiulan that Shengbao was busy preparing the expedition and would be leaving for the mountains right after Clear and Bright Day. (*A time for tidying and sweeping family graves, usually in early April.*)

He's bound to go to market, Kaixia thought. I can meet him in Huangbao and the two of us can very naturally take a stroll along the road on the eastern plain. There aren't many people we know there.

"Ma, I'm going to market," Kaixia told her mother that morning.

The widow was surprised. "What for? I thought we were planting beans today."

"I have to buy a notebook."

"What kind?"

"How many kinds are there? For homework."

Her mother gazed at her suspiciously, then said, "Hm. Go ahead."

While the widow swept the cottage and cooked breakfast, Kaixia sat by the window in the spring sunlight, combing and braiding her thick glossy hair carefully before the mirror. Lowering her head, the twenty-one-year-old girl followed with pleasure the line of the braids as they passed the swell of her breasts and extended down to her waist. With the expertness instinctive in all women she appraised the effect of her primping was likely to have upon Shengbao. Finally satisfied, she tossed the two braids behind her back.

After breakfast, carrying a bamboo basket in which her mother had placed some thirty eggs, Kaixia went out of the gate of the persimmon-tree compound. Raising her head with its glistening dark hair, she looked for Shengbao. But she saw only his thatched cottage, silently squatting beneath the elm and poplar trees that were just beginning to bud. Her mother followed her to the compound gate.

"Go early and come home quickly," the widow cautioned. "Don't dawdle away the whole day. In the afternoon, we still have to plant those beans.

"Yes, ma," said Kaixia. Shengbao hasn't left yet, she thought to herself. I'll go on ahead and wait for him in Huangbao.

Her small feet, clad in plaid cloth shoes with button-down straps, trod lightly on the raised path between the paddy fields. Kaixia was happy, gay, like the dandelions and daisies growing in profusion by the side of the road.

With the approach of Clear and Bright Day, both banks of the stream had changed into colorful spring garb. It was a time of red peach blossoms and green willow tendrils, of flying larks and skimming swallows. Burgeoning wheat sprouts, warming in the sun, emitted a verdant fragrance. The barley was already putting out heads. Crystal-clear water flowing in the creek beside the road gurgled as it hastened along on its journey to the distant sea.

The government had urged a spring-time irrigation. But many peasants who were still farming alone hadn't been able to decide, their minds fettered by the old feudal superstition: "Irrigation in spring, no grain in summer." Shengbao's mutual-aid team had set an example for the other peasants. They had irrigated their land and spread chemical fertilizer, and now the leaves on their wheat were a lush dark green that rivalled the pines of Mount Chongnan.

Leaving the path between the paddy fields, Kaixia set out along the Huangbao road. Peasants — pushing barrows, driving donkeys, bearing reeds on their shoulders or boards on their backs, toting shoulder-poles, holding baskets, carrying chickens — moved along the dust road to the market town in an endless procession beneath the warm rays of the sun. Some had already changed into light spring garments; others still wore their padded winter clothes.

Kaixia walked very slowly. Peasants travelling alone or in groups of two and three passed her from behind. Some turned to look back and declared to their companions with a laugh: "That girl must be waiting for someone. She walks staring at her toes."

"Is it any of your business? Nosey!" Kaixia said under her breath, sweeping them with an angry glare.

Small groups of Frog Flat peasants who were preparing to go into the mountains also passed her by. They were talking about the things they intended to buy — curved sickles, straight sickles, felt leg wrappings, hemp sandals... One man said he already had a curved sickle, he would just buy a straight one. Another responded that Shengbao said it wasn't necessary for each person to buy a straight sickle; two or there could share one among them; cutting thin branches off the stalk of the bamboo broom wasn't like cutting the bamboo trunk — it took very little time. "Shengbao said", everything was "Shengbao said." He seemed to have become their authority.

As Kaixia listened, her heart felt smooth and comfortable, as if it had been ironed. "Shengbao can manage," the peasants said. "He's bold but painstaking."

"Ah! Kaixia." The voice was old Ren the Fourth's. "Are you going anywhere, or aren't you? You're walking like you can't decide."

"I'm thinking about something," the girl replied hastily, blushing.

The old man's stubble-covered lips split in a grin, and he walked on, his bow-back swaying.

What's keeping Shengbao? Kaixia wondered. She wanted to look over her shoulder, but she was afraid someone she knew would see her and laugh. After a few more steps, she thought: Maybe Shengbao has a lot to do in Huangbao, maybe he's there already?

"Going to market, Kaixia?" Blabbermouth's leering voice struck her like a blow in the back. She didn't have to look; she could picture his lecherous stare. That avid gaze was enough to frighten any respectable girl.

Blabbermouth hurried a few steps to catch up. Now he walked by her side, deliberately pressing the white sleeve of his shirt against the blue sleeve of Kaixia's simple cloth tunic. Distastefully, she drew away.

"Here, let me carry your basket."

"No need. I can carry it myself." Kaixia shifted the basket from her right hand to her left.

The persistent Blabbermouth circled to her left side and again reached for the basket.

"You don't have to worry about those eggs. I can't eat 'em raw."

Kaixia moved the basket back to her right hand. Her face stiffening, she said coldly, a note of warning in her voice: "You walk along properly. Quit grabbing and skittering about. What will people think?"

Blabbermouth neither blushed nor looked sheepish. Though he gave up trying to take the basket, he wasn't discouraged. He would find some other way to render service to Kaixia.

"Is it worth making a special trip into town just to sell those few eggs? You must have other things to do also."

The girl didn't reply. She felt uncomfortable, as if some fiend were walking at her side. Of all the luck, she thought, running into this mug. If he didn't help Chairman Chenshan on the civil affairs committee, I'd be a lot less polite... She forced herself to be patient, for the chairman's sake.

"You also have other things to do at the fair." Blabbermouth tried again.

"Yes."

"What are they? If you're too busy, I can help — "

"No need."

Kaixia quickened her pace. One by one, she caught up with and passed those who had passed her before. She wanted to shake off Blabbermouth. Kaixia couldn't bear the hungry way he stared at her face, her braids, her bosom. She had made up for Shengbao, not for Blabbermouth. And the leering, simpering tone he used — as if she were some hussy with a bad reputation. The filthy dog! she thought furiously.

But Blabbermouth was blithely unaware. Matching his stride to Kaixia's, he went right on talking and smirking, trying hard to give everyone on the road the impression that here, beyond a doubt, was a young couple going to market. He told the girl that in the Huangbao culture center there was a series of illustrated posters explaining the new Marriage Law, and also a chart on the new method of midwifery. On market days, many, many people went to see them. As for himself, he made a point of going every time he went to market, because it improved his mind and taught him something scientific. He strongly recommended that Kaixia also go.

Shameless wretch, the girl swore to herself. Even if you improve you mind and go to the Huangbao culture center every day, you'll never find a girl. Eat your heart out!

But she didn't say a word. She just let Blabbermouth ramble on. Repressing her rage, she flew along like the wind. Only after she crossed the big Huangbao bridge and passed the grain, hay and animal market outside the town's south gate, did she finally manage to lose Blabbermouth in the noisy milling crowds. Kaixia pushed on through the south gate into Huangbao proper. When she saw that Blabbermouth was no longer at her side, she heaved a sigh of relief.

She had come to meet Shengbao. But where was he? Should she wait for him at the big bridge? No, that wouldn't do. She had seen Chenshan at the animal market by the bridge, buying piglets. That chairman had urged her so often to go into industry, she didn't want him to know that she was talking to Shengbao behind his back.

Bad luck. Rotten luck, thought Kaixia, standing amid the crowds. I rushed to get here, but for what?

At the food purchasing department of the supply and marketing co-operative she sold the eggs her mother had given her. She drifted down the market street, lined by awnings held in place by rope and bamboo poles, and drifted back again. Should she stand somewhere and wait for Shengbao, Kaixia wondered anxiously, or should she continue to wander around until she "accidentally" met him? She couldn't miss the chance. In another few days it would be Clear and Bright, and Shengbao would be going into the mountains.

Kaixia made three circuits of the Huangbao market street, which was heavily thronged with peasants. Looking for a ruddy young face with large eyes and thick brows in that moving sea of straw hats and cloth turbans was very tiring. Kaixia was getting a headache. She changed her plan and went to the crossroads of the south gate street to watch for Shengbao there. Not a sign of him. Where could he have gone? Kaixia was beginning to get a trifle discouraged, and a trifle annoyed with Shengbao. Was he just being obstinate where their love was concerned? Couldn't he co-operate a little, be more considerate? Suddenly another thought struck her. Even if she met him, suppose he had Yuwan, Huanxi or some of the others with him, all in a hurry to do things? How could she get him off to the east plain road?

He's busy. He must be busy. How could it be otherwise? He's going to take a group of men into the mountains. What shall I do? The more Kaixia thought, the more discouraged she became, and the more she felt there was no point in waiting.

But she continued to wait. She thought: I'll just stay here till noon.

Damn. The bristly-faced Chenshan, carrying two squealing piglets in a hamper, was coming her way. Beside him in a black cloth cap trotted Blabbermouth, fawningly begging the chairman for some favor. Kaixia hastily hid herself in the crowd, and they walked by without seeing her. After they had passed she came out again. She could hear the chairman's big voice saying:

"There's no use in you having any ideas about Kaixia. She's not meant for a country boy. She'll be leaving soon."

"Where's she going?" the neatly dressed Blabbermouth asked in surprise.

"Don't you bother about other people's affairs," Chenshan instructed him. "Just mind your own business and you'll get along fine."

Kaixia couldn't hear the rest of the conversation, for the chairman and Blabbermouth walked on toward the farm implements department of the supply and marketing co-op.

She thought the chairman's answer was very clever. He had given her the good idea of going into industry, and he was helping her keep the secret. Chenshan was as shrewd as they come.

For a moment, particularly because Shengbao was making her stand on a street corner and wait for him in vain, for a moment her mind ran riot. The chairman was so concerned about her welfare, and here she was deceiving him. It was too discourteous of her. Kaixia felt ashamed, repentant. She felt unworthy of the chairman's care. Although she was alone, the honest girl blushed.

Standing by herself in the market crowds, Kaixia again wondered whether there could be anything behind Chanshan's interest. Nonsense. What cause had she to doubt him? Had the bristly-faced peasant ever made any requests of her? He couldn't be thinking of matching her up with his youngest brother. The young fellow was already engaged to a girl in another village. The couple had come to

Huangbao where they had their picture taken together, ate in a restaurant, strolled the streets, and bought materials for their wedding clothes. All they had to do now was register. Kaixia was sure that the chairman's kindness to her was prompted only by the best of motives — his sincere concern for her future and for the country's industrialization.

This attitude coincided entirely with Kaixia's own.

She decided to go home, she wouldn't wait for Shengbao. This was final. Unhesitatingly, she made her way through the crowds of peasants and crossed the big Huangbao bridge. The traditional code of conduct had once again overcome modern love.

On the road back, deeply stirred, she said to the absent Shengbao, wherever he was: I wish you success, I wish you victory. I hope you find the kind of girl you want. As for me, I'm leaving.

Suddenly her nose tingled and tears welled to her lovely eyes. It wasn't that she was weak, and it wasn't that she was backward. When you sacrifice your love for a lofty ideal, tears are entirely reasonable. Just think. If you suddenly uprooted a tender sprout of love which you yourself had raised in your heart, how could your body help but bleed a few drops of emotion? Only if there was no end to them, only if the tears couldn't be stopped, could they be called the dirty water of weakness and backwardness. With a delicate finger Kaixia wiped away the two tears that had formed in the corners of her eyes, and continued toward home.

She was positive now that Shengbao was on the streets of Huangbao, swallowed up by the peasant crowds. She hadn't been able to talk with him. What a pity. What a pity.

Head down, she walked on. There were not many people going to market on the road now, so Kaixia didn't bump into anyone, even though she didn't look where she was going. As she trudged, she wondered about the mystery of love. Although she had decided to be a new-type woman, she was still just a country girl after all. The change in the situation and the various unexpected elements made it very difficult for her to analyze a thing as complex as "being in love."

Forget it, she said to herself. I won't think about it any more, for now.

She looked up and suddenly she saw him. Shengbao, together with Yuwan, was coming toward her down the broad highway. Kaixia was overjoyed. All at once the whole earth and sky became bright and shining. How delightfully soothed her heart felt.

What had she been thinking a moment ago? In the wink of an eye she forgot everything. Could it be that she hadn't been thinking at all?

stratagem. Shengbao would be forced to plead for her hand without delay. Once he stated that he was against her becoming a textile worker, she wouldn't go no matter who urged her.

But when at last she raised her head, Kaixia was dumbfounded. Shengbao's face had turned ashen, and he wore a sarcastic smile.

"Fine. Take the entrance test, by all means," he urged courteously. Suddenly he had become cool and distant, with an unforgiving look in his eye.

Kaixia's heart sank. Her brain felt paralyzed. It couldn't function.

"Fine." Shengbao concentrated his thoughts on going into the mountains. "I'm busy," he said politely. "Yuwan's waiting for me in Huangbao. We can talk about this again some other time." He rose quickly and, even before his voice had died away, started off.

"Shengbao, how can you act like this? Let me finish," the girl shouted after him frantically, still hoping to save the situation.

But he continued walking with his basket of eggs. "Next time," he called back over his shoulder. "I'm too busy now."

From the small path, he returned to the highway and strode away.

Ai!

SATIRIC VERSE

The Chinese are among the world's most natural and spontaneous versifiers. From *The Book of Songs*, compiled in the seventh or eighth century BC, we can see that they were rhyming their verse a thousand years before the poets writing in Latin or Arabic adopted rhyme forms. Whether it is in their genes, or something in the nature of the language itself, the Chinese are constantly producing rhymes — of course in poetry, but also in folk aphorisms, in word games, in daily speech, and frequently in political comment.

Outstanding in this last category is Yuan Shuipo.

Yuan Shuipo (1916-1982)

Yuan Shuipo was born in the beautiful ancient city of Suzhou (Soochow) in south China in 1916, where he received his early schooling. After a few years in a Shanghai university, when the war against the Japanese invaders broke out in 1937 he plunged into revolutionary literary activities. For over twenty years starting in 1940, he made pungent observations on domestic and international affairs in colloquial verse.

His satiric poems were carried in the left-wing press in Kuomintang times, and were very popular among liberals. After the establishment of the People's Republic in 1949, they reached a much wider audience, and appeared in a number of collections.

An editor and critic in his later years, he was also a council member of the Writers Union and a national committeeman of the Federation of Writers and Artists. He was expelled from these and all other posts after the "Cultural Revolution" because he was one of the few writers to have sided with the "Gang of Four".

He died in 1982, unhappy and scorned.

The sample poems chosen here were taken from the Yuan Shuipo collection entitled Soy Sauce and Prawns, *published in Beijing in 1963. They span a period from 1945 to 1960. Written in a deft variety of styles, they are devastating comments on current news items. Their bitter sarcasm cries out in furious indignation at the cruel inequities then being inflicted on China and the world.*

SOY SAUCE AND PRAWNS

FOR THE SAKE OF THE FASCISTS' HEALTH

News item, December 1943. Herbert Morrison, Britain's Secretary of State for Home Affairs, has ordered the release from prison of Oswald Mosley, leader of England's fascist party, "for the sake of his health."

It's like saying:
If wolves chase us,
Throw them our babies.

It's like saying:
If a robber's purse is empty,
Give him a pistol.

It's like saying:
If a murderer's hands itch,
Open the prison door and set him free.

Ridiculous, of course,
Who would be so insane?
Yet some have done just that.

Herbert Morrison
Released Mosley,
For the sake of this fascist leader's health.
Italian planes and guns
Slaughtered barefooted Ethiopians,

For the sake of Mussolini's health.

In a Munich banquet hall
Chamberlain "fed" Hitler all he demanded
For the sake of the Fuehrer's health.

Millions of youths pounded to bloody bits,
Europe, democracy, locked in concentration camps,
All for the sake of the fascists' health.

You're so solicitous
About their health.
You wine and dine them
Plump and fat,
While everywhere the people
Long for their death.

Well, just because
They are still healthy,
Just because
They're not all dead yet,
We're going to unite, shout,
Wipe them out.

Only when
They're healthy no longer,
Only when
We've rid the world of fascists,
Only then
Will we stop.

PUSSY CAT

December 1943.

Fire hose, swords,
   Marked the warlord era;
Artillery, rifles;
   Chiang does it better.

Toward Chinese students
  A wolf's ferocity,
Toward foreign bosses
  Feline docility.

Boot-licking pussy,
  Eyes that adore,
"Money please, money,
  More, more, more."

THEIR CREED

1946. A barb against the troglodyte philosophy of the Kuomintang rulers.

"Only we believe,
Only we venerate:
  Everything old, ancient, antique,
  All that is static.

"New equals wicked,
Future means finis;
We've terrible doubts of our sons' tomorrow,
We dare not think of our grandsons' day.

"Only we believe,
Only we venerate:
  Stagnation — our pleasantest state,
  The grave — ultimate in safety,
  Paralysis — our best legality,
  Retreat — our utmost normality,
  Slavery — our highest ideal.

"Only we believe
That only we are right."

FRENCH FARCE

News item, May 1954: Laniel government prohibits performance of Ballet Russe in France.

Russian ballet here in Paris?
Pull the curtain, *mon Dieu*!
The thought's too terribly terrible,
It's just too frightfully *affreux*.

Ulanova, *mon Dieu*!
Don't let her get on stage.
A *femme* extremely *dangereuse*,
Wall Street would simply rage.

A shakily ailing weakling
Jumps at the drop of a pin,
That gentle prince of "Swan Lake"
Might stave the cabinet in.

No Ballet Russe in Paris,
Such caution deserves praise,
Whose Iron Curtain is it?
"Free World"? — ironic phrase.

"ARTISTIC FREEDOM"

June 1957. On seeing a photo of a "pavement artist" and reading a report of an "art exhibition" in the London Times.

A middle-aged man kneels on the curb
In London's Trafalgar Square,
Drawing pictures with colored chalks,
The dirty pavement his art gallery.

Cold wind ruffles his sparse hair,
Fog seeps through his muffler;

Passers-by toss him glances of contempt, or pity,
But few drop a penny in his upturned old hat.

A beggar who's learned to paint?
Or a painter who's learned to beg?
"Artistic freedom", a tenet of the "Free World",
Includes the freedom to decorate its gutters.

Of course, fortune blesses other favorites too,
Even more creative freedom is found in the city zoo;
There, "paintings" by black apes form an exhibition grand,
Hairy simian paws have replaced Gainsborough's hand.

SOY SAUCE AND PRAWNS

News item, May 1959. The United States has prohibited the trans-shipment of a cargo of Chinese canned prawns and soy sauce destined for Canada.

Neither canned prawns nor soy sauce
May America's borders cross;
Canadians, amazed, confused,
Are irritated and amused.

Soy sauce endangers security,
The reason's there for all to see,
So deeply red it's purple nearly,
— Criminal nature proven clearly.

And as to Chinese big prawns canned,
They obviously must be banned;
In armor cased from tail to head,
When boiled they turn a fiery red.

An Iron Curtain America blinds,
Hysteria grips the White House minds;
"Strategic goods" — what if they're edible?
Such idiocy is scarcely credible.

BABES TO THE BARRICADES

News item, October 1959. The House Un-American Activities Committee is investigating Communist influence in California schools among children between the ages of five and seven.

Infant subversives,
They're news, they're hot,
Will they revolt
Or will they not?
(Naturally, their teachers too
Must answer legal process due.)

Outer bluster,
Inner dread, Everyone
A potential Red,
Seek then under
Every bed.
(Big and small
Suspect them all.)

No matter if
They're five or six,
Those Communists
Are full of tricks;
Preserve our precious
Liberty,
Put kids and teachers
Under lock and key.

HYPOCRISY INCORPORATED, USA

February 1960.

Foxes pray and wolves read scriptures,
Poisonous snakes offer tooth-ache pills,
Gory paws are drenched in perfume,
Fashionable gangsters wear fancy frills.

Murderous rockets called "Honest John",
Atomic bombs as "clean" as clover,
Invasion's name becomes "defence",
War's face is thickly powdered over.

Afterword

Virtually nothing was written during the notorious "Cultural Revolution" (1966-1976). Its conclusion coincided with the death of Mao and the end of the Mao Zedong era. We close our *Sampler* here, on the eve a new period, a time of reform and opening to the outside world. The literary works which have since been created deserve a compendium of their own, and this, no doubt, will in time be produced. But that is outside the scope of our already voluminous *Sampler*.

图书在版编目(CIP)数据

中国文学集锦：从明代到毛泽东时代：英文/施耐庵，茅盾等著；沙博里(Shapiro，S.)编译.—北京：中国文学出版社，1996.3
ISBN 7-5071-0345-5

Ⅰ.中… Ⅱ.①施… ②茅… ③沙… Ⅲ.文学—作品集—中国—英文 Ⅳ.I21

中国版本图书馆 CIP 数据核字（96）第 02520 号

中国文学集锦：从明代到毛泽东时代
沙博里　编
熊猫丛书
*
中国文学出版社出版
（中国北京百万庄路 24 号）
北京外文印刷厂印刷
中国国际图书贸易总公司发行
（中国北京车公庄西路 35 号）
北京邮政信箱第 399 号　邮政编码 100044
1996 年第 1 版（英）
ISBN 7-5071-0345-5
03400
10-E-3079S